Praise for
Jung to Live By

"I found the book a clear and lively introduction to Jung. The author has kept his reader clearly in mind as he wrote and this enables him to communicate the essence and spirit of Jungian thought effectively to his readers. One gets the feeling that Mr. Pascal knows his Jung well and is creatively enamored of Jung's work and this enthusiasm communicates itself to the reader in his book."

—**John A. Sanford,** Certified Jungian Analyst, and author of *Soul Journey: A Jungian Analyst Looks at Reincarnation; Healing and Wholeness;* and *The Kingdom Within*

"Pascal has written a helpful and practical introduction to Jung's thought in many realms. His connecting of Jungian psychology to Buddhist philosophy helps link East and West in what can only be described as the spiritual dimension so many of us are concerned with. An important contribution to clarifying Jung, the book reveals much of the wisdom and relevance and old-fashioned common sense this titan of our times offers us."

—**Alice O. Howell,** author of
The Dove in the Stone: Finding the Sacred in the Commonplace; Jungian Symbolism in Astrology; and *Jungian Synchronicity in Astrological Signs and Ages*

JUNG TO LIVE BY

EUGENE PASCAL, Ph.L.

WARNER BOOKS

A Time Warner Company

Diagrams on pages 19, 34, and 58 are adapted from *The Psychology of C. G. Jung*, © 1973 by Jolande Jacobi, Yale University Press, New Haven, CT. Adapted with permission.

Warner Books, Inc., 1271 Avenue of the Americas, New York, NY 10020

A Time Warner Company

Printed in the United States of America
First printing: October 1992
10 9 8 7 6 5 4 3 2

Library of Congress Cataloging-in-Publication Data

Pascal, Eugene.
    Jung to live by / Eugene Pascal.
        p.   cm.
    Includes bibliographical references.
    ISBN 0-446-39294-4
    1. Psychoanalysis—Popular works.   2. Jung, C. G. (Carl Gustav),
1875–1961.   I. Title.
BF173.P29   1992
150.19'54—dc20   92-10439
                                                                    CIP

Cover design by Morris Taub
Cover art by Paul Klee
Book design by Leo McRee

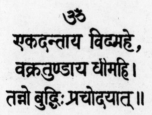

Dedicated to
Ma,
Thérèse Martin, Pio Forgione
and
Julia Blackbourn

Contents

This depression—the handicaps, the encumbrances which are weighing upon us—perhaps it is the very thing which will bring out vital issues from our life and fire our heart with new consciousness. . . . I often look upon the struggles I have gone through as my greatest blessing, and I think every truly thoughtful person can say the same thing. The hours of trial are the hours that make us strong. . . . Thus hard conditions may be for you like a little bit of flint striking upon you to ignite the fire of real life.

Today on all sides we hear people complaining about the misery of existence and there is held before us so constantly the picture of a world going to pieces that almost we believe it is so. Is it not time for some men and women to become imbued with another concept, to create a different picture which will show us that we are placed here by a Divine hand and are fulfilling a Divine purpose? Such an attitude would change the whole meaning of life for us.

Thomas Carlyle,
Heroes and the Cult of Heroes

Introduction

The ground-breaking work of Swiss psychiatrist and depth psychologist Carl Jung laid the foundations of dozens of contemporary ways of seeing the world and human nature. The women's movement. The men's movement. Growing public interest in the importance and role of myth, thanks to the work of Bill Moyers and his interviews with the late Joseph Campbell. Studies in comparative religion. The intensified search for a new mythology in the space age that is upon us. The new, much-discussed application of symbolic meanings regarding addictions, alcoholism, sex changes and evolving family structures. Many terms of common contemporary speech (introvert, extravert, complex, persona, collective unconscious, archetypes) stem from Jungian psychology. In bookstores one sees a plethora of publications with Jung's name mentioned in the title, much as a decade or so ago one saw books entitled *Zen and the Art of Whatever*.

Jungian psychology is being increasingly recognized by a growing audience as a universal and easy way to clearly understand not only human psychology but also many other subjects, including the Bible, fairy tales, Navaho sand paintings, tarot cards, Oriental religions, shamanism, alchemy, parapsychological studies, world literature, stages of life, social and cultural phenomena, and a host of other areas of human interest.

If Jung remains relatively unknown to the larger public, it is because of his somewhat inaccessible and peculiar stream-of-consciousness writing style as well as a less than covert campaign to discredit him, conducted mainly by the Freudian camp and other schools of psychology antagonistic to depth psychology in general which deals with all levels of the unconscious mind. Their efforts have come to naught, thanks both to Jung's genuine genius and to the assiduous work of his students who have authored books, penned in an everyday idiom, based on his insights and observations.

Carl Jung was a thinker who was truly ahead of his time. Born in a country not known for making tempestuous waves on the world scene, Jung seemed to reflect the quiet, calm, step-by-step, fastidious Swiss approach. Slowly but surely his work has entered areas and disciplines of coping with everyday life, many times without acknowledgment of his direct influence or indirect inspiration. Many people take the Myers-Briggs type indicator test, read about the Goddess and her influence, participate in a twelve-step program, join a men's identity group, or use visualization to rid themselves of cancer and other diseases, not knowing that in the early twentieth century Jung formulated these revolutionary concepts. It is high time that credit be given where credit is due, not in order to make Jung into a celebrity but rather to make his valuable and helpful insights more accessible in our attempts to reduce human suffering. Let us take a closer look at this astute doctor of the soul.

Carl Gustav Jung (pronounced "Yoong" in German) was born on July 26, 1875, in Kesswil in the canton of Thurgau in Switzerland. When he was four years old, he and his parents moved to Basel, a city in the northwestern part of the country bordering on France and Germany. His maternal family were Baslers. His paternal ancestors had come to settle in Switzerland from Germany in 1822. His German grandfather was a professor of surgery at the University of Basel; his father was a minister in the Reformed Church. It was rumored that his German grandfather was the natural son of the poet Goethe, but Jung seemed not to have taken this rumor seriously.

After studying medicine in Basel, in 1900 Jung became an assistant professor at the Psychiatric Clinic at the University of Zurich. He remained at the clinic for the next nine years. In 1902, during a leave of absence from the Psychiatric Clinic, he went to Paris to study psychopathology with Dr. Pierre Janet at the famous La Salpêtrière Clinic, where he remained for one semester. He then returned to Zurich to do research under Eugen Bleuler, director of the Burghölzli Clinic, which allowed him to have some research papers published. His reputation grew thanks to these initial publications, and he received many invitations to lecture abroad.

In 1903 he married Emma Rauschenbach, who collaborated with him in his studies in depth psychology until her passing in 1955. Together they had raised a family of five children.

In 1905 Zurich University offered him a position as instructor in psychiatry, which he accepted and kept for the next four years. Then in 1909 he set up a private practice as a physician and psychotherapist and spent much time in personal research and study.

It was in 1907 that Jung and Sigmund Freud first met and that Jung became interested in Freud's work in psychoanalysis, which he saw as confirming his independent observations and discoveries in psychopathology. Jung and Freud began relating closely both personally and professionally. During this period, Eugen Bleuler and Sigmund Freud sponsored the *Yearbook for Psychoanalytic and Psychopathological Research* and named Jung as its editor.

In 1911 Jung founded the International Psychoanalytic Association, becoming its first president. A year later the initial signs of a rupture with Freud were visible when Jung published *Transformation and Symbols of Libido* (now renamed *Symbols of Transformation*), in which he openly took issue with Freudian theories. The definitive break with Freud and his school of psychoanalysis came in 1913.

The year of the breakup was a deeply emotional turning point for Jung as well as for a disappointed Freud, who had thought of Jung as the "crown prince" of the Freudian school of therapy. Returning from his last meeting with Freud in Vienna, Jung gave up all teaching engagements in Zurich to focus entirely on research into the nature and dynamics of the unconscious psyche. Four years later, in 1917, he published *Two Essays on Analytical Psychology* (the name Jung chose for his own school of thought) based on his studies and experiences since his break with Freud. His other publications dealt with entirely new concepts in the area of depth psychology.

In the spring of 1920 Jung felt the need to study the psyches of non-Europeans to broaden his understanding and to test his intuitions about human nature, so he sailed to Algiers in North Africa and traveled for several months along the road to Tunis and points south into the desert oases. In the beginning of 1925 he visited with the Taos Pueblo Nation in the American Southwest. The next year he toured East Africa, mainly in the Mount Elgon area of Kenya. Through these travels he learned that the unconscious psychic manifestations of people around the world, regardless of their geographical habitat, are strikingly similar. This insight prompted him to pursue more research in ethnology and the comparative study of religions.

He next turned his attention toward Asia and the Far East with the help of the sinologist Richard Wilhelm, director of the China Institute in Frankfurt, Germany, and translator of and commentator on Chinese classical works of philosophy and literature. In 1930 Jung wrote a psychological commentary on an ancient Chinese Taoist text entitled *The Secret of the Golden Flower*, in collaboration with Wilhelm, who had translated it.

In 1933 Jung began a friendship with the German Indologist Heinrich Zimmer that lasted until the latter's death in 1943. Jung learned much about Asian-Indian thought, religion and psychology from his friend, and in 1944 he edited Zimmer's last work, *The Way to the Self*. With Karl Kerenyi, the Hungarian mythologist, in 1942 Jung collaborated on a work titled *Essays on a Science of Mythology*, which argued that myths reveal patterns of human consciousness.

Besides his active psychotherapeutic practice in Zurich, Jung spoke at several U.S. universities, and was awarded honorary degrees from Fordham, Clark, Yale and Harvard. In January 1938 he went to India, as a guest of the British government for anniversary celebrations of the University of Calcutta. While in India he was awarded Doctor of Literature degrees from the Hindu University of Benares and from the University of Allahabad and a Doctor of Science degree from the University of Calcutta. Later in the same year he received a Doctor of Science degree from Oxford University and was appointed a Fellow of the Royal Society of Medicine.

In 1945, due to illness and overwork, Jung gave up the position in medical psychology that he had held for one year at the University of Basel. He also had to abandon his medical practice but was able to devote his energies to further research and writing. Swiss compatriots named him winner of the Literary Prize of the City of Zurich in 1942. He was awarded an honorary doctorate by the University of Geneva in 1945 when he was seventy years old, and another honorary doctorate in 1955 at age eighty by the Federal Polytechnic Institute of Zurich.

Toward the end of Jung's life his interests in parapsychology were renewed. For him parapsychology was part and parcel of everyday psychology. His later writings focused on his investigations in religion and alchemy as ancient methods of psychological transformation. His thirty-odd books and ninety or so articles have been translated into almost all European languages and into an increasing number of non-European languages as the vital import of his discoveries reaches around the world. All the details of Jung's life are well described in his highly recommended autobiography entitled *Memories*,

Dreams, Reflections and in a biography by Barbara Hannah titled *Jung: His Life and Work*.

The reprintings of his works increase year after year. Shortly before reaching the age of eighty-six, Jung died on June 6, 1961. He was buried in the local cemetery in the village of Küsnacht just outside of Zurich, where he had lived and had his private practice for many years. The Jung Institute, which trains analysts, is just down the road from the Jung residence.

Both Jung and Freud were pioneers in the field of depth psychology. Students of Jungian psychology who train to become analysts at one of the many Jungian Institutes around the world study the basics of Freudian concepts but learn to see them as limited, shortsighted, one-sided and doctrinaire. Throughout his life, Jung maintained that he was glad he was Jung and not a "Jungian." He never wanted to codify his discoveries since he himself was continually in the process of observing something new about the human psyche, a living, evolving entity that could not be pinned down into neat categories or systems.

He constantly reiterated to his students that as analysts they must eject from their minds everything they had learned about the general principles of depth psychology. Instead they must focus entirely on the uniqueness of the individual patient who comes for a consultation.

It is hoped that the sketches of ideas and explanations in the chapters that follow will not be seen as "codifications" of Jungian psychic observations, but rather will be understood as aids in the task of becoming who we inherently are.

The aim of this book is to demystify Jungian psychology, to put Jung's ever-evolving concepts into clear, simple language so that the power and freedom they can bestow will reach people around the globe, even those without any background in the field of psychology. In a time when satellite communication has turned our disparate towns and villages into one global village, Jung offers a viable method of intercultural understanding.

Jung could interact without the slightest difficulty with people from every level of society and all walks of life. He was able to tune in to the uniqueness of these individuals. Jungian psychology, in its closeness to the Mother Nature in us all, is for young as well as old, rich as well as poor, college graduates as well as nonacademics. It is a useful everyday tool for everyday life, on the path to a secure peace of mind.

More than thirty years after his death, C. G. Jung continues to influence an ever-growing, worldwide audience. People are tired of superficial solutions and Jung points the way on the journey to real self-awareness and deep inner transformation. Jung is indeed a psychologist of the twenty-first century.

E. P.

Taos, New Mexico
August 15, 1991

Chapter 1

The Nature and Structure of Consciousness

Jung called his observations of human nature "analytical psychology," and this book sets forth his main ideas so that a layperson, without any background whatever in psychology, may easily understand them and use them in practical, everyday ways. Jung's unique insights can help alleviate psychic suffering in the world wherever people are open to his universal therapeutic approach to restoring psychic balance. *

Jung never wished to found the Jung Institute of Zurich because he felt that study of the human psyche could in no way be a fixed, static, "institutionalized" phenomenon to be squeezed into set categories. He saw the psyche as a phenomenon to be lived and to be learned about through personal experience. He adhered to the old Roman proverb "Vivere deinde philosophare," which translates as "Live, then philosophize!"

"Traduttori tradittori" ("Translators are traitors") is another proverb from Italy to which Jung paid heed. When we "translate" the living psyche into print and delineate its patterns and dynamics, we betray its true nature. Psychology talks about the psyche, but the psyche expresses itself as a living entity

---

* The word "psychic" throughout this book is used merely as a synonym for "psychological," with no connotation of ESP (extrasensory perception).

within every one of us. We ought not confuse a photo for the person photographed, but very often we do. The task Jung is proposing to us is that we each journey into our own psyche to acquire a direct knowledge of who we are at the deepest levels.

Jungian analytical psychology encourages us to personally encounter and experience all that is deep within us, and offers age-old, universally applicable methods for understanding the challenging mystery that we are. The goal of Jungian psychology is to make conscious what has hitherto been unconscious within us. This journey must begin with a look at the nature and structure of consciousness.

As our physical bodies are composed of parts, so are our psyches. This basic fact about ourselves often eludes us. But if we quiet our minds and steadily gaze inward at the movements of our minds for a period of time, we will notice that consciousness is not a single unit. It has three distinct parts: waking consciousness, dreaming and dreamless sleep.

The first level, *waking consciousness*, is dominated by our ego, or, simply, the center of our field of awareness. Our ego is related to a certain body-sense, and to an awareness of cerebral thinking and to imagery accompanied by feelings and sentiments of all kinds, physical and emotional. Our ego creates a sense of personal boundary and of separateness from others and from the world at large. Our ego-consciousness can focus outwardly or inwardly, on both outer and inner worlds. It allows us to get across a street adroitly without getting hit by a car. It serves very practical purposes in the three-dimensional world of which it is an integral part.

The second category is *dreaming*, an activity we associate with unconscious processes. We dream while we are asleep or we can daydream while awake. The reality of sleeping dreams and daydreaming is quite different from that of waking consciousness. Dreams seem to come from a different dimension or dimensions, and they speak a language all their own. The fact that we daydream implies an interpenetration of the two states of consciousness.

Our egos seem to be a point of reference for us that can relate to waking consciousness, to the outer world and to the dream states and dramas or activities of the unconscious inner world.

When asleep, we are sometimes aware that we are dreaming, and unconscious processes are observed more closely from an inner perspective. On occasion we can become aware of a third category, a *dreamless sleep* state during which the unconscious seems to become devoid of any contents. In this state we truly go blank. No images or dream stories appear in this very peaceful, serene state, yet somehow we continue to exist. We are very probably most energized by this state during sleep.

These three states of consciousness, waking, dreaming and dreamless sleep, are expressions of what we are. The word *psyche* (pronounced "sigh-key") is Greek for "soul," and psychology is "the science of the soul."

Ultimately pain is a neutral thing. It is not an "evil" in itself. For example, if we walk barefooted across a floor and happen to step on a tack, the pain that results is merely a signal that something has taken place that needs to be dealt with urgently. Pain awakens us, communicating an important message. We should pay heed to what it is trying to convey.

When all is said and done, there is a deep wound we all feel in having our psyches and consciousness divided into three parts. This division deprives us of wholeness, the feeling of being totally integrated, and is the cause of much of our "free-floating," existential pain. The word *sanity* comes from the Latin *sanus*, meaning "whole" or "healthy." Psychology helps us achieve reintegration of the various disjointed parts of our psyches and consciousness so that we may become whole, or sane, again.

Carl Jung did not create anything new to help alleviate human suffering or to assist human psycho-spiritual growth and evolution. What he did was to contribute his introspective abilities and his piercing powers of observation of the myriad subtle movements of the human psyche as it obeys certain universal natural laws and patterns. The human psyche is interconnected, interrelated and in a continuum with all other manifestations of Nature. The entire thrust of Jung's work focused on what has always been part and parcel of the human psyche from the very beginning of human existence on the planet. He minutely studied all the forces, patterns and dynamics that make human psychic life what it is.

Jung considered the psyche so much a part of the world of Nature that he recommended that we keep abreast of the newest discoveries in physics in order to better understand our own psyches. *Physics* is derived from the Greek *physis*, which means "Nature." So when we scrutinize the play of the forces of Nature, we are also learning about the energies and dynamics of human psychology.

People in modern Western societies find it hard to see their unity with trees, animals, clouds, rivers, sunlight and air, not to mention other human beings. We forget that our ancestors called all that we live in a "universe," not a "duoverse" or "trioverse." There was a reason for their choosing this significant word, but since we have come to believe that our ancestors were not as informed as we are, we have disinherited ourselves of their wisdom. How can we believe in ourselves if we do not believe in the well-established intelligence and achievements of our human forebears? It takes an incredible amount of insight to see the hodgepodge of phenomena as constituting a "universe" (a "uni-churning": *versare* in Latin means "to stir" or "churn" or "pour"). More and more scientific discoveries in the new physics are corroborating the intuitive observations and findings of our remotest ancestors.

Through his compelling insight, Jung allows us to discover the perennial dynamics of our psyches with all their hidden resources and powers. He helps us interpret the painful signals which are so often confusing but are, nonetheless, full of pertinent news and life-affirming meaning. None of us wishes to suffer. And we need not suffer if we learn to pay attention to pain's meaning instead of trying to avoid it at all costs.

Before learning about the operations of our personal psyches and how to orchestrate their dynamics, we must learn about mind, or psyche, in general.

We know the nature of the sun by its hot rays that we see and feel warming our bodies. Likewise, the psyche may be apprehended and understood from all its effects, from literally everything that has emanated from it, including the arts, the sciences, architecture, societal and cultural structures, folklore, philosophies, religions, customs and traditions of all kinds. Most psychology books teach only abstractions and theories regarding the psychic realm. By comparison, the science and art of depth psychology are able to come within reach not only of academic and scholarly specialists but also of anyone willing to observe the workings of the psyche in all that mankind has created.

From this standpoint, the psyche may come to be understood even by those who do not make the long, arduous voyage into the deep inner recesses of their psyches via dream-work. One need not sit in a mountain cave for years on end in deep meditation to attain self-knowledge, or lie on an analytic couch, because everything humanity does in the outer world blatantly reveals the nature of the human psyche deep within. Essentially we simply need a burning curiosity and a certain fascination concerning the mysteries of the human psyche and what it has produced through the ages—the good and the bad, the outer and the inner, the sophisticated and the crude.

To commune with and relate in a more intimate way to one's personal unconscious psyche, one must spend much leisure time, just as one needs time to cultivate any kind of meaningful relationship. As a popular adage has it, "What we love is what we have time for." If we really love all the various parts of ourselves the way we think we do, there will always be ample time available for the exploration and discovery of the wondrous Nature that we are deep down within.

In all of life's unpredictable changes, we begin with the psyche and end with the psyche. The psyche suffers and the psyche heals itself. All that we experience in life is done with our consciousness, our psyches. Let us take a closer look at the psyche and what we can learn from it.

Chapter 2

The Functions of Consciousness, Otherwise Called Typology

Penicillin is a species of mold that has well-known antibiotic properties. But for generations people threw away moldy bread instead of ingesting it as a natural antibiotic to cure infections of all kinds. They died by the thousands. Meanwhile, in South American countries the pre-Columbian natives created "antibiotics" by purposely putting corn cakes under wet clay pots so they would get moldy. Though they suffered from various infections, they survived because they knew that eating these moldy corn cakes would make them well. Without that knowledge, people in other cultures suffered.

If we look at life long enough, we will see that ignorance or lack of awareness is at the source of all of our suffering. Many times we can be so ignorant as to not even realize that we are ignorant. But all our sorrow, no matter how great, can be overcome in a place deep within our unconscious minds. This inner haven is absolutely free of ignorance, fear and want, a perfect musical silence at the epicenter of the wrathful typhoon assaulting our lives. This book aims at teaching the art of bringing our minds to this state of tranquillity using Jung's insights and discoveries.

This chapter looks at how we can acknowledge our ignorant sides, thereby revealing the potential buried beneath our lack of awareness. Our blind spots, according to Jung, are accounted for by typology, which describes the particular way our individual psyches process human experience: how they *perceive* reality and how they *evaluate* what they perceive.

Jungian Typology

Typology declares that consciousness functions in two ways: perceiving and evaluating. We perceive reality with our *sensation* function, using our five senses—sight, sound, smell, taste and touch. We may also perceive reality with a "sixth sense" called *intuition*. With sensation we see corners, but with intuition we see around corners. With sensation we can only read the lines as they are printed in black and white. With intuition we can read between the lines.

For example, a sensate stockbroker married to an intuitive homemaker always asked his wife where to invest. He needed only to mention a few possible stocks, and without knowing a single detail about them, she always picked a profitable investment. She did not know or understand how she managed this feat, and neither did her husband. They simply smiled all the way to the bank each time, as she was rarely off target.

We can evaluate what we perceive with the function of *thinking*. With thinking we use logic and intellectual analysis to ascertain the true character of a person or the true nature of a thing or an event, and to figure out how they work.

We may also evaluate our experiences of persons and happenings by use of our *feeling* function, our pleasant or unpleasant reactions to people, places and actions. Our feeling function is different from emotions, sentiments or affect. The German word that Jung used to name this evaluative function was *Einfühlung*, which means "feeling into"; it is also the term for "empathy" in German. The feeling function accepts or rejects as good or bad, appropriate or inappropriate, whatever our consciousness perceives through sensation or intuition.

Unfortunately, within a given individual the four functions of consciousness are not equally developed, and this is at the root of most of our problems. In each of us one function predominates, helped by one or two others. One or two functions generally remain undeveloped. This is our personal typology. Sometimes circumstances force us to develop a certain function over another that is more natural to us because of the pressing one-sided influence of our parents or of the culture we live in. Some societies are very thinking and technically oriented. Others are more feeling and "musical." Some cultures are sensate-oriented and "down to earth," while others are intuitive and mystical. All make up our world and all are valid. The Scots do not function the way Egyptians do, Egyptians do not function the way Romans do, and Romans do not function the way Polynesians do. And we can be thankful for that! Ideally, however, we need an equal opportunity to develop all four functions of consciousness. Unfortunately, the ideal and the real are two distinct things.

Nothing in Jung's psychology is rigid or dogmatic. For didactic purposes, the psyche is described in precise and neat categories, but these are only meant to be practical approximations and sketches of individual typologies and traits of consciousness. Despite all the various systems that study the human psyche, we must never forget that each individual's psyche is as unique as a person's thumbprint and genetic material. No two psyches are exactly alike. Jung taught his students to put aside everything they had learned in their study of psychology when a person came in for a consultation and to focus entirely on that person's uniqueness.

Typology as a descriptive tool is meant only as an aid in personal self-exploration. Studying a road map before taking a trip across country is a completely different experience from the adventure of the trip itself, but it is easy to see how useful

(YANG)
EGO CONSCIOUSNESS

(YIN)
THE UNCONSCIOUSNESS   Figure 2.1

advance study of a road map can be. Learning about typology is like familiarizing yourself with the road map. The adventure of living and growing with your own and others' typologies is yet to unfold.

Jung believed that each individual's personal consciousness functions in a dominant way. He found that if thinking dominates our conscious mind, then feeling will remain undeveloped in the unconscious, and vice versa. If sensation governs our conscious mind, then intuition will remain undeveloped in the unconscious, and vice versa.

Jung liked using a Chinese symbol called *tai-chi-tu* (Figure 2.1) to depict the oppositional and complementary energies or qualities of Nature in all of us—the feminine and masculine, night and day, passive and aggressive. In Chinese these energies are called *yin* (dark, earth, feminine) and *yang* (light, sky, masculine).

Jung used the symbol of the *tai-chi-tu* to depict the interaction of the conscious and unconscious domains, the *yin* and

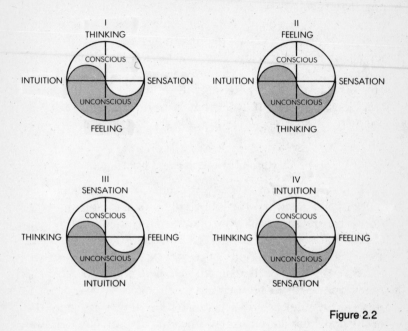

Figure 2.2

yang aspects of our psyches. For his purposes he flipped it sideways from the way it is usually presented. The upper, light, yang side for Jung represents the ego consciousness, and the lower, dark, yin side the hidden, unknown unconscious psyche. Each side contains within itself a bit of its opposite.

Each part of Figure 2.2 depicts one of the four functions in the dominant position, with the other three in various states of development in the conscious/unconscious continuum.

Notice that in example 1, with thinking on top as the main function of consciousness and feeling as the inferior function lodged in the recesses of the unconscious, the two perceptive functions of intuition and sensation hover on the borderline between the conscious and the unconscious. Known as *helping functions*, one of them might be more conscious than the other or both could be equally consciously developed. In rare cases even both prospective helping functions have been known to remain in an undeveloped state. There are no fixed rules, however, and this makes for individuality. There are all sorts of individuals, some operating with only one function made conscious, others with two, others with three, and rarely anyone with all four operative in the conscious sphere.

The Role of the Inferior Function

Neurosis, the clinical word for psychological and emotional suffering, occurs when the growth of one's natural main function is frustrated, possibly by one's parents or cultural milieu. If a natural-born thinker is forced by circumstances to operate with the inferior function of feeling, he or she will turn out to be a maladjusted, ill-adapted, muddled, confused personality. If one of his or her helping functions, sensation or intuition, is emphasized and accentuated by family or society, he or she could fare better in life, since the helping functions are more easily brought to consciousness than is the fourth, the undeveloped or *inferior* function that is buried far down in the unconscious.

The problem is that each person believes that his or her own particular main function is the best way to approach life—for him- or herself and everyone else in the world! This is because one learns through experience to distrust one's own inferior function as a way of coping in life, since it usually works badly. As a consequence, one disparages one's faulty inferior function as well as the people having this same function as their dominant one. For them it may work well, but that does not matter to the individual who distrusts his own inferior function, seeing it as an entity that has always been a stumbling block in life.

This phenomenon explains why individuals and groups look

down on one another—why a husband and wife, or neighbors, or siblings, or whole cultures may be perpetually at logger-heads. The thinker generally considers feelers to be inferior beings. Feelers mistrust thinkers, believing the worst of them. Probably more divorces result from these inner dynamics than from any other circumstance.

Sensates believe intuitives are flakey and unrealistic, and intuitives view sensates as unimaginative, boring rhinoceroses! Such dislikes and aversions poison countless daily encounters at the workplace and social gatherings.

Life is further complicated by the fact that opposites, besides repelling each other so violently, also attract! This explains why feelers often marry thinkers, and intuitives often mate with sensates. The proverbial battle of the sexes could very well be, in part at least, an oppositional difference of func-tional typology. The practical explanation for this is that in their one-sidedness each desperately needs the opposite "other" as a counterbalance and complement.

Usually the marriage partners or significant others do have a helping function in common, which eases communication between them and hence their relationship. Thinkers and feelers have to use their helping sensation or intuition, which-ever they have in common, to get across to each other. We must learn to see that opposites need each other because each supplies a piece of the picture that the other just does not see or evaluate or understand thoroughly.

In Asia, a story about a group of blind men standing around an elephant provides a picturesque example of this phenome-non. One grasps the elephant's trunk and says the elephant is like a snake. Another, seizing the tail, states that it is like a rope. A third, taking hold of the ear, declares that the ele-phant is like a big leaf, and a fourth, poking the elephant's side, asserts that it is like a big drum. All are correct. What the blind perceivers and evaluators need to do now is to listen to each other to get the whole picture because none of them has got it as yet.

If we look at marital, racial and international conflicts and disputes closely and dispassionately from the vantage point of functional typology, they may be seen for what they are: stark and glaring differences in typology. What we do not understand is what we fear, and what we fear we generally run away from or attack. It's the timeless "fight or flight" response.

If I, a thinker, fear using my feeling function because it always trips me up, I will begin distrusting and hating the feeling function in myself and in everyone else. By extension, I will begin dreading and consequently distrusting and disliking feeling persons and feeling ethnic and national groups.

This dynamic operates in all directions: Feelers may misunderstand and thus fear and detest thinking persons and groups; sensates may misjudge and thus fear and disdain intuitive persons and groups; intuitives may misinterpret and thus fear and spurn sensate persons and groups. This is an oversimplified picture, but if used as a rule of thumb it will greatly help elucidate individual and group dynamics, as well as the reasons for most of our likes and dislikes.

Fear and hate, deadly self-destructive psychological poisons, are both products of ignorance—ignorance of the dynamics of human psychology in general, and of typology in particular. If ignorance is the major cause of our suffering, then it is expedient for us to learn not only how our own individual psyches function but how psychic energies operate in humanity as a whole.

Each individual, each ethnic group and each nation with its collective typology has a unique contribution to make in perceiving and evaluating life's challenges on a personal, local, national and worldwide scale. Understanding this fact will lessen age-old mutual frictions and irritations. Each nation or ethnic group is like one of those blind men making statements about the elephant.

When we understand the all-prevailing influence of typology on the human community, we can go beyond an arrogant tolerance of others. We will be able to see that we are all minute parts of a whole body of global consciousness, each of us with our various typological aspects and diverse contributions.

Whatever we resist will persist in any case, psychologically speaking, and we will literally energize it with our resistance.

If a sensate obstinately resists all intuition, he or she will be plagued with all kinds of wild hunches flooding into consciousness—for example, "clairvoyant insights" that never pan out—creating a "loser" personality.

If intuitives stubbornly resist sense data at all costs, their conscious minds will be inundated with vivid and troublesome imagery. Their bodies will experience an array of weird sensations and hypochondriacal symptoms.

The thinker who pigheadedly resists feeling will say inappropriate and silly things or act stiffly, bloodlessly and undiplomatically when she or he should be otherwise, creating the impression of an "ice queen" or "ice king."

Feelers who mulishly resist proper thinking are besieged with wrong analyses, bungled interpretations and false conclusions about everything under the sun. They become "scatterbrains."

This psychological tripping-up always is caused by an undeveloped, unconscious, unwieldy typological function tightly anchored in the unconscious. Our inferior function acts as the proverbial thorn in our (psychological) side.

On the whole, the unconscious and the inferior function or the undeveloped helping function(s) lodged in it are optimally complementary and compensatory to everything in consciousness. While we are awake, the fourth, or inferior, function works badly and in troublesome ways. We see the fourth function operating well, however, in our nightly dreams. This is precisely why remembering our dreams is so helpful, because in our dream life we have access to whatever helpful dynamics are lacking in our ego-waking state.

Ego-consciousness is merely the tip of the iceberg. The bulk of the iceberg and the ocean in which it floats symbolize the vast unconscious mind. All of psychic life wells up from these unconscious depths, and this is why we daydream and spend one-third of our earthly lives asleep so that we can reconnect with our energizing psychic roots. This recontact with the matrix of our conscious mind restores and balances our conscious mind, supplying us with whatever is missing in waking consciousness. The prime reason for remembering dreams is to gain access to an aspect of our psyche that we need to assimilate and integrate into ego-consciousness if we are to live our lives in a fuller, more satisfactory fashion.

What's Your Type?

If you wish to determine your typology, a Jungian analyst can administer professional tests such as the Myers-Briggs, Grey-Wheelwright or the newest and updated Singer-Loomis. In lieu of one of these, you may easily test yourself with the help of a popular introductory book titled *Please Understand Me*, by David Keirsey and Marilyn Bates, available at most bookstores. It helps readers ascertain their personal typologies in an unconfusing, simple and entertaining way.

An experiential approach—in other words, self-observation—is ultimately the best and surest way to determine your typology. It far surpasses any test. Self-observation of our daily modes of functioning keeps us alert, and more conscious and more sensitive to who we are. Since it is the inferior function that always fouls up our everyday life, simply observe if you fail most in perceiving reality via sensation or intuition or in evaluating reality via thinking or feeling. Ask yourself the following questions.

In your experience, do others tell you that you do not perceive objective reality very well? That you miss the obvious? That you are a dreamer? That you always show up late for appointments, if at all? If so, your sensation function is causing you trouble, and you are probably an intuitive type. If people accuse you of not being able to read between the lines, of not being able to see behind the facades people present to you, of taking everything literally or of being gullible, then you are most likely a sensate type.

If your mate or friends accuse you of sticking your foot in your mouth and saying inappropriate things, of being cold and of being staunchly moral but unethical, you most probably are a thinking type. If you are hopeless at making logical inferences à la Sherlock Holmes, are a rotten mathematician, misinterpret other people's intentions and motivations and gush effusively at everything that happens outwardly or inwardly, or if you keep the gushing all bottled up, you are undoubtedly a feeling type.

A thinker might say that if we are at war with a dangerous enemy who could soon get the upper hand, we should use a nuclear bomb on all the enemy's major cities. The feeler will cry out, "And what about the civilian population and our embassy and consulate personnel and those of other ally countries?" It is thinking that provides moral rules and regulations, cold and rigid "Thou shalts" and "Thou shalt nots." The feeling function, however, prefers ethical behavior which is pliably contextual; for example, thou shalt not kill, but if a mugger is about to murder an innocent victim, it is justifiable and honorable to kill the would-be culprit if no other means of prevention are possible.

Which evaluative approach appeals to you more? Both thinking and feeling stances are necessary to live life prudently and conscientiously. Thinking provides rules and structure, but feeling makes the structure resilient and supple enough to withstand the "quakes and tremors" that are the behaviors of society's members. Enlightened living is truly a balancing act. To which side of the scales do you tend to tip?

Intuitives see an array of possibilities and out of them a probability, whereas sensates register only what is before their eyes. A true intuitive, however, will most likely see the one probability among the many possibilities that is not presently "visible." This will utterly amaze the sensate, who is solely caught up in concrete actualities of the here and now. The sensate in turn will be on the boat that the intuitive will have missed entirely, because intuitives generally do not see what is right in front of their noses. In which manner do you tend to perceive reality?

Life is basically a question of typology. When our egos comprehend that the behaviors and attitudes of our psyches are just as real and as substantial as our physical bodies and that they constitute the personality that we are, we will come to understand why certain things always seem to happen to us. If we wish to change our destiny, we need to transform our character, which is the same in great part as our personal typology. We accomplish this transformation first by focusing on the natural main function more, and toning it up. Next comes developing the two natural helping functions, consciously leaving the fourth, inferior function alone for the time being. The fourth usually will surface on its own during our mid-life shifting of gears, when we slow up in certain areas and pick up speed in others, and when we need to adapt to life's changes in a totally different way. Until then we need only rely on a spouse or someone else close to us for their complementary input from our inferior but their main function. What is termed our mid-life crisis generally involves a birthing and upsurgence of our undeveloped third and fourth inferior functions dug up from the unconscious. This phenomenon startles us at first since we begin perceiving and evaluating our outer and inner worlds in totally but refreshingly new ways.

Our typology also affects the work we choose to do in our lives, the careers in which we feel most satisfied. For instance, an intuitive thinker might prefer physical science research, computers, engineering, technical work or management of people. An intuitive feeler may prefer a career in art, music, literature, health care, therapy or religious service. A sensate feeler is more likely to be comfortable with a career in teaching, office work, sales, health care or supervision of people. A sensate thinker is happiest in work that provides technical skills with objects and facts, such as business, law enforcement, banking, production, construction or business administration.

The Attitudes of the Psyche

When we speak about our conscious or unconscious spheres, we are really talking about psychic energy systems. Energy ebbs and flows, progresses or regresses. When we are awake, the outer world forces our psyches to stream outwardly to deal with it; when we are asleep, the flow turns inward toward the interior world of the unconscious realm. All of us experience this throughout our lives.

Jung brought to our awareness and clarified for us what he called typical and dominant *attitudes* of our psyches, which work in conjunction with our typological functions. Certain people, when awake, are more interested in and attracted to the inner psychic world, viewing the outer realms as an intrusion into their field of consciousness. Individuals who are naturally drawn more to the inner world Jung called *introverts*. Other individuals seemed to him to more readily let their psychic energy flow onto the outer spheres of life, experiencing any incursion of the internal world as an intrusion into their field of awareness. People to whom the outer world has more appeal he termed *extraverts*. Extraverts are simply more interested in outer persons, things and events than in inner persons, things and events.

These two terms, introvert and extravert, coined by Jung himself, have become part and parcel of everyday Western speech. Unfortunately, both terms have come to have negative connotations. If one accepts these connotations, one cannot "win" either way, as an introvert or an extravert.

In popular parlance, introverts are wallflowers and extraverts are loudmouths. According to stereotypical extraverted thinking, introverts who like solitary walks in the woods might eventually become serial murderers. According to stereotypical introverted thinking, extraverts are people who dress in bright colors, are loud and exuberant in speech, and always get excluded from proper and elegant cocktail and dinner parties.

For Jung, who coined the two terms to describe subtle facets of human nature, *introversion* and *extraversion* are merely neutral descriptive terms designating the two basic movements of the psychic energy of consciousness. In strict Jungian usage, the terms in no way correspond to what most people mistakenly imply when using them.

All the expressions mean is that the two types of people, introverts and extraverts, react differently to a given event due to the direction of the flow of the energy systems of their psyches. Introverts are shy vis-à-vis the outer world, and one could say extraverts are shy with regard to the inner world. Introverts are more restrained in performing externally directed tasks that require personal involvement, and extraverts are reserved in coming to terms with inner realities with which they need to grapple. Jung's terms are by no means meant to be judgmental or derogatory. The two attitudes of introversion and extraversion delineate inborn qualities of psychic interest. That is all. Some people are more interested in the inner world, others in the outer. No character evaluation is implied by the use of the two terms.

A person with an extraverted attitude predominantly orients him- or herself by external, collective norms, what we call the spirit of the times, and is generally poorly adjusted to the demands of the interior world. Extraverts focus thinking, feeling, sensation or intuition in relation to others and events in the outside world, and they tend to lose themselves in the outer persons, objects or events. It is no crime to lead one's life in this manner, but, as with all things, it does have its drawbacks.

The introverted attitude impels one more into relating to inner psychic experiences. The introvert operates on mainly personal, subjective factors and consequently adapts less, if at all sometimes, to the external environment, which he or she considers to be only of secondary interest. The introvert's first spontaneous reaction to an outer stimulus is to recoil. This is not paranoia. The outer world's impingements simply take the introvert by surprise.

It is up to each of us to determine the natural flow of our psychic energy. Introspection and constant self-observation come more easily to introverts in this endeavor. Extraverts seem to prefer outer determinants such as written or oral typology testing.

While the four functions—thinking, feeling, intuition and sensation—indicate the *way* we process human experiences, the two attitudes of introversion and extraversion reveal the *direction* of the flux and flow of our psychic energy, as expressed in thinking, feeling, intuition and sensation. Consequently we can speak of an introverted thinking type or an extraverted thinking type. Both use analytical or discursive reasoning, but concerning absolutely different things. The introverted thinker is occupied with inner philosophical speculations, while the extraverted thinker is involved in Sherlock Holmesian out-in-the-world problem solving and understanding.

Introverted feelers may be madly in love with you, but it's "none of your damned business" as far as they are concerned, and that's all there is to it. Extraverted feelers, in their propensity to exhibit and express evaluative feeling, "say it" with flowers and poetic greeting cards and with invitations to the opera and candlelight dinners by the sea. They must communicate their feeling reactions at all costs. If it feels good, they must do it. If it does not feel good, they won't do it.

Introverted intuitives populate the monasteries and mountaintops of the world, "mystical" places that are "close to the gods." Extraverted intuitives are to be found playing "games" at the racetrack or stock market, or at psychic-reading parlors, chasing their fancy wherever it flutters.

Introverted sensates listen to fine music, surround themselves with art and beautiful objects and delight in the effects of haute cuisine since they are interested in the impact of these things on their senses. Extraverted sensates manufacture and provide the music, art objects, haute cuisine and marvelous stereo equipment that the introverted sensates take so much pleasure in.

However, in reality there are no pure types such as the ones I have facetiously portrayed above. Life would be unbearably boring if there were only eight, or sixteen or even thirty-two or sixty-four types of people. When we describe types, we are depicting abstract patterns of consciousness that facilitate an understanding of human behavior and human beings. We are people and not patterns, but when we imply that a person is "very French," or "very Russian," or "South American" or "Australian," everyone catches on immediately. It is similar with typological functions and attitudes. A person is somewhat of an extravert and more or less a thinker, intuitive to a certain degree, disturbingly unfeeling, and so forth. Types are not absolutes, and we individually most definitely are not.

Jung made the interesting observation that if the principal function was introverted, the opposite, inferior function would be extraverted, and the other way round. If the main function was extraverted, the inferior function would be found to be introverted. Take a look at Figure 2.3.

In example number 1, introverted thinking is the dominant function, and the inferior function is extraverted feeling. In practical terms, this person's unconscious output of dreams and daydreams will be colored by extraverted feeling that operates well at the unconscious level. The inferior function of extraverted feeling, when this individual is awake, will not function well and will be a source of all kinds of personal foul-ups—grouchiness, outbursts of temper, displays of a maudlin sentimentality, etc. But in the thinker's unconscious dream-productions his feeling function will indeed work efficiently. This type of person would not be good in a public relations position, as the feeling component is the least developed in ego-consciousness and usually manifests itself in a primitive,

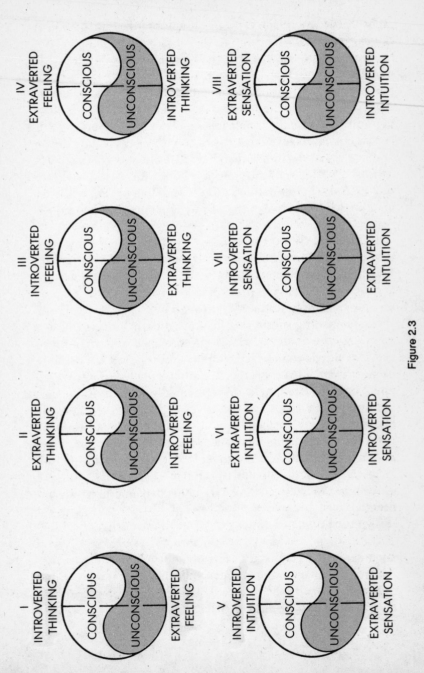

Figure 2.3

archaic way when it does make an appearance during waking hours.

Introverts, no matter what their main function, customarily work best alone, when the outer world does not encroach too much on their attention. Extraverts work most advantageously in an outer environment that is very challenging and stimulating and that demands their full supply of psychic energy.

It is crucial to remember that a cool thinker's feeling dream accesses a sound, on-the-mark feeling evaluation of his or her human experiences. On the other hand, the thinking dream of a person whose main function is sensitive feeling will offer an unbiased, objective, logical analysis of any given psychological situation.

In similar fashion, the sensate dream grants uncanny intuitives access to hitherto unnoticed, concrete details of reality, whether inner or outer. And the intuitive dream of down-to-earth sensates will give them precognitive or prophetic information or simply allow the dreamer to "read between the lines," providing subtle insights missed during waking hours.

As far as human relationships, romance and friendships are concerned—areas in which "chemistry" is a key issue—extraverts are ironically predominantly attracted to introverts, and vice versa. Thinkers are captivated by feelers and feelers by thinkers. Sensates and intuitives find each other mutually fascinating. In a nutshell, opposites attract and "fall in love" with each other, and—to make life more intriguing—they also repel! Polarity seems to be the essence of life. If we seriously look at all the mishaps in our relationships, intimate as well as casual, we will see that this dynamic plays an important role.

Typology explains many of our spontaneous likes and dislikes of other individuals. In romantic relationships it is as if an individual were looking for a complementary personality akin to his or her own unconscious, but one that is represented outwardly in another person. Thus we are constantly drawn to a specific type of individual love partner.

Since it is very laborious to integrate into one's conscious personality the "other half" that lies dormant in one's unconscious psyche, it is much easier to find those very features in an outer romantic partner who supplies us with the missing pieces. In friendships, these strictly oppositional characteristics are not so much in demand. As an example, two thinkers can be friends, one having sensation as a secondary function and the other perhaps possessing intuition as a secondary function. In a simple friendship, often the secondary functions are interestingly oppositional and exert an attracting complementarity.

Typology is neither black nor white nor definitive in any way, and relationships and careers are not mechanically predetermined. However, generally speaking, in any given individual, if the main function is extraverted, the inferior function will be introverted. The two helping functions will be more or less extraverted and/or introverted depending on the extent to which they have been made conscious by circumstances. If not very developed and therefore lodging in the unconscious, the helping functions will be more colored by the attitude of the unconscious, inferior function. A person with an introverted main function will have to relate to the outer world with one or both of the helping functions that can become extraverted.

The functions themselves seldom appear in pure form. They usually manifest as mixed types. Figure 2.4 illustrates this point.

As with the four functions, if an attitude that is thrust on a child is not natural to that child's innate psychological constitution, neurosis (psychic suffering) will ensue most assuredly starting at an early age. The attitudes of introversion and extraversion are much more rigidly fixed by nature than the four functions, which can more easily be brought into conscious development than can the two attitudes.

A born introvert can only feign an extraverted attitude, and depression inevitably accompanies this lack of being oneself.

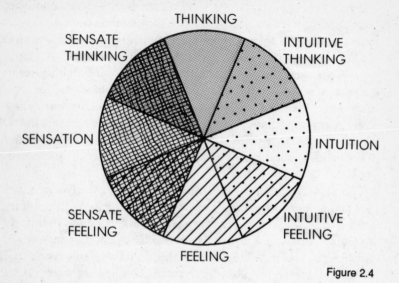

Figure 2.4

Similarly, the born extravert can pretend to be introverted only with much concerted effort, and will experience a similarly caused depression. The law of averages is that Mother Nature probably brings into being a global population that is half introverted and half extraverted, but countries and groups of people develop collective characteristic patterns. In the American culture, for instance, about seventy-five percent are extraverted thinkers and twenty-five percent are introverted feelers. A greater percentage of males have thinking as their dominant function; the same is true of females as feeling types. Interestingly, introverts in relatively more introverted New England on the whole fare better than introverts in more extraverted California; the New England psychic atmosphere and climate are somehow more accommodating to the attitude of introversion. The overall culture in the United States, however, makes an extravert feel more at home than it does a born introvert. Feeling at ease with one's attitude and temperament is very much affected, whether positively or negatively, by one's psychic environment, whether it be family or culture. Often simply resettling in a culture more in tune with one's individual typology can eliminate much useless neurotic affliction.

In the overall development and evolution of a child, more extraversion is required in the schooling period and later in the establishment of a career and a family—in general, the demands of growing up. In mid-life, a more introspective, soul-searching, introverted attitude normally is required for the emotionally sensitive confrontation with the realities of old age and the eventuality of death.

Born extraverts therefore have an easier time in early life and a more trying time adapting to the tempo of later years, when energies are impelled to turn inward. The early years are generally a more arduous experience for the introvert than for the extravert, since introversion normally goes against the demands of living in society during this early period. Born introverts must be coaxed into understanding why it is to their advantage at certain times to turn their psychic energies to outer concerns. They must simultaneously be allowed ample opportunities for vitally needed introverted activities such as reading, walks in Nature, listening to music, painting and drawing, even playing alone if they wish or just daydreaming. An old Roman proverb says: "Moderation in all things and moderation in moderation." It is hard to strike a happy and artful balance in granting introverted children their rightful freedom to be who they are. At the same time they need sympathetic encouragement in adapting to the impositions of outer, everyday life in the framework of school and society.

Extraverts re-energize and re-create themselves by throwing themselves into enjoyable outer ventures and activities, while introverts re-create best by delving into their favorite inner explorations and musings. These nuanced dynamics must be honored.

In my early teaching days I was assigned to a study period that was the very last class of the day. One afternoon a young student raised his hand and asked if he could sit at the window and just "look at the rain" instead of focusing on his homework. He was very introverted and needed to recharge his psychic batteries by daydreaming if he was going to be able to continue the extraverted task of doing his demanding homework. I told him that ten minutes of looking out the window at the falling rain would be okay, but after that he really ought to focus again on his studies. He was happy as a lark to hear my reply. Many times ten minutes of "inner work" is all introverts need to handle the intrusions of required extraversion. This anecdote is a perfect illustration of the French expression: "Reculez pour mieux sauter," roughly translated as "Regress in order to progress better." Introverts especially need to engage in such "regression" frequently during a busy day.

Nightly sleep is the regression that we all need in order to pick up the next day where we left off. The need for mini-doses of introversion throughout the day is extremely important for very introverted people pressed upon by an exceedingly extraverted world. This cannot be stressed enough. Life is full of starts and stops in any case, so allowing introverts brief moments of quiet and solitude ought not to be seen by bewildered extraverts as a waste of precious time or as a neglect of social duties. If deprived of introverted moments, introverts will close down altogether, performing with grinding inefficiency if not seeming incompetence.

In the heyday of his confrontations with British imperialism, Mahatma Gandhi, an introvert, took time out daily to sit at his spinning wheel. Spinning is very hypnotic, allowing one's hands to keep busy while the ego-consciousness bathes, as it were, in the waters of the unconscious. In his contact with the unconscious, occasioned by spinning, Gandhi found the creative wisdom, subtle strategies and inexhaustible energy to combat a colossal outer foe.

In modern, naturally more introverted Japan, office workers in some large corporate buildings can go to a quiet meditation room for fifteen minutes or so—just to empty out the conscious mind—mainly in order to be more productive and alert at work in their efficiency-oriented culture. Asia is more introverted than the West, but this does not mean that extraverted Westerners would not profit by stopping the outward surging of their workaday minds for brief moments during the day in order to perform more competently and adroitly and with less stress and strain, nervous conditions and heart ailments. Aptitude and efficiency are really symptomatic of a rested, tension-free, re-energized mind. Even die-hard extraverts need their morning and afternoon coffee breaks to catch their psychic breath.

A Dinner Party

To help summarize the various colors and shadings of typology (something that, of course, cannot ultimately be genuinely systematized), let's consider the dinner party thrown by a Washington hostess who invited seven people. The guest list was as follows:

1. A talented lawyer
2. A distinguished engineer
3. A noted stockbroker
4. A taciturn, enigmatic musician
5. An eminent scholar
6. A quiet art collector
7. A famous poet (who forgot about the invitation altogether)

These eight characters are merely fleshed-out examples that will facilitate our understanding of typology.

Our *hostess* with the "mostest" is a woman knowledgeable in the affairs of the world, the right kind of lighting, the best of champagne to make everyone feel "buoyant" and like having a good time. She has on-target, gut feelings about seating arrangements and an instinct about whom to or not to invite. She is a natural public-relations person, with a constant

stock of quiche in her deep freezer and a small chamber ensem-
ble on call at all times. She picks up her tailor-made gowns in
Paris on her way to winter skiing vacations in Montreux;
she summers—where else but in St. Paul-de-Valence; *noblesse
oblige* is one of her finer visceral qualities. She is very probably
an *extraverted feeler* with more than a dash of panache.

The talented lawyer is a man whose focus is on outer rules,
regulations and hard-nosed facts. He has committed to memory many laws and cunningly manipulates them as they connect to a client's misdemeanors and follies, a feat for which
he is generously rewarded. He sees how events and facts tie
together, spotting causes and effects in all that he perceives,
and he knows how to hide certain information smoothly and
beautifully. He always has polished shoes, pressed suits and
starched shirts, and he wears a pristine business suit every day.
He is probably an *extraverted thinker* with strong *sensation* and
possibly *intuition* as helping functions.

The distinguished engineer is a practical problem solver and
trouble shooter. Call her when two islands need a bridge
between them, or when an aqueduct must traverse uneven
terrain. Or when exported fruit trees need to be genetically
altered and adapted to a foreign environment. How could we
have a three-minute egg in ten seconds if she had not invented
the microwave oven? With her earthly *extraverted sensation*
function, the objective reality of a problem is deftly discerned
and scrutinized, and the helping functions of *thinking* and
feeling are brought in to deal with concrete facts in a practical
way. The earthy extraverted sensation function gave birth to
Coca Cola, Kentucky Fried Chicken and McDonald's, as well
as many a Swiss bank account connected thereto.

The noted stockbroker wheels and deals at a fast pace on Wall
Street. She has extraordinary hunches about which stocks will
rise and which will fall. She just knows if people are giving
her a genuine hot tip or are passing on a false lead. She is
remarkably lucky at Las Vegas casinos but, alas, not so lucky
in love. She's a fast talker and can convince anyone about

anything, especially her well-heeled clients, who know her sixth sense has never proved wrong. She is clearly an *extraverted intuitive* type, with *thinking* and *feeling* as her helping functions.

The taciturn, enigmatic musician is a beguiling mystery. Though he looks utterly apathetic to most of the guests, one suspects this individual is cosmically tuned-in to the music of the spheres, but we don't know for sure until he is asked by the hostess to play the violin to accompany the cappuccino and Viennese pastry in the drawing room. His magical, rapturous strings make you forget your own name, as the hostess leans over to whisper that the musician has been secretly and passionately in love with you (yes, *you*) for a decade, if not more. The *introverted feeler* keeps everything inside, but the violinist's helping functions of *sensation* and *intuition*, being more extraverted, can give us a clue, if keenly and closely espied, to these all-powerful currents that run so deep.

The *eminent scholar*, our *introverted thinker*, is probably discussing pre-Socratic philosophy as the real motivating factor in Alexander the Great's Eastern campaigns, greatly impressing the opposite typology of the extraverted feeling hostess, who is full of effusive adulation for the mesmerizing genius of her scholarly guest. He reminds her so much of her late third husband! He employs his helping functions of *sensation* and *intuition* (the same helping functions that are shared by our extraverted feeling hostess) to impart his ideas with eloquent verve.

The *quiet art collector* has experienced sheer carnal ecstasy in the *nouvelle cuisine*, the *Beaujolais fin*, the Chippendale dining room, the new *trompe l'oeil* and *faux marbre* decor and now the violinist's rendition of a lost Paganini masterpiece. The whole evening has been physically and neurologically therapeutic for this *introverted sensate*, who was virtually entranced and gratified down to the marrow of his bones by the exquisite choice of guests and the matchless taste of the hostess and her new live-in chef.

The absence of the famous but charming *introverted intuitive poet* (guest number 7), never known to reside in time or space, was noted by all. His recently published tome of lyric poetry was a smashing success, thanks to his earthy and gutsy literary agent, who filled in for him at the last moment and who gained at least five pounds at dinner. The poet phoned the next day to excuse his absence; after all, his helping functions are *thinking* and *feeling*, which have the superb knack of appraising a situation and rectifying an unforgivably gauche faux pas. He will be invited again, no doubt, because he is so incredibly fascinating to talk to, when his muses remind him to show up, that is.

We do not expect a cat to bark, a dog to meow, a bird to moo, or a cow to chirp. But, strangely enough, we do assume that all other human beings will always and everywhere express optimal, highly differentiated functions of feeling, thinking, intuition and sensation, as well as thoroughly developed attitudes of introversion and extraversion. In short, we expect others to be perfect—in all their relations with *us*. This flagrant expectation is highly delusional and unrealistic, to say the least.

An understanding of typology can spare us many disappointments in life and hence much of the suffering that can be caused by false expectations. Most of us are attempting to be what we are not, and we foolishly long for others to do the same. Knowledge of typology makes us more practical and level-headed, and it inspires simplicity, a powerful force that allows us to revel in who we are and to accept and enjoy others exactly and unconditionally as they are.

Only now at the end of the twentieth century are Jung's astute observations of the human psyche beginning to become more widely known and appreciated by a growing international public, who are applying them in practical, daily situations to healing and wholeness-producing ends.

The following is a case in point: In a reading class for children, when a certain number of the students made absolutely no progress at all the teacher gave herself and the students a simplified version of a Jungian typology test. The results revealed that the teacher was an extraverted thinker and that the nonreaders turned out to be introverted feelers, the teacher's opposite typology. When the introverted feeling students were put into a class with an introverted feeling teacher, all the former nonachievers began reaching their goal. Typology and its collective consequences follow us everywhere, into our classrooms, our bedrooms and our workplaces.

The practical application of typology covers all of life's stages. Jungian psychology is not only for the second half of life, as some uninformed non-Jungian "experts" have declared on occasion. Typological principles begin in infancy, and the various Jungian institutes around the world train student therapists in a Jungian approach to child psychology. Jung's analytical psychology is not for just one age group; it is for all age groups and people of all national backgrounds.

With a knowledge of Jungian typology, we can more easily handle countless encounters in everyday life. A simple conflict in an office between an *extraverted thinker* with *sensation* as a second function and an *introverted feeler* with *intuition* as a second function can leave both parties frustrated and depressed, perhaps until a third party intervenes. A third party's typology can act as a bridge of communication and understanding. This peacemaker's typology could feasibly be "ambi-verted" (equally extraverted and introverted) sensation or intuition as a main function with highly developed thinking and feeling as helping functions, so he or she can communicate to the main functions of both other parties. Figure 2.5 illustrates.

We sometimes try to get something across to another individual that seems to fly over his or her head. When it's something very simple, we cannot fathom why the other person is not understanding what we are so plainly saying. Along comes a friend or associate to whom we relate what we are trying to communicate. That person in turn repeats what we have just recounted, with his or her particular typology, to the first

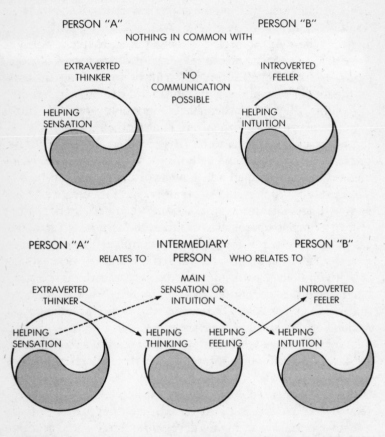

THE INTERMEDIARY PERSON'S TWO HELPING FUNCTIONS ARE EQUALLY DEVELOPED. PERSON "A" TRYING TO COMMUNICATE WITH PERSON "B" MAY HAVE FEELING AND INTUITION TOTALLY UNDEVELOPED. PERSON "B" TRYING TO COMMUNICATE WITH PERSON "A" MAY HAVE THINKING AND SENSATION TOTALLY UNDEVELOPED. PERSON "A" AND "B" HAVE NO TYPOLOGICAL LINK-UPS TO EACH OTHER AND SO THEY NEED THE INTERMEDIARY PERSON AS A BRIDGE OF COMMUNICATION.

Figure 2.5

person, who then surprisingly gets the idea. The number of times this happens in everyday life is uncountable—and frustrating.

If ignorance is the cause of all suffering, then the antidote must be knowledge. Knowledge of typology specifically will safeguard us from much frustration and aggravation in interpersonal relationships along with a certain degree of patience.

If only the various races and ethnic groups of our planet could realize that the source of much mutual misunderstanding, mistrust and mutual suspicion is essentially a question of collective typology, then more effort would be made in trying to communicate via third parties whose typology could act as a harmonizing agent and communicative bridge between the two disparate typologies. In many instances Japan has "interpreted" America to other Far Eastern nations, successfully acting as a go-between, and other examples abound in international affairs. Let us not forget that what we call culture, national politics and religious and social movements are created by the psyche and a particular typology that expresses itself through the members of each particular social, ethnic or religious collective.

Among religious groups, the typology of the founder generally becomes the ideal typology for all present and future members of that sect to emulate and mirror. Since the founder's typology is supposed to be modeled exactly, certain members who possess natural typologies diametrically opposite to the founder's may not feel comfortable with the religion they were born into. These typologically different members then create a new religious movement or sect, a new version that will be typologically different from the original founder's. In the history of Christianity, Eastern Orthodoxy and Roman Catholicism went their separate ways in A.D. 1054, due to theological and cultural (read "typological") differences; Protestantism and Roman Catholicism diverged four hundred years later, also for typological reasons, among others. These divisions were in part politically and theologically motivated, but we

tend to forget that typologically defined psyches are what produced particular theologies and political views in the first
place.

On television a few years ago an allergist from Buffalo, New
York, showed a film of a little boy punching his mother. The
boy was tested for allergies, because his mother had noticed
that he engaged in violent behavior after ingesting certain
foods and beverages. Tests showed milk to be the most aggra-
vating irritant to the child; when milk was removed from his
diet, he became calm and nonviolent. The allergist went on
to say that she found it was not extraordinary things like
processed foods with chemical additives that drastically altered
behavior. In her dealings with problem children, she found
that the more ordinary foods, such as milk and wheat, were
most responsible for mood and behavior modification.

The interviewer then switched to a professor from M.I.T.
to get his expert commentary on the allergist's statements
and the outrageous filmed behavior of the allergic child. The
M.I.T. professor basically said the following: "There is no
evidence for this. No one should change their child's diet with
the idea of controlling behavior until this has been proven
scientifically." The allergist retorted: "We don't have twenty
years for this child to stop assaulting his mother. We test for
culprit foods, we take the child off that particular food and his
violent behavior ceases. When he is given that culprit food
again, the child resumes violently beating his mother. You
scientists spend twenty years trying to find out the whys and
wherefores, but we allergists working with problem children
and their parents need immediate practical results."

Here are two typologies that will never see eye to eye,
because they are looking at the problem from very different
perspectives. The allergist seems to have strong extraverted
intuition as well as extraverted sensation, practicality aligned
with thinking. The professor appears to be an introverted
thinker who assumes something to be invalid until he himself
can understand how that something works, as if validity de-

pended on his personal understanding. He obviously has little intuition, groundedness or common sense.

Our inferior function is our blind spot. If we look over the events of our personal lives carefully, we will notice that our inferior function has always proven to be the proverbial thorn in our psychic side. If we could come to understand that our own inferior function may work perfectly well in some other person's psyche, we would benefit from consulting with that person precisely to get a perception or evaluation based on his or her superior function, instead of engaging in endless debates and disputes.

Typology is one of Jung's greatest contributions to the world of psychology. Many ask what objective evidence there is that typology exists. I usually reply, as the allergist did, that people in therapy usually do not have twenty years to find proof for typology. Their own experience of typology ought doubtless to be validation enough, once it is pointed out to them and once they observe its dynamics operating in themselves and others. Their own experience of the workings of their personal typology should offer them the possibility of expanding and acquiring a clear-cut, unconditional acceptance of other people and the way they function. A life led without constant negative judgments of others and the deep peace that this brings to one's heart is all the proof that anyone would want or need.

The more you honestly apply Jungian psychology to your life, the less abstract it will appear and the more commonsensical and practical you will find it to be. It is truly an agent of healing.

Chapter 3
Masks for All Seasons

In Oscar Wilde's *The Picture of Dorian Gray*, a portrait of a handsome young man is hung in a room of an elegant large mansion. This young man slowly becomes a reprehensible character. The portrait eventually is stored away in the attic. His personality changes from bad to worse, and, stranger still, he never ages. At the end of the story, he ventures up into the attic and unveils the painting to find that his portrait no longer depicts the young and dashing man that he was, but rather an old man with the face of a monster. All the ugliness of his personality had never shown on his physiognomy but had mysteriously affected the portrait's features tucked away all those years in the attic. The very sight of it throws the man into shock and, falling down, he dies. The painting uncannily resumes the handsomeness of his younger days as the corpse's face assumes the hideous appearance formerly displayed on the portrait.

Wilde's novel dramatically depicts the concept Jung termed the *persona*. Of course, the realities of the human psyche have existed from time immemorial, but Jung gave us a contemporary vocabulary to better understand these age-old psychic aspects in a clearer way.

The word *persona* is a historical term, the name of the large carved wooden masks worn by the actors in Greco-Roman theater. The Latin expression is *per + sonare*, meaning "to sound through." The theatrical mask, besides identifying the good guys and bad guys to the audience of antiquity, served as a primitive megaphone to carry the voice of the actors to the top bleachers of the amphitheater. In short, these masks, or personas, facilitated communication between the individual actor and the spectators.

The differentiation, or focusing, of ego-consciousness gives rise to the persona, which is the form of an individual's general character and attitude toward the outer world. The persona is a kind of bridge or buffer between one's subjective ego (the center of one's field of awareness) and the outer, objective world.

Jung's definition is as follows: "The persona is thus a functional complex that has come into existence for reasons of adaptation or personal convenience, but by no means is it identical with the individuality. The persona is exclusively concerned with the relation to [outer] objects" (*Psychological Types, Collected Works*, vol. 6, par. 801). "The persona is a compromise between individual and society as to what a man should appear to be" (*The Relations Between the Ego and the Unconscious, Collected Works*, vol. 7, par. 246).

Put more succinctly, the persona is a compromise between what society expects of us and our own personal identity, between individuality and self-image. Lawyers in a corporate environment are to appear at work in navy-blue or dark-gray suits, as the colors brown and green are definitely "out." If a lawyer showed up at his corporate firm in a see-through cellophane suit and ponytail, his colleagues might have a difficult time taking him seriously as a "big-time" corporate professional. When outfitted according to society's expectations, including adopting appropriate speech, body language and demeanor, he identifies himself and his status or position and facilitates professional relations with his boss, peers and clients. "Facilitates" is the key word. Within the parameters of his specific occupational expectations, a person's individuality might be expressed by his choice of tie, his office furnishings, or where he takes clients to lunch, all of which make up his professional personality. His persona makes him plausible in the social role that he is playing.

A severe problem arises if this man forgets to "change clothes" (i.e., his persona) when he goes home to his family. His wife and children do not want him to be "corporate" in the family setting. If he cannot coo-coo and shmooze with the new baby but can only shake hands in a smart, businesslike fashion, feelings of icy-cold alienation will poison the household. Being a husband and father requires special personas. To vary his persona under different circumstances, he must not be "on automatic." He must be relatively conscious of the situation and the emotional and aesthetic expectations of others.

If the corporate world of big business seems demanding of adult individuality, peer pressure impacts even more on our adolescents and consequently stifles genuine individuality. This is a major factor in understanding what are commonly called "growing pains" (a condition clinically known as teen-age neurosis). It is imperative, therefore, that teenagers be offered absolute acceptance at home of their God-given singularity (to be distinguished from "collectively contrived singularities") in an unconditionally loving atmosphere, since elsewhere these conditions may not prevail.

Figure 3.1 depicts a person whose main typological function is sensation which must filter through the persona to the outer world. The persona personalizes the developed functions of the individual. It is a kind of overlay of ego-consciousness that relates it to the outer world.

If you are invited to a square-dancing party, it is inappropriate to arrive dressed like Queen Elizabeth or Prince Phillip on a royal visit—we need always to heed outer collective conditions. The folks at the square-dancing party in no way expect anyone to arrive in a gilded horse-drawn carriage with

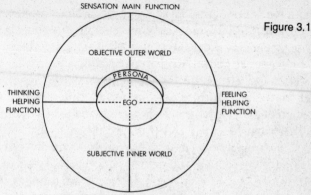

Figure 3.1

THE DIAGRAM ABOVE IS THAT OF A PERSON WHOSE MAIN FUNCTION IS SENSATION. THE *PERSONA* IS THAT ASPECT OF EGO-CONSCIOUSNESS THAT RELATES THE EGO TO THE OUTER WORLD. THE EGO ITSELF RELATES TO BOTH INNER AND OUTER WORLDS.

footmen. They might be dazzled and awestruck but probably not too open to relaxed, casual communication. Collective limitations have to be respected if we truly wish to relate to a particular group of people. "When in Rome, do as the Romans do" is generally sound advice with regard to the persona.

When Mahatma Gandhi left South Africa and arrived in Bombay by ship to begin his political career there, he disembarked and greeted the clamoring crowds dressed as a common Indian coolie, or porter. He had packed away his British-style barrister's tweeds and starched white shirts, suitable to his lawyer's position in South Africa. He put on this Indian persona to be more approachable to the oppressed poor. As he was Indian by birth, his new persona, which was not farfetched and which suited him nicely, facilitated communication in a particular cultural and political context. The crowds adored him because they saw him as one of their own.

Whatever happened to Norma Jean Baker, once the mask of Marilyn Monroe covered her from head to foot? She appears to have been a classical victim of a mechanical persona. She was trapped and smothered in the role of Love Goddess, to the detriment of her own individuality. A well-balanced consciousness can always freely dispose of a particular persona, adapting itself to the requirements of the moment, and exchanging one distinct persona for another more suitable one when necessary. Norma Jean was never allowed to be anything other than Marilyn, and this type of situation can only lead to catastrophe. She must have suffered tremendously.

What are some of the myriad personas so typical of our own culture? We need only look at all those popular images of characters that fascinate us on television, in films and in public displays of all kinds: Joan Baez, Pearl Bailey, Lucille Ball, Archie Bunker and his wife "Dingbat," Bugs Bunny, Charlie Chaplin, Nat King Cole, Bill Cosby, Bette Davis, Sammy Davis, Jr., James Dean, Donald Duck, Clark Gable, Greta Garbo, Arsenio Hall, Rock Hudson, Michael Jackson, Indiana Jones, Mickey Mouse, Miss Piggy and Kermit, Prince, Elvis Presley, Rambo, Diana Ross, Frank Sinatra, Snow White, Superman, Dionne Warwick, John Wayne—"immortals" all. All are inimitable personalities, and they all somehow reflect personas our Western culture easily relates to.

Women entering professions dominated by men were initially expected to dress and act like men. The only persona they were allowed was a masculine one, but as long as a woman tries to come on as a man, she is going to be "inferior." It is the same situation as a feeler trying to behave like a thinker, or vice versa. Women sporting masculine personas might be more acceptable in "masculine" careers, but one wonders if they will ever be accepted as women. A woman with a forced masculine persona, for example, gray tweed suits and high-neck tie-blouses, is a victim. It need not be so, and fortunately things are progressing in a better direction in this regard.

The goal of Jungian psychology is to learn to be oneself, a task that sometimes implies social confrontation that might raise another's consciousness, not to mention one's own. Happily, women's groups and publications are addressing these fundamental not-just-women's issues. The feminine is different and complementary to the masculine; it is not inferior, since "difference" does not imply inferiority or secondary status.

A persona is considered healthy and appropriate if it expresses three basic factors. First, the persona ought to express the person's true individuality and uniqueness, not an imagined or concocted one. Remember, there are no clones in Nature. God apparently has an infinite supply of imagination. Each of us has an image deep down of who we most genuinely are, and nonsticking, replaceable personas will best reflect all the roles that we need to play in life and all the facets of our multidimensional personalities. "To thine own self be true" is sound advice; if followed, it will lead more times than not to good psychic health.

Second, our uniqueness ought to adapt to a moderate form of conscious conventionality. Society's demands must be met at least halfway if we are to be taken seriously in a particular cultural or social setting or to appear plausible in a certain professional role or even some ordinary relationship. If the local shoe-shine boy were to speak in perfect Oxfordian English, he assuredly would raise many a suspicious eyebrow. An incongruous persona is the very essence of solid good humor in all climes and cultures. A healthy persona ought to bring forth more than just a hint of the individual behind it. It ought to help in expressing that unrepeatable individuality as much as possible.

Third, a persona has to respect physical and psychological parameters. For example, a dark-skinned person with dyed platinum blond hair would not be respecting his or her genuine ethnicity. Many spouses try to turn their mates into something that they simply are not. The perfect example of this is a retired Florida woman dressing her eighty-year-old husband in the clothing of a thirty-year-old playboy of the silent screen era or a man who wants his wife to dress and act like his favorite television actress and cater to his wildest fantasies of seduction.

Worse still is when parents want their child to be an extra-verted thinker, for example, when in fact the child is by nature an introverted feeler. True adaptation to the environment is always accomplished with one's natural main function and never with one's inferior function. A particular persona may be forced upon a child by its parents, peer pressures or cultural demands, and, no matter how one looks at it, this can only lead to serious consequences and utterly unnecessary suffering in the long run, for the child who cannot be him- or herself and for the parents who are always disappointed in what Fate imposed on them, namely, a child whose typology is radically different from their own.

Compulsive or addictive behavior is always associated with one's inferior function. Stifling the innate temperament and crushing the natural expression of the main attitude and func-tion lead ultimately to a compulsive character disorder and an outright neurotic way of life. When an artificial persona expresses the inferior function and/or attitude, it sadly takes on all the compulsive inadequacies of primitive, undeveloped, unconscious factors. There is no controlling of the inferior function which is now like a fish out of water.

Such unfortunate, oppressed individuals always create an unpleasant impression and leave us with a puzzled feeling about them as we subliminally perceive that something is askew, false or mechanical in their responses, in their ways of dressing and in their use of body language. They appear to blunder through everything in life, never quite fitting in anywhere, with little or no awareness of behavior that is appropriate to a given situation. Lady Luck always seems to pass them by because their natural main function was never allowed to function as they tried to express their individuality to the outer world. They have proverbial "loser" personalities through no fault of their own.

Human dignity is by and large the product of a naturally

spontaneous expression of who we intrinsically are. Some of us must dare to be who we are. Native and African Americans, Asians, Mexicans, and other ethnic minorities in America are finally taking up this dare and consequently are being more themselves and becoming less neurotic.

Outer imposition of a false persona is only half of the problem. Inner impositions coming from the depths of the unconscious always also pose a greater problem if the individual mistakenly believes that his or her natural ego-consciousness and individuality are not suitable for one reason or another. This inner-produced negative attitude can undermine a happy adaptation to the environment in a completely insidious, unconscious way. The result is the very same, however, as a false persona imposed from without. Some people believe they have to drive a certain type of car to be acceptable, to speak with an affected accent, to act like an intellectual when in fact they really despise academia and so on and so forth.

The skin of our bodies, if healthy and supple, allows the cells and tissues underneath to breathe and flourish; however, nonresilient, clogged skin prevents oxygenation of the same tissues and cells. Likewise will a natural, organic, well-functioning persona enable our inner selves to "breathe" and allow a smoothly flowing relationship to flourish between our individuality and the outer world. When a persona is overidentified with, it loses its elasticity, resilience and permeability, and becomes ineffectual in our relationships with others on almost all levels.

We must accept the fact that no matter who we are and what personality we put forth in facing others, the law of averages dictates that, whatever we do or say, one-third of the world will absolutely love us and relate to us, one-third will hate us off the bat, and one-third will not care one jot about us either way! Try as hard as we may, we simply cannot be all things to all people. There are too many unpredictables in human expectations and interactions.

One thing is certain: If the mask freezes over and cannot

come off, the individual beneath will sooner or later just smother and waste away, and invariably experience deep psychic misery. For individuals well adjusted to their various environments and comfortable with who they really are, the persona will act solely as a practical instrument facilitating communication that is spontaneous, smooth and natural.

Sensitive souls and those ashamed of their individuality find it convenient to hide their real nature behind the camouflage of a contrived persona. Self-appreciation and a mature audacity are needed by those who are more unique and less ordinary than others. Both qualities may be cultivated with the moral support of loving parents or friends, whereby all fear of being different can become dissipated. A compassionate relationship with a therapist can provide the same moral support.

There are indeed many physical and psychological factors that condition and impinge upon individual and collective persona expectations. If I am only five feet tall and live in a society where the average height is six feet and over, I will appear limited to the outer world. Trying to act like a tall basketball player would not fool anybody, and compensating with an arrogant haughty persona will not make me endearing, facilitate communication or foster positive relationships. I simply have to "bite the bullet" regarding certain limiting inborn characteristics, and develop other qualities of personality that will make up for my physical shortcomings. Kindness, considerateness, good humor and charm make for an exceptional personality. Grandeur of soul is just as impressive as tallness of physical stature and can be disarming to those who meet the standards for height but who fall short in basic spiritual qualities.

As for inner psychological conditions affecting persona, the classical example in extraverted America is that of the extreme introvert who somehow must "fit in" at all costs. As a rule the extreme introvert overcompensates and puts on a social mask of an offensive type of extraversion, that of a stereotypical enthusiast or loudmouth who is annoying and irritating to all concerned. We must realize that if one is an introvert, there are subtler and better ways to communicate with an exaggeratedly extraverted environment. Say it with flowers! Say it with a soft smile. Be friendly in a quiet way with kind attentiveness to the needs of others. An introverted, alert presence can be quite eloquent, probably making you more mysterious, intriguing and refreshing for the person relating with you. Dare to be yourself—slightly different but not offensively so. It can be very alluring. Remember that opposites attract as well as repel.

Chapter 4

Realm of the Complexes

Freud called the "subconscious" an epiphenomenon of the ego, which is an academic way of saying that the subconscious is produced and created by what the ego rejects. This is also a typically extraverted way of seeing things. For Freud the subconscious is created by forgotten memories and by material that is suppressed (consciously) and repressed (unconsciously).

Jung, observed that the "unconscious" contains not only forgotten memories and suppressed and repressed material of all kinds, but also material that we subliminally perceive and feel and a host of other entities. In addition, Jung believed that a newborn child enters the world with many inherited psychological factors, including the makeup of the unconscious and modern studies in genetics have made the same point.

Memory of our immediate and more remote evolutionary ancestors is biochemically transmitted from one generation to the next. In one study of this phenomenon, a worm is trained to do a feat, such as crawling around the top of a drinking glass. When the worm is cut in two, the head grows a new tail, the tail part grows a new head, and we now have two trained worms. DNA is taken from both and transferred into a third, untrained worm, which then surprisingly and suddenly knows how to perform the feat originally learned by the first worm.

Modern studies of adult identical twins separated at birth illustrate the point in human terms. Many books and documentaries record the startling similarities in the lives of twins during the years they lived apart, totally unaware that the other existed. As a composite example, at birth one might have been adopted by a family in New York and the other by a family in California. Possibly at age thirty-five they come to know that they have a twin, and they contact their other half. Catching up on what occurred in their childhood and adolescence, they discover that they both lived on an Orchard Street, at age five both fractured their left elbow in the month of August, at age ten both had a fox terrier named Poochy, at age eighteen both graduated high school with honors in French, and at age twenty both married a girl named Helen, who gave birth to a baby girl they named Celine!

Energy is never destroyed, according to modern physics; it just eternally changes form. It is difficult to fathom the metaphysical implications of this formidable concept. Jung reiterated throughout his career that to fully understand the human psyche we must constantly keep apace of the latest discoveries of contemporary physics. Our psyches are part and parcel of Nature, a truth people in Western societies especially tend to forget.

The Collective Unconscious

In the realm of the unconscious Jung observed various layers, each reaching farther and farther down away from a personal level into an area that is utterly impersonal. At these deepest transpersonal levels the various layers or zones are not easily differentiated and appear to blend with each other. In Figure 4.1, a diagram of a wave on the ocean illustrates this important point.

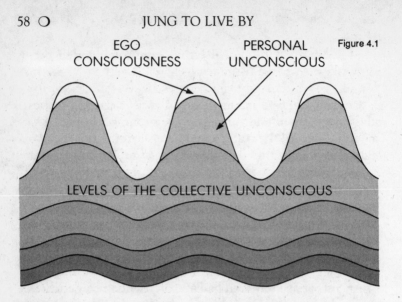

EGO CONSCIOUSNESS

PERSONAL UNCONSCIOUS

Figure 4.1

LEVELS OF THE COLLECTIVE UNCONSCIOUS

THE VERY LOWEST AREAS REPRESENT AREAS OF THE COLLEC-
TIVE UNCONSCIOUS THAT ARE NEVER MADE CONSCIOUS.

Most people are shocked to discover that they can share an
impersonal state of collective unconsciousness with all other
human beings. Extraverts in particular tend to revolt at the
idea. We more easily accept that a personal unconscious contains personal material specific to the ego and to our own life
history, such as forgotten memories, suppressed and repressed
contents, and subliminally perceived and felt material concerning our own intimate life. But stating that there is a
collective unconscious shared with billions of others can incite
accusations of mysticism or of insanity. I remember a young
student reacting loudly to this concept, saying, "This collective unconscious is just a theory of Jung's!" I asked her if she
had ever noticed anything utterly impersonal welling up from
deep down inside her, something of a mythic, fairy-tale-like
nature that had nothing whatever to do with her personal
historical existence. She conceded that her fantasies and
dreams did at times produce mythical, fairy-tale-like stories

and pictures that had no connection whatsoever to her personal life experiences. I rested my case.

These deeper layers of our unconscious communicate with
our ego-consciousness via mythical and poetic images, stories
and feelings that consist entirely of elements and characteristics of the human species, the voice of uninfluenced primal
Nature, filtering up to our human ego-awareness. They are
not part of an individual's personal development and history
but rather of the development and history of the human species
as a whole.

The deepest layers appear to be indifferent to egocentric
concerns and purposes and to operate in ways that are beyond
the ken of our egos. Jung called the collective unconscious
the objective psyche, and wrote that it had a purposiveness of
its own, intentionally warding off the occasional one-sidedness
of our egos and directing things toward the completeness and
wholeness of the psyche in general. This is a much more
positive view of the inner world than the gloomy Freudian
vision of a subconscious stuffed with psychic refuse.

Our ego-consciousness, when intensely and one-pointedly
introspective, experiences certain patterns that emerge from
these unknown depths of our being. We feel their effects very
strongly as *complexes* (a word coined by Jung) and *symptoms*,
as well as *symbols* and *images* that we experience in dreams,
fantasies and visions of all kinds.

"What has gotten into her?" "I'm just not myself today."
"He is beside himself." These cliché phrases, used and heard
day in and day out, mean something very specific.

Complex Psychology

Jung initially wished to call his own school of thought "complex psychology" before he named it "analytical psychology,"
demonstrating the importance he gave to this aspect of the
psyche. Jung himself defined complexes as "psychic entities

which are outside the control of the conscious mind. They have been split off from consciousness and lead a separate existence in the dark realm of the unconscious, being at all times ready to hinder or reinforce conscious functioning" (*A Psychological Theory of Types, Collected Works*, vol. 7, appendix, par. 923).

In popular Western culture, we know and speak about inferiority complexes, superiority complexes, the Napoleon complex and so on, but very few of us have clear ideas of the makeup and dynamics of these autonomous forces called complexes.

A complex is a very sensitive but highly manipulative force in the unconscious. In therapy, where complexes are dealt with viscerally and not intellectually, the analysand (the person on the journey of self-discovery) is usually asked simply to watch a complex as it arises from the depths, as it pushes the ego out of the way and assumes total control of the personality. With constant unbiased, nonjudgmental observation the complex is seen to consist of a core element that is highly charged with emotion and personal meaning. Highly autonomous in nature, it is surrounded by or linked to many associations of the same emotional tone and images pertaining to one's personal history. These feeling-toned images and associations cluster around a core element, usually an image of mother, father, money, self-worth, power or other powerful driving or motivating force.

This core element, a sort of encapsulated energy system, personal or collective, positive or negative, is sparked into action by specific externally or internally produced stimuli of all kinds, such as a word, a thought, a conversation or even a movie. When stirred and awakened into action, the complex will dominate the whole personality. When a complex is triggered (a single innocent word in a conversation may do it!), the ego descends into a passive seizure as the ascending complex brings up an unforeseen foreign personality or personality traits. It is akin to a possession. When we are in the grip of *archetype* *original pattern or model from which all things of the same kind are copied*

an unconscious force such as a complex, we are said to be in a state of identity with it. We become just as unconscious as it is, and being unconscious always causes chaos in our lives.

We all have complexes, or rather, complexes have all of us! Sometimes helpful, sometimes not so helpful, there are positive complexes and negative complexes, which simply indicate that something exists in the unconscious which is incompatible with ego-ideals, is unresolved or conflictual. Then again, complexes can represent a positive stimulus to greater creativity and achievement. They always denote something sensitive and unintegrated in the individual unconscious psyche. But Jung, in an important observation, noticed that without the complexes of our unconscious, psychic activity would come to a standstill. They create psychic life by the magnetic tension they produce among themselves and other aspects of the individual psyche.

We need to look more closely at the archetypal, mythic core of the unconscious to get a fuller understanding of these dynamic, vitalizing complexes. At their cores, complexes are archetypal. The word *archetype* comes from the Greek *arche*, meaning "primal," and *typos*, meaning "imprint, stamp, pattern." Complexes, typical eternally recurring human patterns of behavior, are the direct expressions of these archetypes hidden in the deepest strata of the unconscious.

Coping with the Complexes

What can we do to prevent a negative complex from causing us or others pain and grief? In theory, we have to deal effectively and sensitively with all the forces of our unconscious minds, a bit of advice more easily talked about than put into practice. Empathy for these aspects of ourselves is the hardest of attitudes to cultivate, but it is not impossible. We sorely need empathy for these sensitive, split-off parts of ourselves if we are to succeed in becoming free of their unruly control. Empathy comes easily when knowledge of psychological dy-

namics and circumspective wisdom are present, not to mention common sense, that rarest of commodities.

According to Jung, complexes are the royal road to the
unconscious, not dreams as Freud believed. Complexes are
ready to act twenty-four hours a day in both our waking and
sleep states. The very mention of such words as "mother,"
"father," "money," "love," "divorce" and "death" can trigger
a mass of memories, painful or otherwise, that have clustered
around the impersonal archetypal core of the complex. When
hit, the complex sparks off strong emotions and moods, and
generates autonomous patterned behaviors of all varieties.

Knowing that a complex exists and that we are in its grip
does not enable us to control it. The pain it evokes will
continue until we diffuse its impact by constant effort of will
or until the explosive psychic energy encapsulated in it is
transferred to a higher emotional understanding of the heart.
The most efficacious healing balm is active empathy for all
the sensitive spots within our psyche. We have to talk to our
hurts, as if they were real persons. They are real persons in a
strange sort of way since they have personalities all their own.
This dialogue is indispensable. No one can do it for us; we
must do it ourselves. It requires a bit of imagination and the
willingness to be "mad" for the duration of the dialogue.

Transformation can sometimes occur by simply outgrowing
the complex, by expanding one's consciousness into a more
mature, more encompassing one. As an example, our mother
or father stops getting under our skin when we finally mature
out of childish dependency on them into adult independence.
The passage of time, aging or just some intense learning experience or inner realization often brings this about.

In Alice in Wonderland, by Lewis Carroll, as Alice is being
chased by the wicked Queen's army of playing cards, at one
point Alice just stops in her tracks, turns around and shouts,
"You are nothing but a deck of cards." Her sudden realization
removes their power over her and they all fall flat.

A negative complex can similarly be resolved by development of inner "distancing" through such practices as meditation.* Higher consciousness always gives better perspective on things. Simply put, we can usually grow out of certain complexes, while others remain sore spots throughout our lives. When the latter is the case, we need to exercise constant healing empathy via soothing dialogue, which is something different from destructive self-pity or feeling sorry for ourselves. As long as the complex is in the depths, it remains impervious to willpower or the coercive influence of consciousness; it can even attract more current memories of mishaps to cluster around it, providing it with more disruptive energy and strength.

A person who is unaware of his or her fear of heights has nothing to work on. In this case the fear "works" unnoticed on him or her. Fear of heights can only be dealt with once the ego recognizes and acknowledges it.

We modify, mute or even disempower our fear of heights or any other complex by engaging all four of the functions of Jungian typology. We come to terms with a complex through actual conversation with it. We have to see that the mythical, archetypal core can be separated from the personal memories clustered around it and can be "spoken" with as if with a hurt, oversensitive child. It's useful to consider the ancient Greek myth of Icarus, who wore wax wings, flew too high toward the sun, had his wings melted and fell to his death. Things always exist as pairs of opposites. The higher we fly, the farther we may fall. Otherwise put, the higher and more unrealistic our idealism, the more readily we may plummet back down to hard, concrete reality. One thing produces the other. We must begin dealing with life's issues symbolically and with more penetrating insight and wisdom.

* See *How to Meditate*, by Lawrence LeShan, Bantam Books, 1974, or the cassette format by St. Martin's Press, New York, 1987.

One important therapeutic activity is to use our imagination to give the complex a persona and to talk with it (with our extreme idealism, for instance) in an empathetic way. Jung first introduced this approach into the world of psychotherapy, calling it active imagination.

When we interact with a complex as we would with another person, a redistribution of psychic energy occurs within the individual psyche. Fears, apprehensions and touchiness become diffused through the simple process of talking it out. Chapter 12 contains more details on this very practical technique.

We must talk sympathetically and caringly with our inner Wicked Witch of the West, our inner Mr. Scrooge, as they too are in need of love and can be softened and transformed by constant exposure to the most powerful force in human existence, namely unconditional love and acceptance.

Charles Dickens's *A Christmas Carol* is the perfect example of the transformation of a miserly, egocentric complex, all accomplished on an inner visionary level, through Ebenezer Scrooge's forced encounters with himself. Mr. Scrooge, whether he liked it or not, was engaged in a no-holds-barred kindly dialogue with the spirits of Christmas Past, Present and Future. The spirits, aspects of his own psyche, *cared* about him enough to contact him. ("Care" comes from Latin *caritas*, connoting "charity" or "love".) The new ways of looking at life that these unconscious spirit forces gave his ego are what thinking, feeling, sensation and intuition can do for our complexes as well. They enable us to perceive and evaluate things from different, more advantageous angles.

Complexes are blind, unconscious forces or subpersonalities, and they need to be educated to a higher, broader way of seeing things, such as the Spirits of Christmas Past, Present and Future accomplished with Scrooge. He could not help but change after being exposed to their genuine concern and what they had to show him.

If ignorance is the source of all suffering, then learning and education on all levels, not just intellectual, are the essential therapeutic remedies we need.

Scrooge's psychic energies were focused on money as a substitute for love. In his youth, his fiancée had left him because of his growing greed and addiction to the power that money symbolized for him. The therapeutic activities of the three Christmas spirits exposed him to a higher perspective on his life, graphically demonstrating how miserable his miserliness and greed had made him. The encapsulated complex-energy was then subsequently able to flow away from money (symbolically the ultimately unsatisfying, false security of power) and instead flow toward caring relationships with those around him, in a decisive shift from logos (power) to eros (relatedness to others). Fundamentally, he came to see how pitifully vulnerable, insecure and lonely he was by nature, and how his complex of greed and power was symptomatic of this basically useless condition.

The power of money merely compensated for a devouring feeling of powerlessness. His fiancée had left him because she realized he was more in love with money (power) than he was with her. We symbolically seek outside of ourselves qualities that we feel we are lacking within. Searching for inner realities in the outer world, however, simply does not make sense.

People with a poor self-image and feelings of worthlessness mistakenly believe that having something of worth will empower them to be something of worth. Being and having are, of course, two entirely different things. Scrooge most likely did not think very much of himself, nor did he see himself as lovable or worthy of his fiancée's love. We allow ourselves to be loved only when we feel we are lovable. When we feel unlovable, we unwittingly alienate people who wish to show us love, as Scrooge did with his fiancée. He eventually learned empathy for his distraught, powerless vulnerable self. He outgrew his lack of self-worth and insecurities, thanks to the spirits, all of whom allowed him to love himself a bit more. As a consequence of his own inner growth he also began to experience empathy for others who needed love as badly as he did. We can only begin truly loving others once we have learned to love ourselves, warts and all!

The task is to talk with our unredeemed personality traits perseveringly over long periods of time in the same sympathetic way that the three spirits did with Scrooge. It may take years, but it can be done. We had best not do it in public, however, for obvious reasons!

There are dozens upon dozens of complexes, both positive and negative, that can be enumerated in their colloquial American nomenclature: the pioneer, the boy scout, the goody-goody, the bull in the china shop, the martyr, the creep, the savior, the do-gooder, Peter Pan, the incorrigible optimist, the Casanova, the tightwad, the star, the lover, the vamp, the Sherman tank and the space cadet, among others. These powerful archetypal figures compel us to act out unwanted, unmanageable, highly patterned and stylized actions and compulsive behaviors. Clinically they could all be classified as compulsion neuroses, depending on their intensity. They become a neurosis when we no longer have any choice in the matter and find that we have stopped being able to choose but rather must act out these autonomous "characters," no matter what.

Some we hate and some we love. Contradictions, ambivalence and inconsistency seem to be who we are until we consciously understand the nature of our own complexes and, with resolve, determination, caring and educated know-how integrate them as much as possible.

A rule of thumb of depth psychology says that whatever is in our unconscious (unknown to our ego) is initially experienced outside in projected form. We do not see the complex inside— we see it projected outside of ourselves in other people. However, when we do finally see it as coming from within ourselves, we can at least begin exercising some power over it, since we ultimately can change only ourselves and hardly ever other people.

If we remain unaware of the complexes in the depths of our own unconscious, we will continually experience them outside in projected form as evil persons or spirits that persecute us from all sides. The clinical term used for this state of affairs is persecution mania, or paranoia. The threatening person or thing is merely an outer "hook" attracting projections, from the depths of our personal unconscious. This happens unwittingly, without the slightest awareness on the part of our egos. The exaggerated hostility that we often see in others is usually our own projected hostility. The same is true in the case of intense friendliness or admiration, if the complex is a positive one.

All of us, young or old, must overcome distorted perceptions or illusions that produce false beliefs or delusions. We do so by gathering and focusing our attention on hard psychological facts; this is the "reality cure" for many of our psychic ills.

The Ego Complex

Jung designated the ego as an *ego-complex*, as he saw the ego as a reflection of the many processes and contents making up ego-consciousness, held together by the gravitational force of their relation to consciousness.

"I do not speak simply *of the ego* but of an *ego-complex*, on the proven assumption that the ego, having a fluctuating composition, is changeable and therefore cannot be simply *the* ego" (*Spirit and Life, Collected Works*, vol. 8, par. 611).

The ego-complex must assimilate into its realm of awareness the repressed and unconscious contents of the hidden, troublesome complexes. Many times an experience called "a grace from the gods," as in the *Alice in Wonderland* story, or a particular shock, as with Scrooge and his spirits, is the only thing that can resolve a given complex. Our intellects or willpower can accomplish only so much. Generally a strong emotional experience is able to free us from possession by a complex. A strong affect or emotion, such as a complex is composed of, can be offset only by an affect or emotion that is stronger than it is. In Scrooge's case, a tallying overview of his life and the fear of impending death, among other things, frightened him into a change of heart in a sort of shock therapy.

We have heads but we rarely use them. Rather, we let them use us, which produces a great amount of uncalled-for suffering. Conversing caringly with the troublesome and bothersome cast of characters within us, making them look at things from different angles, is the secret to freedom. It is that simple and that difficult. The "healing spirits" are in all of us. We need only invoke their assistance for them to jump into action.

Since there are complexes of greater and lesser strengths, our dialogue and interaction will also have to be of greater or lesser intensity and doses. Other people affect us and we them in our daily lives; we are changed and so are they, simply by interacting. The same dynamic holds true among the various parts and split-off subpersonalities of which our psyches are composed.

A complex may be so strong and unconscious as to totally envelop the ego-complex, creating a state of blurring identification between the two. For instance, a person may have a positive father complex and literally become possessed by his or her father's thoughts, attitudes, aspirations, opinions and words. This is a pathetic state in which the psychic umbilical cord has not been cut. Our unconscious in the form of dreams will come to our assistance in such a dilemma, but we must learn to trust the healing power of dreaming. A dream may show our father as stupid and portray him in a negative light, as the unconscious attempts to depotentiate a blind positive complex. More on this healing mechanism will be elucidated in chapter 11.

Some persons identify with such archetypal figures as God or the devil, great world leaders or even animals. This is what clinicians call psychosis. In contrast, the less lethal positive or negative father complex is classified as one of the many forms of neurosis.

Neurosis—or, more graphically put, psychic crucifixion—is the product of unintegrated negative complexes. As described above, interacting through dialogue—what Jung called active imagination—is how we can hope to deal with an identified complex. The complex appears in fantasies and dreams as one of an endless array of characters and subpersonalities. In our imaginations we ought to relate feelingly and thinkingly with the figure representing our individual complex. We do with it what the spirits did with Scrooge; we talk with it and ask it to express what it feels and thinks. We point out to it its blind spots as we see them, offering it our point of view from the level of the three-dimensional world in which we live. After weeks, months or years we may disarm it in this way, often with results that lead us to more self-assuredness and more satisfying and compatible relationships with others, because we no longer project complexes onto them. The results may also offer more opportunities to do and to choose more freely in life. Or we may simply reach a reasonable compromise with our personified compulsions. Unfortunately, the outcomes are not guaranteed.

The more unconscious identification there is, the less is our ego able to assert itself against the flood of inner compulsions or against the onrush of outer reactions from others due to our projecting onto them. The undefined, undifferentiated ego-complex does not have the ability to distinguish between inner and outer, subject and object. Consequently, children, unconscious adults and neurotics are all prey to manipulations by individuals or groups. Projection of complexes onto others gives them power they in fact do not really have. Children, unconscious adults and neurotics are also victimized from within by various compulsions due to activated complexes.

Psychic maturity implies the ability to distinguish between the awarenesses of ego-consciousness and those stemming from our unconscious complexes. This is what "differentiation" means. Believing we are our father, another powerful figure or a Cinderella figure prevents us from adapting adequately to inner and outer reality, from making sound decisions and from having meaningful relationships—the things we humans cherish most. Assuredly, the road to maturity is not easily traveled. When we escape identifying with our complexes, we not only develop a discriminating and stronger, more well-defined ego, but we also tend to participate in the creation of a more conscious, more finely focused collective culture at large. Everyone benefits from our personal individual growth in consciousness. Since a healthy, discerning and sturdy ego-complex can fend for itself in onslaughts from inner complexes or outer events, this state of affairs makes for better relations with all concerned.

Seeing the Opposites in Complexes

Most neurotics show strong attachments to complexes despite the severe suffering created by them, though they may pretend to want to get rid of them at all costs. The real dilemma neurotics face is their fear of conflict, of a head-on confrontation with their complexes. Dealing with our complexes requires boldness, tenacity, a certain pluckiness and the willingness to suffer the uncertain consequences of such a confrontation. Dropping one's infantilisms and puerile obsessions implies a sort of psychic death, something that all of us instinctively flee. Peter Pan, the eternal youth in us, has to die if we are going to mature psychologically.

Ironically, an inferiority complex is generally a superiority complex turned inside out. We feel inferior; therefore we see people being superior all around us. If we believe others to be superior to us, how else can we feel but inferior? Conversely, a superiority complex for the most part camouflages and compensates for acute feelings of inferiority; subsequently we see ourselves surrounded by inferior people wherever we go. If everyone else is inferior, how can we not feel superior? In point of fact, in attending to either type of complex, it pays to remember a simple psychological truism, that no one is generally better or worse than anyone else, as we all have good characteristics and bad, which differ only in category and in intensity from those of other persons. Learning this basic truth about human nature can spare us being controlled by inferiority or superiority complexes.

When a complex surfaces, so do the conflictual opposites that compose it. For instance, we always see juxtaposed independence vs. dependency, worthiness vs. unworthiness, competence vs. incompetence, superiority vs. inferiority, assertiveness vs. passivity, graciousness vs. envy, self-confidence vs. insecurity. We usually discover that one of the polar opposites had been repressed and now resurfaces tormentingly. When the complex was still in a repressed state, we did not feel as if stretched out on a cross of conflicted opposites. We did not yet suffer the actual conflict but rather a host of substitute pseudoproblems and symptoms. We were even capable of repressing the real polar conflict into our bodies. We keep forgetting that our minds and bodies, psyche and soma, are two aspects of the same reality.

The most typical sort of complex is one of a moral order, namely an inability to express or a fear of expressing the totality of the various aspects of our instinctual nature. Homophobia, an obvious example, is the inability, for one reason or another, to acknowledge and express our own repressed homoerotic impulses. By and large what we loathe and fear most in others is what we loathe and fear most, albeit unconsciously, in ourselves. In a homophobic complex, strong homoerotic feelings are repressed deep into the unconscious, allowing only the repugnance free access to act out in the outer world. If the homoerotic feelings were ever to be acknowledged by the ego, real, overwhelming conflictual suffering would ensue. Clinging to the complex is one way of avoiding psychic pain. It's a false sort of logic: Better to see the enemy outside than to see it inside. If one sees it inside, then one might feel compelled to confront and grapple with it, and that would take an enormous amount of moral strength, which might be lacking. In short, gay bashing is really a transparent attempt to keep the closet door tightly closed on one's own homoerotic complex. Ultimately this type of tactic to control one's complex does not work since putting one polar opposite against another simply energizes the opposite that is suppressed. It will in the end surface with a vengeance. It is best to allow both poles of a complex to enjoy the light of consciousness, where they can come to terms with each other. Simple forgiveness toward oneself and others is more often than not the necessary antidote to such a conflictual dilemma.

All of the above descriptions may lead one to think that Jung's observations concerning complexes tally with those of Freud. This is far from the truth.

The Complexes Make Us Who We Are

What distinguishes Jung is his discovery of the *collective* unconscious as opposed to the *personal* unconscious. The collective unconscious was seen by him as the deposit of the archetypal patterning forces of human behavior and experience. He saw them as inherited, biochemically transmitted characteristics and predispositions of patterned psychic functioning. Connected with this collective stratum and its powerful agents, a much broader meaning and more important function may be attributable to complexes. For Jung, complexes are dynamic points of psychic life that make human beings who they are. If we did not have these dynamic nodal points within us, psychic life would come to a fatal standstill.

Contrary to Freud's views, Jung believed psychic pain caused by complexes offers no evidence of any pathological disturbance, principally because no human creature lacks complexes! As Jung wrote: "Suffering is not an illness; it is the normal counterpole to happiness. *A complex becomes pathologi-*

cal only when we think we do not have it" [emphasis added] ("The Practice of Psychotherapy," *Collected Works,* vol. 16, par. 179). Jung's view will come as liberating good news in overwhelmingly Freudianized Western nations. Freud's contention that complexes represent illness and pathology is, in contrast to Jung's, cynical and pessimistic as well as shortsighted.

Jung viewed complexes as part and parcel of the human condition, of the psychically healthy as well as the ill. For Jung a troublesome complex "only means that something incompatible, unassimilated, and conflicting exists—perhaps as an obstacle, *but also as a stimulus to greater effort,* and so, perhaps, as *an opening to new possibilities of achievement"* [emphasis added] ("A Psychological Theory of Types," in *Modern Man in Search of a Soul,* p. 79). For Jung, complexes are a challenge to greater evolution.

In the old, outworn Freudian view, complexes are repressions from childhood. Jung's observations are broader, more nuanced and astute. In his therapeutic work, he observed many complexes resulting from repression, but he also noticed that there were others that never were in consciousness in the first place.

Jung observed that if a complex displays mythical or universally human characteristics, we may conclude that it has arisen from the collective unconscious; if personal and individually acquired characteristics are expressed by a complex, we may safely say that it is a product of the personal unconscious.

Mythical complexes appear to emerge out of the deepest layers of the unconscious, what Jung called the collective unconscious. He stated the following: "While the contents of the personal unconscious are felt as belonging to one's own psyche, the contents of the collective unconscious seem alien, as if they came from outside. The reintegration of a personal complex has the effect of release and often of healing, whereas the invasion of a complex from the collective unconscious is a very disagreeable and even dangerous phenomenon" ("The

Psychological Foundations of Belief in Spirits," *Collected Works*, vol. 8, par. 591).

According to Jung, whatever their origin, complexes belong organically to the very nature and structure of the human psyche, and they are not to be automatically considered as pathological elements. All in all, elements surfacing from the collective unconscious are not considered pathological. Pathology results from an individual's unconscious conflictual reactions concerning archetypal issues that emerge from the collective unconscious.

When a person interrelates with a particular complex through dialogue with it, the clusters of repressed personal historical associations eventually will fall away, laying bare the timeless, impersonal archetypal core. The individual can then see the core of the conflict as a perennial human problem and not solely as a personal problem. They say misery loves company. This is because we actually get more perspective on our own issues when we can observe the very same problems outside of ourselves in others.

One of the reasons that Alcoholics Anonymous groups work so well is that in the company of other alcoholics one can get more distance and perspective on one's own affliction by the mechanism and dynamic of impersonalizing (to be distinguished from depersonalizing) observation of others who are in the same boat. Alcoholism is then seen as a human problem, as a disease, and not only as my problem.

Philosophy is the Ultimate Medicine

A poignant story from Buddhist legend tells about the tragedy of a young and pretty Indian woman named Kisha-Gotami illustrating that no one can help us except ourselves. As a young girl she always dreamed about being married, having children and engaging in a happy household and family life. She lived in a society in which marriages are arranged by the parents, but she was more than satisfied when her parents chose a young man that she herself would have picked. They were happy with each other from their first moments together, but a year after their wedding tragedy struck. Her husband died in an accident and Kisha-Gotami tried desperately to console herself by focusing all of her energies on her new baby, who looked exactly like her husband.

One fatal morning soon after her husband's demise, the young widow woke up to find her baby lying lifeless beside her. Her grief was infinite, and she went mad. She walked holding her dead baby through the highways and byways of her village, holding her dead baby, unwilling to release the decaying corpse for a proper funeral. Though countless friends and neighbors tried to convince her to hand over the dead child, she would not relent. When some tried snatching the dead child from her arms, she ran away and began raving if anyone approached her.

An old woman told Kisha-Gotami that a very wise and powerful holy man was camped on a nearby mountain, and that it was rumored that he performed miracles of all kinds and even brought the dead back to life.

Kisha-Gotami ran at full speed up the mountain to see the Buddha sitting serenely in the shade of a banyan tree, instructing some of his disciples. She implored him on her knees to bring her baby back to life by use of his miraculous powers.

He told her empathetically that he would surely help her, but she must first accomplish a simple task. She must go back down to the village and beg for a few grains of mustard seeds and bring them back up to him on the mountain. These grains must come, however, from a house where no one had ever died.

She rushed away, still clutching her baby and at the first house she saw she begged for some mustard seeds. These were readily given to her, as mustard seeds were a common household item. As she was departing she remembered to ask if anyone had ever died in that house, and the woman answered that only last week, her old father-in-law had died in the very premises. Kisha sadly gave back the seeds and went on to the next house, only to find that there too a death had recently taken place. And from house to house she went throughout the entire village, and the neighboring village as well, disappointed at every turn, as she discovered that Death had stalked every door.

She climbed back up the mountain without any mustard seeds and knelt before the Buddha, placing the dead baby at his feet. She said but two words, "I understand," and wept. The scriptures go on to tell how she became a dedicated disciple of the sacred teachings that free one from suffering and how she even attained nirvana at the end of her days.

When we understand that philosophy (love of wisdom arrived at through personal effort and experience) is the ultimate medicine for all our psychological ills, we shall free ourselves from the bonds of sorrow. What is needed is philosophy in the sense of a lived, visceral experience like that of Kisha-Gotami. The incredible dilemma in our own Western extraverted culture is that there is a negative reaction to anything philosophical since we are so addicted to immediate high-tech fixes of all kinds that cost only the price of an audio cassette or a weekend workshop, guaranteeing total liberation or your money back. We are so frightened of facing life's issues square in the face, of patiently and caringly working through our psychic wounds instead of around them. "Denial," as they say, "is not a river in Egypt!"

Courage and bravery were well-prized virtues among Native American cultures, but none of their inner moral strength seems to have carried over into ours. It is pitiful to see courage and bravery invalidated in the context of pop psychology that urges us not to repress any feelings, especially the negative ones, to "let it all hang out," to whimper and whine and complain like small children. They urge and cater to expressions of weak-minded feelings over those positive states of being that can be cultivated to stop our feeling so sorry for ourselves. *

Whatever happened to the concepts of heroism, valor, fearlessness and virtue (*virtus*, in Latin, means "spiritual strength")? These attributes in no way suppress or repress negative feelings. If we spend more time cultivating such positive attributes as stoutheartedness and simple nerve, negative ones simply will not have the opportunity to manifest themselves. Virtue, it is said, is its own reward. Virtues are therefore a form of preventive medicine. Pretending we have them is not very efficacious, however.

Negativities can be transmuted by cultivating positive qualities. This takes time to accomplish. If there is darkness in a room, all we need to do is switch on a light. We might need help, from a counselor, spiritual leader or friend; even an ordinary task like driving a car requires a few lessons.

In the story above, the Buddha as a friend and facilitator headed Kisha-Gotami in the right direction, and she was able to move from her painful intimate loss to loss as a general human issue. He helped her successfully move from a particular to the general. This is the way of wisdom. This gave her distancing. Wisdom is what makes us rise above life's miseries, not unrealistically but rather in the same timely existential way that Kisha-Gotami did. She confronted the main challenge of her life as she went from door to door. Little by little wisdom awakened in her like the morning sun.

True release from suffering is never effected by harping ad infinitum on the personally toned material of a painful complex. Freedom comes when, bearing our scars, we are able to rise above the personal to the level of the transpersonal, to the level of the timeless archetypal core.

To more fully understand this profound subject of com-

---

* See *Time*, August 12, 1991, "Crybabies: Eternal Victims. What's Happening to the American Character?" pp. 6–18, reported by Ann Blackman, Tom Curry and Edwin M. Reingold.

plexes, we must plumb in depth the world of the archetypes. Only then will we be able to see complexes in a fuller scope as life-renewing and life-promoting in their capacity to bring unconscious forces and their energies to strengthen and enliven everyday waking consciousness.

Chapter 5

The Powers That Be

The contents of the personal unconscious are mainly the affect-laden and feeling-toned complexes described in chapter 4. The material of the collective unconscious are called *archetypes* (pronounced "arka-types"). To fully understand what a complex is, we must understand the nature and dimension of the archetypes, those eternally influential and dynamic patterns happening always and everywhere in typical human ways of being and typical acts of human behavior.

Strictly speaking, we human beings never really experience archetypes per se, since they are located in the inaccessible reaches of the collective unconscious. What we do experience are *archetypal images* in our personal unconscious that are emanations of the archetypes deeper down in the collective strata. The archetype itself, an invisible nodal point, does not belong to the psychological but rather to a psychoid realm of consciousness, bordering on the metaphysical dimensions of our being.

Jung used the term "archetypal" to describe all psychological realities of a biological, psycho-biological or image producing character that are typical, stereotypical and universal. The ability of a newborn child to suckle is archetypal, as are smiling, frowning, crying, all those recurring qualities, behaviors and gestures that make us human. Some one-sided extraverted psychologies say that these qualities are programmed from outside, since they believe the human psyche is a "clean slate" at birth. Jung claimed that there is an archetypal genetic potential in the child without which no "programming" could ever take place. Innate in geese and ducks, as in most animals, is the archetypal urge to relate to a mother figure. When the natural mother is removed, humans working with the birds for all practical purposes become the "mothers" of the chicks. This "urge" to need a mother is an example of what Jung called an archetype.

The rituals of social interactions, mating games, ways of perceiving and evaluating what we perceive, attitudes, ideas, cultural assumptions—all are archetypal since they are typical and eternally repeated behaviors among human beings. Archetypes allow birds to fly north in summer and south in winter, and to know exactly what to do during mating season; they do not need how-to manuals, thanks to inherited, built-in archetypal instincts.

The concept of the collective unconscious and its dynamics irritates some people tremendously, probably because the idea of a collective unconscious seems to diminish the possibility of being unique and supremely free. Nothing could be further from the truth. Truth is always paradoxical. Everything about us is as unique as our thumbprint and DNA, but, then again, we are all just human as well. As with all paradoxes, this one is hard to swallow. If we look around a room at the light bulbs and lamps, we can easily deduce that the light energy or electricity is the same in each one. This image provides some understanding of the nature of the collective unconscious. Each of us is a distinct, separate, unique "bulb" of a certain wattage and trademark, but the animating principle in each of us is the same "electrical energy." This concept may strike a severe blow to our egocentricity, but if we look within deeply and intensely enough, we will see that it is true. We are equally personal and impersonal at the same time. We can become truly personal only when we begin differentiating and sifting away the personal from the impersonal elements within ourselves. One way we do this is by coming to terms with the world of archetypes, those blind patterns or that instinctual behavior that silently rules over us most of our lives from within the hidden depths. They make us operate "on automatic" in an impersonal way until we bring individual personal consciousness into play and shine it upon them. We must cooperate and work along with these archetypes in a spontaneous but conscious way, and not in a halting, self-conscious way. This takes much practice, however.

We can perhaps understand our individuality more clearly if we understand the word's derivation. "Individuality" comes from the Latin *individuus*, meaning "undivided" or "whole," "something not fragmented." We claim our individuality by becoming whole, by owning up to all the parts that compose us, and by consciously helping in their harmonious orchestration.

As our bodies have parts, so do our psyches. The more superficial parts of our psyches are personal, but the deepest strata of the unconscious are distinctly not so personal at all. Paradoxically, this deepest area is where we get the humanness we share with all other human beings. We become individuals—"undivided beings," "unfragmented beings"—by incorporating all those psychic parts of ourselves, whether only semiconscious or totally unconscious, into a conscious whole. We may be surprised to learn that we also are that deepest stratum called the collective unconscious, which is truly very impersonal in nature, though "other-worldly" might perhaps be a better term.

We are all really like portable radios picking up a transmitted broadcast from the archetypes deep down, according to the capacity of the particular type or brand of radio that we are. Some are shortwave radios, some are AM and some FM. The archetypal "broadcast" becomes individualized by the type of radio it sounds through. Personalization manifests only on the surface of collective consciousness; below a certain depth all appears essentially as impersonal. To use another image, the waves on the sea are personal, while the sea itself is collective and impersonal.

Projections of the Unconscious

Let us take a closer look at those patterns of human life that emanate from the collective unconscious. It is a general rule in depth psychology that whatever the contents of our unconscious, personal or collective, we initially experience and first view them outside of ourselves in projected form. This phenomenon of projection is how we first encounter factors that are in reality more inside ourselves than outside. In fact, most of what we observe in others and in the world around us are really projections of unconscious contents onto our outer environment, like a film shot from a projector onto a screen. Projections occur without our even being aware that they are happening. They color and falsify what is objectively outside of our heads with material that is our own personal property. Literally everything in the depths of our unconscious psyches is seen outside of ourselves in projected form until we finally become aware of the subtle mechanism of projection and realize that much of what we think we are seeing in others is mainly deep within our own unconscious minds. This concept is immensely important because it will spare us much unnecessary misunderstanding and hardship in our relations with others. It will help us avoid distorted perceptions created by unconscious overlaying of projected qualities onto the people in our lives. What we project on other people can be positive or negative.

Six thousand years ago, according to Jung, the clear desert sky over ancient Mesopotamia between the Tigris and Euphrates rivers served as the first Rorschach test. This test consists of a series of twelve ink-blot "pictures," if they can be called that, invented by a Swiss doctor named Rorschach. They allow the administering psychologist to peer into the unconscious of his patient. Whatever the patient sees in the haphazard configurations and blots of color or black and white is really inside his or her unconscious mind. Objectively, blots of haphazard configurations appear on a white background. Subjectively, however, a variety of projected forms, shapes and even persons with specific characteristics are seen in the blots of ink.

So, six thousand years ago in Mesopotamia people began seeing things in the night sky. One person saw a ram, another saw a bull, a third saw a set of twins, a fourth espied a crab, a fifth noticed a lion, and a sixth person spotted a young virgin up in the sky—and most probably none of them had been drinking anything stronger than mint tea! They went home and told their friends, who began seeing things themselves: a weighing scale, a scorpion, a centaur, a mountain goat with the tail of a fish, a man pouring water from a jug, and a pair of fish swimming in opposite directions.

After a while, each person succeeded in making the others see what he or she had seen. To make matters more interesting, several suggested that they were sure that the gods and goddesses were intimately connected with the strange wheel of animals and humans seen high above in the clear desert sky.

In dealing with this subject, Jung was not discussing astrology but rather depth psychology and the phenomenon called projection. It is worth reiterating: Whatever is in the depths of the unconscious is initially experienced and seen outside in projected form. Projection happens automatically, unknown to the ego seeing the projected qualities. What is seen subjectively by one person as a snake on the ground may be seen objectively as a rope by another. The first person is projecting; the second one is not.

Soon the nightly visionaries of ancient Mesopotamia began attributing patterned qualities, attitudes, special functions and various aspects of human life to the zodiacal phenomena they saw in the heavens. They were convinced that some were fiery or intuitive, some earthy or sensate, some airy or thinking, and some watery or feeling. These ancients related how some of these celestial entities liked each other and complemented each other. Earth and water went best together, as did fire and air. Some of these deities caused strife and disharmony when they got together. Water put out fire, fire boiled water and so on.

What the ancients observed in the sky, according to Jung, were the contents of the collective unconscious, namely the archetypes, those "powers" that pattern and give meaning to human life on earth.

Gradually, besides the initial twelve figures, hundreds upon hundreds of archetypal images were seen and experienced in projected form upon the firmament in the likeness of gods and goddesses and shapes of every variety. Only the wise guessed that these many mythic gods and goddesses seen high above were really the components of the soul (psyche) of humankind here below.

Each culture has its gods, goddesses, demigods and "divine" beasts (for example, the American eagle, the Chinese dragon, the Plumed Serpent of Mexico and so on) whether projected upon the heavens or not. All of these archetypes take on the coloring and costumes of the individual culture but are basically the same universal archetypes, humankind's typical ways of perceiving and reacting to life's situations since primordial times.

Plato spoke about the World of Ideas, each ethereal Idea being a formative agent of an earthly entity. In Plato's World of Ideas "chairness" is what expresses itself in all the myriad types of three-dimensional chairs on earth. For Plato, the Ideas were luminous models of supreme perfection. In Jung's observation, the archetypes were bipolar, having positive and negative, light and dark sides to them.

Many people believe that it is not within the realm of psychology to discuss anything touching upon the metaphysical. According to these sectarian purists, postulating the existence of archetypes falls under this category. Such people are generally superficial extraverted sensates who wish to impose their typology on everyone else. Human psyches are metaphysical by their very nature, the proof of which is the proliferation of all the religions and philosophies that have been produced by human psyches throughout the ages. Everything the human psyche produces gives us precise information about it, including religious and philosophical ideas. Would we expect an anthropologist to go into the bush to live and study a lost tribe but not pay attention to that tribe's metaphysical ideas, simply because the anthropologist was personally an atheist and did not believe that such topics have any relevance? That would not be a very objective scientific approach, to say the least. The same holds true for the realm of depth psychology.

As a depth psychologist, Jung was interested, not in the postulated archetypes per se, which he left in the hands of metaphysicians, but in the archetypal images in the psyche that he assumed to be emanations of the invisible archetypes themselves. Psychic experience in all of its ramifications is what Jungian psychology is about.

In the history of psychology, Freud wished to squeeze everyone into his Oedipus myth theory wherein the child falls in love with the parent of the opposite sex and, out of jealousy, wishes to eliminate the parent of the same sex. Jung responded that this was Freud's own personal psychology, which he projected onto all of humanity. In Greco-Roman and other mythologies there are dozens of other archetypal myths describing child-parent relationships that have no connection whatsoever with the mythic pattern of Oedipus. Have these other myths no descriptive and diagnostic value? If so, why not? Freud also believed religion was a pathological illusion and, with typical disdain, he treated it as such. More than likely he was in revolt against his own past personal delusions of a religious nature.

Historically, the parting of the ways between psychology

and philosophy really only began in the early nineteenth century. Throughout human history, psychology was an integral
part of philosophy, which was the study of how to avoid mental
pitfalls in the acquisition of Wisdom, considered the healing
balm for all psychic wounds. Jung literally saw everything that
emanated from the psyche as worthy of serious study. He did
not believe that one ought to impose the yardstick of one's
own typology, petty personal interests or cultural and tribal
prejudices in evaluating the manifestations of psyche as they
appear around the world. For him even what is now commonly
called parapsychology is a natural part of psychology since
"extrasensory perception" is only another term for "well-devel-
oped intuition," one of the normal functions of typology. To
repeat, everything created by the human psyche tells us about
the nature, structure and dynamics of the psyche at large
and very simply about who we humans most truly are. As
multifaceted and multidimensional creatures, why should we
not investigate the full range of who we are?

With regard to the archetypes of the zodiac (with Greek
equivalents of the Roman name given in parentheses), we can
plainly state that Mars (Ares); Venus (Aphrodite); Mercury
(Hermes); the Moon Goddess Diana (Artemis); Apollo the
Sun; the four asteroid goddesses Minerva (Pallas Athena),
Vesta (Hestia), Ceres (Demeter) and Juno (Hera); Jupiter
(Zeus); Saturn (Kronos); Uranus (Ouranos); Neptune (Poseidon); Pluto (Hades)—the entire pantheon and untold others
are actively patterning our lives from deep down in the collective unconscious. We are not speaking of planetary bodies in
our solar system, but rather of those archetypal patterns of
human qualities and human ways of being that were unwittingly projected into the sky by our ancient forebears and seen
as gods and goddesses, as powers on high.

We experience some archetypes as more dominant than
others. Some individual psyches appear more lunar than solar,
more yin than yang, more receptive than active, more reflec-

tive of energy than energy-producing. Some are more contractive (Saturn) and others more expansive (Jupiter), some more aggressive (Mars) and some more congenial (Venus). The "gods" and "goddesses" in everyone represent harmonious and/or contradictory qualities that make human life what it paradoxically is and all that we may ever hope to become. The gods and goddesses are indeed images of what we too may ultimately become. The African who ritually dresses up as Yemaya, the Sea Goddess, is "play-acting," yet recognizes that he or she truly incarnates all the qualities of that particular goddess and is not separate from her. Does not St. Paul say: "I am crucified with Christ; nevertheless I live, yet not I, but Christ liveth in me" (Galatians 2:20).

The world of mythology, which is really the world of depth psychology, can be rather confusing to the neophyte, and for this reason I believe that systematized astral mythology is a good place to begin one's studies of primordial patterns. Alan Oken's *Complete Astrology* is an excellent book on the twelve archetypal zodiacal symbols and the deities connected with each. The student of Jungian archetypal psychology need only focus on the part that describes the psychological qualities and the mythological functions of the various deities, and the areas and events of human life symbolized by the twelve "houses" or areas of human activity. This advice to read Oken's book is not to be construed as a recommendation to go consulting tea-leaf readers and fortune-tellers or to begin following one's daily horoscope in the tabloids. I recommend it only as an easy means to become acquainted with those images of the psychological qualities that pattern human consciousness that were projected onto the night sky by our ancestors of antiquity.

After this initial acquaintance with the celestial archetypes, I recommend studying a serious book on the mythology of your particular ethnic group, since the archetypal images that appear in your psyche in dreams, fantasies and behaviors will be colored and personalized by your national and ethnic back-

ground. Mars in Africa may look quite different from Mars in
China, but he is nevertheless the god of strength and force
wherever he is encountered.

Many in the "new worlds," including North, Central and
South America, and Australia, have more than one ethnic
background and would do well to acquaint themselves with
the mythologies of their respective ancestors. We must not
forget that our ancestors live on genetically in us. This idea is
strangely distasteful to people who wish to erase all differences
among the races, because to them "different" means "superior"
or "inferior," when in fact all that "different" means is "different." Such people want to homogenize themselves into Cana-
dians, Americans, Brazilians, Argentines or Australians.
There is a fear of appearing foreign and different in certain
new cultures. Strangely, if one even suggests that the entire
history of one's ethnic group is just under the psychic surface,
certain second-generation immigrants feel more than uneasy,
yet they do not mind reducing all of their present behavior
and states of mind solely to childhood traumas and even events
of "past lives," ideas which have more of a psycho-cultural
impact in the modern world than most are willing to admit.

"Different" does not mean or in any way imply "inferior"
or "superior." In any case, once the archetypes of a particular
ethnic group are studied, they will be seen to be the same,
only in "different" guise, as all the archetypes existing in
other national groups. As the French say regarding males and
females: "Vive la différence!" which means "Thank God for
the difference in the sexes!" We may also say the same for the
archetypes and the way they manifest themselves in a unique
manner in each ethnic group. Differences just make life more
interesting, and not necessarily conflictual. They become conflictual only in conflicted minds.

If we become intimately acquainted with the mythological
figures of our own psyche, we can readily feel at home in most
of the countries of the world. Once educated about this deeper
level of psychic life, we learn to look past the outer trappings

of a foreign psyche and begin viewing its universal archetypal layers of patterns, which recur in the same way always and everywhere on the planet. Human beings are indeed human first and foremost, no matter what their background or place of geographical origin.

The deeper we journey into the unconscious, the more we will have to learn the language of archetypes or, more precisely, the language of archetypal imagery. A Chinese proverb says, "One picture is worth a hundred thousand words." Archetypal images are relatively limited in number, as they correspond to the typical and fundamental experiences of humans since primordial times. They appear relentlessly in all mythologies, fairy tales, religious traditions, "mysteries" and rites of passage, which are all descriptions of universal human experience.

Living the Archetypes

The psychological dilemma plaguing most of humanity is that *the archetypes live us instead of us living them.* Unless we become aware that there are such things as blind forces or archetypes in our unconscious, unless we become cognizant that we are in their grip, we will remain in a state of identity with these blind, unconscious, archetypal forces. If our egos are in the grip of an archetype, our behaviors are unconscious and thus become slaves of our archetypal impulses. This is not a favorable state of affairs because if we are unconscious— "on automatic"—we usually create all kinds of problems for ourselves and those around us. Being unconscious and being ignorant of this fact are what cause most of our human suffering. We have got to wake up to our deeper realities and dynamics if we are going to stop being menaces to ourselves and everyone else.

If we find ourselves dominated by a particular blind archetypal force, Mars, for instance, we can unwittingly be aggressive and pushy, despite our better judgment and good intentions. We may be very surprised to arrive home one evening after work and find a Dear John or Dear Jane letter from our mate, who has had quite enough and wants no more of us.

Since archetypes have a positive as well as a negative side, the way to control the negative side is to activate and accentuate the positive side. Mars, positively speaking, is strength and represents a pioneering and enterprising spirit ever forging ahead in the enjoyment of making new discoveries. By accentuating the positive, we do not eliminate the negative, as it always will be there, but we can manage to keep it under control. First we must make conscious those unconscious dominants. By acquainting ourselves with all the mythological stories connected with each deity, we can engage in a living dialogue with the "gods" and the "goddesses" that exist in all of us. Communicating with the personified forces within is how we come to terms with them, even though it is an exercise that takes some getting used to, as was discussed in the previous chapter on complexes.

The typical Western male has great difficulty integrating into his everyday understanding the idea that "goddesses" and the feminine qualities they represent can reside in his psyche. But men can truly be Venusian and women can truly be Martial. The Moon Goddess can dominate a man and Solar Apollo can dominate a woman. The gods and goddesses do not live in the same dimensions that our egos do, and it is up to our ego-consciousness to give these unconscious entities guidance and direction and to set up parameters for them in our three-dimensional world. To be sure, men will express Venus in a masculine way and women will do so in a feminine way, but romance is romance. If the impulse for romantic involvement remains an unknown entity, if Venus remains ignored and unacknowledged, then, like everything else in the unconscious, she might make us behave compulsively concerning relationships. And compulsions, as we know, always lead to pain and woe, generally sooner rather than later.

As Jung said, "Archetypes were, and still are, living psychic forces that demand to be taken seriously, and they have a strange way of making sure of their effect. Always they were the bringers of protection and salvation, and their violation has as its consequence the 'perils of the soul,' known to us from the psychology of primitives. Moreover, they are the unfailing causes of neurotic and even psychotic disorders, behaving exactly like neglected or maltreated physical organs or organic functional systems" (*The Psychology of the Child Archetype, Collected Works*, vol. 9, part 1, par. 266). The gods and goddesses of antiquity are not dead, despite what our ministers, priests, rabbis, mullahs and some psychologists want us to believe.

Archetypes (the deities) are not airy-fairy irrelevant concepts; they are the fundamental dynamics of the conscious mind, hidden in the psychic depths. They are not outdated philosophical categories from antiquity but the nodal points of psychic energy in every contemporary psyche, impelling us to actions and behaviors and ways of perceiving and evaluating the realities of everyday life in the here and now. These form-giving images also pattern all our emotions. And what can be more real than our fantasies and emotions? Jung believed archetypal propensities, the psychic aspect of our material brain, were inherited with the human brain structure.

Many of our beautiful relationships and many of our uglier ones are expressions of differences in archetypal dominance in the romantic parties concerned. Since they appear to be biologically grounded, they are inevitably at play within us all the time. Even common likes and dislikes can be said to be archetypal, in the same way as two biological species such as dogs and cats are natural enemies unless trained otherwise. Likes and dislikes can cause great harmony or great strife in all of our close relationships, as most of us already know. But if we understand that such things are archetypally based, we will become more lenient and resilient, and we will take our relationships more in stride.

All the patterns of human consciousness are wondrous revelations of the archetypes, or "deities." It is they who give meaning and definition to our lives in connection to our loved ones, our careers and the ways we are creative or re-creative. They fill our lives with affect and emotion. As movies move us and the muses amuse us, so do the archetypes create a never-ending interweaving and portrayal of psychic and mythic imagery in our depths. When Jung spoke of deities, he was not discussing ancient theology but was rather stating that the gods and goddesses of all the various world mythologies are none other than the blind, unconscious forces of the human unconscious psyche that impact on us nonstop every day of our lives, in every human encounter and activity.

The modern sense of meaninglessness is the product of an alienated, one-sided ego out of touch with these enlivening contents of the deepest strata of the collective unconscious, which are ever attempting to well up and break into consciousness to supply us with meaningful, relevant human experience.

When the ego remains caught up in superficial interests and in an infantile, naive way strives incorrigibly to find happiness only in outer persons, places, things or happenings upon which a lot has been projected, we are bound to be disappointed and ultimately feel a dreadful ache of meaninglessness. When we demythologize everything in life, as contemporary society has done, and try to fit all of reality into neat, rationalistic syllogisms and categories, we create a sterile, antiseptic, boxlike world for ourselves in which everything is "understood" and which consequently bores us to death. Persons who are stuck in their heads and who focus only on what is "understood" forget that they have hearts; they lose touch with those archetypal forces that provide deep emotional satisfaction. The deities truly make life enchanting and worth living. The problem is that one-sided, cerebral people do not appreciate the nonrational, which is basically what the archetypes are. Cerebral folk confuse the nonrational with the irrational, a neutral term with a negative term. Consequently they suppress and/or repress everything that is trying to reach ego-awareness from the archetypal realm. The nonrational and symbolic world of unconscious, mytho-poetic archetypes completely eludes them since these left-hemisphered "cerebrals" can perceive reality only in clear-cut, three-dimensional, extraverted, rationalistic terms. This mentality unfortunately has dominated our Western culture. However, those right-brained forces that their hyperrationalism has suppressed are beginning to fight back.

How Symbols Work

The mythic reality of our right hemispherical cortex speaks in what is to cerebral people the foreign, nonrational language of symbols. A symbol (from the Greek *symbolon:* "thrown together") expresses something nonrational and indescribable in ordinary speech and language, since ordinary speech and language can deal adequately only with three-dimensional realities. Our psyches have more dimensions than just three, and the deeper we travel, the more dimensions we encounter. Symbols are the sole language that can describe realities that are not of a three-dimensional nature. Our psyches are not only three-dimensional. They are multidimensional, and symbols are what best express these other, multidimensional parts of ourselves.

The picture of a centaur—half human, half horse—is how a particular Sagittarian-Jupiterian state of consciousness tries to express itself to the human ego. The symbol is a form of psychic energy with specific qualities. Symbols express intra-psychic processes through images. As images rising to consciousness from the depths, they impress their meaning on the ego-consciousness with a rush of psychic energy of a particular caliber and quality and form.

The one-sided rationalist unfortunately is cut off from the flow of natural instinctual life (another way of thinking of archetypal experience) springing from the depths and enlivening ego-consciousness with meaning. The truth is that we humans can face anything in life—including suffering and death—if it has meaning. To find meaning we must take account of and connect with those psychic images and symbols that surge up spontaneously from the archetypal realms via fantasies and dreams. To daydream is natural and healthy. Our daydreams energize us in more ways than one and tell us about our real needs, desires and aspirations, those things that make life worth living.

Each of us has his or her own myth to live by, and our myths can fill our lives with meaning, if we would just look within and avoid abortive rationalistic blinders. Even the silliest, seemingly insignificant fantasies ought to be remembered or written down. At first appearance, they will seem insignificant, but they eventually will provide the pieces to a much larger psychic puzzle. When all the pieces are put together, deeply meaningful pictures reveal themselves, the same archetypal pictures that gave meaning to our ancestors throughout all kinds of adversity and gave them the strength and know-how to make it through life's ups and downs.

Jung told the story of a schizophrenic patient who spoke to him one day in 1906 in a Zurich hospital. The patient said that if he looked up at the sun and moved his head from side to side, he would be able to see the sun's penis wagging to and fro, producing all the winds on our planet. Four years later Jung happened to read a newly discovered two-thousand-year-old Greek text describing a ritual and initiation into the worship of Mithras, the Sun-god of ancient Persia. According to the text, the initiate was to move his head from side to side to observe the sun's phallus producing the east and west winds on earth. The schizophrenic Jung had spoken with could not have consulted this newly unearthed ancient text before recounting his own version of its contents to Jung.

This odd story, as well as thousands of other observations, confirmed for Jung that archetypal motifs repeat themselves ad infinitum over many millennia within human psyches of diverse ethnic and geographical origin.

Our psychic problems are archetypally the same as those of our ancestors, and if our ancestors found solutions and meaning from within their own depths, the likelihood is that we will too, if we know where to look and how to tap those forces. The archetypes are ever the same; the "clothing" they wear changes with the times and culture they find themselves in.

Jung put it succinctly: "A psychoneurosis must be understood, ultimately, as the suffering of a soul which has not discovered its meaning. But all creativeness in the realm of the spirit as well as every psychic advance of man arises from the suffering of the soul, and the cause of the suffering is spiritual stagnation, or psychic sterility" (*Psychology and Religion, Collected Works*, vol. 11, par. 497).

In Jung's view, unhappiness or neurosis is our golden chance for breaking through to a higher, more meaningful consciousness. It is as if the suffering is intended to propel us ahead to new states of being.

The archetypal symbols are energy units and carriers of meaning capable of renewing our conscious lives. Connecting with them allows new impulses to enter from below; it is like finding a well in your backyard during a drought.

In modern colloquial language, the words "myth" and "mythic" have unfortunately acquired negative meanings. In ordinary popular language, a myth is something that is untrue. In Jungian language, however, and in that of Joseph Campbell and others, a myth is a psychological pattern of timeless validity, true always and everywhere in its archetypal nature.

The mythic core of our disturbing complexes, if understood, can be a source of personal meaningfulness in our lives. What was first seen as a down-grading liability can ultimately be viewed as a dynamic asset.

The deaths of Kisha-Gotami's husband and her child tormented her. The core archetype was Death, a reality operative always and everywhere in human experience. She emotionally transcended the personalized pain of loss by coincidentally encountering Death in every home that she visited asking for mustard seeds. Thanks to the Buddha, she was not subjected to therapeutic platitudes or forced into self-pity. She was allowed to see the universality of her dilemma through her personal efforts. This self-help raised her out of her tremendous feelings of victimization. She began seeing the impermanence of all beings, not just those near and dear to her. Philosophical wisdom released her from the morass of her obsessional torment. She was lead deftly and expertly by the Buddha, who respected her unique rhythm in crossing over into a completely new way of viewing things. In a way, she was benevolently tricked into it. The gentleness and simplicity of his compassionate ruse made it work. From then on her life headed in a new direction, departing from attachment to the impermanent joys of life and progressing toward those joys that were permanently imbedded in her soul, joys that no force in heaven or on earth could shake or take away. She must have kept her psychic scars, a reminder of her former, more vulnerable state of consciousness, but these very scars undoubtedly sensitized her to the suffering of others, a necessary step in the evolution of the soul. In hindsight they can be seen as reminders of necessary challenges in her psycho-spiritual journey. Somehow personal suffering seems to be a prerequisite for individual growth.

In lieu of an outer experience such as Kisha-Gotami's, most of us—not as fortunate as she in meeting such a superior guide—may have to rely on an encounter with an inner Wisdom principle to bring about what the New Testament terms a *metanoia*, a change of attitude, a change of heart.

Be the Light

A famous Zen Buddhist saying advises: "If you meet the Buddha on the road, kill him." The idea behind this piece of shocking advice is: It is useless to *see* the Light, since we have got to *be* the Light ourselves! We become the Light by connecting with it inside, not outside of ourselves. In this task analytical psychology can offer some assistance.

To let this Light shine forth, we must go within ourselves to the source of this Energy, to the realm of the "gods and goddesses." Those who have taken this journey report back to us that the quintessence of who we are is Light. "Light" can be understood in left-brain terminology as "the fullness of consciousness, the fullness of awareness."

When the Light we seek flashes up into consciousness, the joy-filled newness that it brings means death to our old way of being. In Christianity, the cross, an instrument of torture, was also a "plus," relaying the truth that death always and everywhere precedes rebirth, and as such ought to be considered "par for the course" of higher evolution. In most religious and cultural traditions of the earth, initiations into new stages of life—from infancy to adolescence, to adulthood, to old age, to life as a disembodied spirit—all are brought about by a ritual of death to what formerly was in order to spring ahead to something entirely new. The story of Jonah in the belly of the whale illustrates this same truth.

Truth, it has been said, is always revolutionary, turning everything—darkness, lies, denials, illusions (false perceptions), delusions (false beliefs)—topsy-turvy and upside down. Hence one has to brace oneself during the truth-finding process that plummets and thrusts us into wellness and greater consciousness.

Jung does not present an easy recipe for creating inner poise and balance, but neither do the multiple cultures of our planet. As with all things in Nature, the unexpected often crops up. Many times no inner help seems forthcoming, as in the case of psychosis, where there is no trace of an ego left, since it has been swallowed up by the archetypal realm. There are times when a Superman from the depths of our unconscious fails to come to our rescue, no matter how much we call out, no matter how many dreams and symbols and fantasies we copy into our diaries and try to understand and integrate into conscious awareness. Who can question the ways of the gods? Sometimes the answer to a prayer is simply a resounding "no."

At this point of impasse, the Jungian stance is to bear with the "tension of opposites." A cross is a tension of opposites. Many times, if one is nailed to a psychic cross, the only alternative left, after all else has been earnestly tried, is to hang there patiently. "Sleep on it" is what we hear in the vernacular. We can muster this resignation, requiring the greatest moral aplomb, if and only if some purpose can be attached to our personal suffering, if our personal suffering can be seen as being vested with some universal archetypal meaning, as happened with Kisha-Gotami.

A religious or philosophical attitude offers much genuine help in this regard. "Religion" is not a dirty word in Jungian vocabulary. The religions of the world are civilizing agents, among many other things. As everything else in Nature, all religions have their positive and negative sides; this is to be expected. In times of crisis, and as "preventive medicine," it is prudent and wise to tap them for their positive values, which are many.

The Latin word for religion is *religio*, which means "tying up, reconnecting, yoking up," much as the Sanskrit word *yoga* means "yoking up, reuniting." What religion or the various yogas help us do is to reconnect our egos to the many layers of our forgotten and neglected unconsciousness, to what is commonly called God-consciousness, to some deep extraordinary godly force of knowingness higher and broader than the ordinary one of our egos.

In one Native American culture, as depicted in the anthropologically accurate film *A Man Called Horse*, male Lakota Sioux engage in an excruciatingly painful sun-dance ritual, a sort of willful "crucifixion" of sorts, wherein two sharp hooks pierce the participants' breasts. These hooks are attached to ropes tied to a tall pole facing the sun. The initiates dance and pull on the ropes by backing off, at the same time blowing on eagle-bone whistles and staring at the sun imploringly. The tireless wisdom seekers continue for as long as it takes to arouse the divine mercy to grant them a vision necessary for the well-being of the tribe. These tribal people obviously view pain as necessary to attracting divine grace and mercy. Why does contemporary America flee from the slightest discomfort, especially in the search for inner balance and wholeness? What did Native Americans and our European ancestors know that we have lost sight of or no longer wish to know?

Countless acts of discipline are endured by shamans (medicine men or women) and other leaders in the world's religions, in their initiations into higher consciousness. We must ask ourselves why we have cast aside time-worn spiritual disciplines and always try to take the easy way out of our problems, a way that usually turns out to fall short of the intended mark and to get us into more calamity.

It is important to mention traditions outside the Judeo-Christian heritage in discussing initiatory suffering because many people wrongly believe it is only the Judeo-Christian traditions, or rather a distorted form of these traditions, that use suffering for the valuable ends it can produce.

In all genuine religious traditions, suffering is undesired but if used wisely can become an efficacious means to a specific, spiritually worthy end. As a liability that is consciously transmuted into an asset, suffering manifests as an abundance and proliferation of a higher consciousness, the acquisition of a transcendental viewpoint, the ability to see things and human affairs "as God sees them."

All initiatory rites, whether simple college fraternity hazing, marine boot camp or full-fledged African puberty rites of passage with bodily scarification and knocked-out teeth, represent a death to the neophyte's consciousness, death to the child and countless infantilisms, rebirth into adulthood and peer group participation.

Without ritualization of hardship and pain, no maturation seems to take place, a concept that the Doctor Spock generation does not fathom. If and when these eternal Spockian children come out of their parent-fostered egocentricities, they might become aware of the deeper parts of their beings. They might even eventually see that there was indeed a price to pay for having been denied the opportunity of psychic maturity. This situation was fostered by a philosophy of overpermissiveness and instant sense-gratification, which led them light-years away from much-needed ego-stability and simple peace of mind.

Suffering and pain are natural aspects of life, not necessarily signs of sickness. Ultimately we do not have problems; rather we have life, which encompasses the opposites of pleasure and pain, positive and negative. Only when we try to avoid suffering at all costs does our resilience and balance give way as we fall prey to complexes and neuroses. Weak egos, cowardice and ignorance lead us to a continuous state of unbearable frustration vis-à-vis life's normal ups and downs.

This is not to say that the world of the archetypes never grants us boons or moments of grace (grace derives from the Latin *gratis*, meaning "free," "with no price to be paid"). In fairy tales, the simpleton usually is the one who stumbles unwittingly upon the hard-to-attain treasure by a guiding act of divine grace. By simply trusting the powers of the unconscious, we too may open ourselves up to helpful and healing grace.

Out of nowhere at times we get flashes of intuition about life's challenges and how to respond to them. Or out of the blue, Lady Luck may come our way to resolve our conflicts and differences. Many proffer explanations for these auspicious occurrences, but no one can be certain about whence they originate. To say that everything is the result of karma (past actions) is to deny the freedom and power of the gods to grant unmerited boons.

The human psyche is still a mystery, and Jung found it no sin to simply say "I don't know" when confronted with an unsolvable or mysterious event in his life or in the lives of his patients.

The Major Archetypes

The following are the major "deities," the psychic drives in the unconscious, the archetypes patterning human consciousness and behaviors that we all must become acquainted with if we are to begin interacting with them to tap them for their positive worth.

All of these patterns and many more reside in every psyche. Some, however, predominate over others. If we pay close attention, we will see them appearing in modern dress in many of our dreams, fantasies and behaviors, not to mention on television or in films.

It must be restated that taking these ancient deities seriously in no way implies an implicit belief in the "religion" of astrology, nor does it have anything whatsoever to do with newspaper and magazine horoscope columns or other modern supersitions.

Astral deities and symbolism present us with mythological motifs in a simple, systematic and practical fashion. They are offered here because learning about the zodiacal gods and goddesses is less confusing than confronting volumes of mythology. The realm of mythology is a vast area of study and can take years to master, whereas the twelve zodiacal signs and deities attached thereto are easily remembered and offer us quicker and easier access to the mysteries of our unconscious drives and dynamics.

Consciousness is basically mytho-poetic. To understand this, we need only look at all the little poetical and mythical stories that are woven never-endingly by our daily and nightly thoughts. The list below is a left-brained endeavor to understand right-brained mythic activity. We ought to approach the enumerated archetypal qualities and tendencies with a

loose, free-associative, naive attitude since the domain of the
gods and goddesses is not as cut-and-dried as waking-consciousness tends to be. As with all archetypes, the "deities"
are bi-polar in nature, representing both positive and negative
energies. They are rarely seen acting alone. (The Roman
names are given first followed by the Greek versions in parentheses.)

1. Mars (Ares). The God of War, associated with fiery
Aries. His sister is Strife. His two sons are Fear and Terror,
and his two battle companions are Pallor and Fright. In a
positive vein he represents strength, self-assertiveness, stam-
ina, courage, élan, a pioneering spirit, protection and inspiration of all new projects and ideas. Negatively, he is the god of
war, untamed passion, unbridled energy, selfishness, bossiness
and aggression. He starts but never finishes, having very poor
impulse control. He pursues personal goals regardless of how
many toes he has to step on. Colloquially he is called the
Pioneer or, in a negative vein, the Sherman Tank.

2. Venus (Aphrodite). Associated with earthy Taurus. The
daughter of the Moon, Venus personifies conditional love,
aesthetics and harmonious bonding. She is a seeker of peace
at any price, and is a provider of food, clothes and home for
her loved ones. She represents luck, sociability and physical
attractiveness. She is the giver of life's gifts and pleasures, and
the inspiration of material and spiritual evolution. On the
down side, she can be ferociously jealous, flirtatious, promiscuous, vain, passive-aggressive, slovenly, clumsy, bashful, slow
to grasp intellectual matters and highly given over to the
senses and bodily appetites. Colloquially she is Earth Mother,
a vamp or, negatively, just plain bullheaded.

3. Mercury (Hermes). Associated with airy Gemini, he
is the son of Jupiter. The messenger of the gods, Mercury
represents the communication arts (writing and speaking),
learning, knowledge, wit, comedy, teaching, authorship, in-
ventiveness, talent and adaptability. But he can also be puerile, ungrounded, superficial, restless, inconsistent, nervous,

unfeeling, flighty and overly caught up in words. Colloquially
he is a Court Jester or, negatively, a Peter Pan who never
wants to grow up.

4. Diana (Artemis). The Moon. Associated with watery
Cancer, she is the lunar sister and daughter of the Sun. Diana
is a virginal mother and fertility goddess. She represents nurturance, ESP, personal magnetism, domesticity, instinc-
tiveness and unconsciousness. She is the goddess of magic and
menstruation, and is fond of children. However, she can be
oversensitive, fearful, extremely conservative, moody, highly
irritable, clingy, prone to lunacy and too attached. Colloquially she can be a fairy godmother or a bitch on wheels.

5. "Invincible Sun" (Apollo). Associated with fiery Leo.
Apollo symbolizes the light of consciousness, reason, nobility,
the self-radiance of divinity, vitality, courage, drama, spirituality, inspiration, generosity and intuition. He can also be
authoritarian, egocentric, proud, hyperactive and nervous,
theatrical, stifling and oppressive. He is a show-off and a
braggart. Colloquially he is a big brother or big sister type or,
more negatively, a benevolent dictator.

6. Vesta (Hestia) and Minerva (Pallas Athena) are co-rulers
of earthy Virgo, the sixth sign of the zodiac. Vesta is the virgin
daughter of Saturn (Kronos). She is goddess of the hearth,
where a sacred fire always burns to cook food and to worship
the deities. She has the reserved dignity of a nun, is dedicated
to duty, possesses modesty, humility, prudence and the virtues,
and lives for the service of others and humanity. However,
she can be petty, narrow-minded and addicted to perfection.
She seethes with anger at the imperfection of others, is concerned with boring details and is overly critical of herself and
others. Colloquially she is a Florence Nightingale or just a
plain old worrywart.

Athena is a virgin warrior goddess sprung from the head of
her father Jupiter (Zeus). She represents wisdom, is a super-
woman, a civilizing agent and bestower of the knowledge of
healing and health. She has a merciful nature and is a settler

of disputes and a teacher of weaving, embroidery, detailed domestic crafts and the science of numbers. Athena invented the ship, flute, clay pots, plough and chariot. Her symbol is the owl, a creature of the air who can observe hidden, night-cloaked secrets. She can be cold, distant, aloof, unfeminine and manipulative, rigid, unsympathetic and picayune. Colloquially she is a freedom seeker and, negatively, a fault finder.

7. Ceres (Demeter) and Juno (Hera) are co-rulers of Libra, the seventh sign of the zodiac. Ceres is an unmarried mother. She symbolizes cereal, grain, food production, nurturing and maternal love. She is mistress of reproductive magic and the harvest, and is concerned with raising and educating children, with caring and bonding. She can be castrating of men, a man-hater, doting too much on her children, unable to be a wife, infantilizing of others and co-dependent on offspring. Colloquially she is a classical "Gal Friday" and, negatively, a fussbudget or yes-man.

Juno is the oldest daughter of Saturn and Rhea, twin sister of Jupiter and his wife, and mother of Mars. She represents womanly stability, commitment, conjugal love, chastity and fruitfulness. She can be jealous, hostile and unforgiving of her promiscuous husband. She suffers from a martyr complex, is fault-finding and bickers. Colloquially she can be described as a Rock of Gibraltar or a classical whiner.

8. Pluto (Hades). Associated with watery Scorpio, the eighth sign of the zodiac. Pluto is the god of the dead, the underworld and transformation. He represents the power of renewal, psychic powers, willpower, healing and sexual magnetism, survival instinct, resurrection and the ability to unrepress contents of the unconscious. He can be very powerful and a great achiever. He can be paranoid, overly secretive, lacking in self-confidence, self-destructive, warlike, domineering, cynical, thieving and a murderer. He can have volcanic and irrational outbursts, and can be very compulsive. When he ascends to the upper world of Earth he is known

as Dionysus. Colloquially he is the classical loyal friend or, negatively, a leech or avenger.

9. Jupiter (Zeus). Associated with fiery Sagittarius, the ninth sign. Jupiter is friendly, kindly, a boon giver, a truth seeker, with many aspirations and a jovial nature. He can be exuberant, philosophical, religious, benevolent, healing, a preserver of justice and an incorrigible idealist. He can express rashness, obtrusive helpfulness, extravagance, incorrigible optimism and self-righteousness, and may be a spendthrift as well as hyperactive and nonintrospective. Colloquially he is the thrill seeker par excellence and, more negatively, a Crusader Rabbit type.

10. Saturn (Kronos). Associated with earthy Capricorn, the tenth sign. Saturn is Father Time, reliable, dutiful, serious, responsible, very structured and disciplined, a planner, sober, tenacious and realistic. He can be uncommunicative, solely goal- and career-oriented, very materialistic, anal-retentive, stingy, heartless, harsh, lonely, conventional, overly conservative, pessimistic, selfish and uncaring. Colloquially he is an overachiever, a miser, a devil's advocate or a closed door.

11. Uranus (Ouranos). Associated with airy Aquarius. He represents the vastness of the sky, independence, originality, freedom, scientific research and tolerance. Uranus displays an electric intelligence, friendliness, democratic spirit and individuation, and he has a keen interest in occultism. He can be very eccentric, explosive in behavior, unpredictable, lazy, annoyingly individualistic, anarchistic, a revolutionary, rebellious against authority, interested in shocking others, iconoclastic and impersonal. Colloquially he is the cosmic friend, although he can be a classical absentminded professor.

12. Neptune (Poseidon). Associated with watery Pisces. Neptune is the Lord of the sea, representing the collective unconscious and its symbol-making capacity, compassion, cosmic values, empathy and unconditional love. He is a dancer, a healer, a mystic, a daydreamer, self-deprecating and an es-

capist. He has an addictive personality, no ego boundaries and a vivid imagination. He has great acting ability, and can be deceptive of himself or others. He possesses great sensitivity and can be a hermit, have a martyr-complex, be into self-denial and hallucinations; he may be a movie addict and an inspiration to others, but also into self-undoing. Colloquially he is a chameleon and a goody-goody, and, negatively, a classic sneak and two-timer.

All of these are stereotypical categories of human qualities. In the human psyche and in human experience they are rarely seen in their pure states. They are generally seen in well-contaminated states, meaning that they are blended with other archetypal human characteristics. As listed categories printed in black and white, they are similar to primary colors, whereas in real life they appear only in nuanced shadings, some complementary and some disharmonious with others. In general the astral categories that precede and follow each other are in conflict. Mars (Aries) conflicts with Venus (Taurus), which conflicts with Mercury (Gemini), which conflicts with Diana the Moon (Cancer), which conflicts with Apollo the Sun (Leo), and so on.

Understanding the human psychic depths can be quite a complicated affair, as reflected in all of the mythologies of the world's cultures. Astral mythology is by far the easiest and least discouraging place to begin our studies on archetypes. We must absorb it very slowly, however, and meditate upon it both inwardly in our own psyche and outwardly in the psyches of others. No perusal of the astrology section of your newspaper's comics pages will do!

Chapter 6

All That We Are

Among all the archetypes that Jung observed there was one that seemed very special. The Self* is an intuited and experienced symbol of psychic totality encompassing both the personal and transpersonal spheres of consciousness. We experience it as a mysterious, paradoxical convergence of all seemingly irreconcilable opposites resolved into a cohesive whole. It is indeed as abstract as it sounds and just as difficult to grasp. Just as our own beings are composed of bodily parts, emotions, mind, soul and spirit, it is possible to see all these conjoined as a whole, though they are seemingly contradictory in their natures. The totality of the union of such disparities is an entity unto itself. In biology this totality has been termed "synergy." In other words, the whole of consciousness is seen to be greater than the sum of its parts; so it is with the Self. The Self, an intimation of our deepest incumbent wholeness, produces feelings of unspeakable satisfaction deep within us.

* The word "Self" and all its forms are capitalized throughout this book, to acknowledge and honor its specialness and sacredness (which is also our own sacredness), realities neglected and unaccented by contemporary materialistic cultures.

The Self: Psychic Center

Ego-consciousness can only intuit the presence of the Self, the union of the entirety of the two psychic systems—the conscious and unconscious. This intuited psychic center is above and beyond our ego-conscious personality, where it is observed as standing out in prominence, if one has eyes to see it. Discovering the Self creates in us a whole new awareness, an entirely new attitude toward Life. Experiencing this coalesced totality is not only the prerogative of well-informed, psychologically astute individuals. Many men and women throughout history have spontaneously come to the same intuitive realization, which has revealed to them that their true psychic center is way beyond the ego personality at a point in the psyche where every aspect of the psyche's dimensions and "frequencies" are able to coalesce. One should not try to come to terms with this supraconscious reality with one's intellect but rather with one's heart. For centuries "heart" has been a layperson's synonym for the deeper levels and broader areas of our consciousness that lie far beyond the limits of ego awareness.

The Self appears to be that out of which the sense of a personal "I" arises and to which it acts as a sort of satellite. The personal "I" is generally experienced as pertaining only to the outer person, to body sense and to the workings of the brain. The little personal "I" appears as a mere reflection of the "Big I" called the Self, which is composed of, encompasses and sums up the various levels of waking, dreaming and dreamless sleep. One can simply call it one's Higher Self, if that is more convenient.

When the Self makes its impressive presence felt, we cease being a captive of the petty, hypersensitive, personal sphere of the ego, and rather feel as though we have somehow acquired a freer, broader, more circumspective and more objective view of life.

The moment when we find this genuine center called the Self, or more precisely when it finds us, we begin distinguishing egotistical desires from genuine needs. We suddenly find ourselves transcending fears, false expectations and ambitions based on habitual delusional thinking. We somehow become more emotionally poised and begin feeling more "at home" and at ease in the entirety of our beings hitherto undivined and unexplored. These new experiences begin to open us up to others without the usual apprehensions and vulnerability that normally accompany intimacy and relatedness.

Jung's intuitive perception and description of the Self bypass the mental grasp of many people, and this is understandable. It is difficult imagining an entity hovering, as it were, between our conscious and our unconscious, composed of both but also transcending both. How to imagine a central point within ourselves that is equally our whole circumference and contains all the contradictory forces of our psyche? The idea boggles the mind, precisely because it is infinitely vaster than the tiny but useful three-dimensional tool called our everyday mind.

The Self can only be intuited and subliminally perceived with our sixth sense. Words fail abysmally to describe it. Be that as it may, it manifests in the psyche as an archetypal image that is bigger than Life itself. This mysterious entity has been endlessly discussed in every culture of the world in the accounts of our eternal quest for what we humans consider to be the most sacred experience in life, namely that of the Great Spirit, to use the Native American term for it.

When we encounter the Self, our ego feels as if it were being observed by something much greater, peering at us from the midpoint and periphery of all that we are. This alien feeling is also astonishingly very familiar, a sort of mysterious center of gravity impinging on the total psyche. The Self per se, like all other archetypes, is a philosophical postulate. Jung postulated its existence, however, because of concrete archetypal images and countless imponderable experiences that have constantly revealed its hidden archetypal presence in the deepest strata of our human collective unconscious from time immemorial.

Symbols for the Self

Images of the Self appear spontaneously in dreams and fanta-sies in the form of symbols of a paradoxical union of opposites. The simplest symbolic form of this is a squared circle, ⊕, called a *mandala* in the East. It is a symmetrical arrangement of four parts around an accentuated midpoint, much like a four-spoked wheel. Mandalic designs are everywhere. For in-stance, logos of many corporations are mandalic in form. The mandalic shape is a symbol of "wholeness." It represents an archetypal image of the Self as a reconciliation of all possible polarities. Mandalic shapes come in endless varieties. The following are a mere sampling of some typical abstract versions:

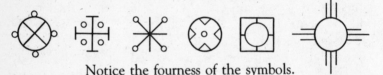

Notice the fourness of the symbols.

When the Self-symbol emerges in our dreams or fantasies, it reflects a transformation of opposites into a higher synthesis, which the uniting mandalic symbol expresses and impacts in a resonating way throughout our whole being, just as a shot of penicillin in an infected bloodstream brings soothing relief to the whole system. Seemingly irreconcilable conflictual ele-ments of the psyche unite and transcend their differences via the impact of the synthesizing mandala-type symbol or a host of other divine images.

Flowers, crosses, wheels, a god or goddess, a Holy City, sacred buildings, even classical marble fountains can all sym-bolize the Self. The examples are too many to enumerate. The important thing about these symbols is their power to restore order and harmony, which then permeate all the levels of our psyche. When these images of the Self emerge from the collective unconscious, filter through to the personal uncon-scious and impact on our ego-consciousness, a feeling of deep, profound peace ensues that is felt as a fortuitous gift and healing grace.

A distraught patient, abandoned by her husband, once reported a simple but mysterious mandalic dream image in which a Chinese elder stood on a green lawn with four trees, each planted singly in the four corners of the garden, equally distanced around him. She did not understand the image intellectually and certainly knew nothing about mandala symbolism, but when she awakened, she no longer felt she was "in pieces," as she had been since her marital breakup. A balanced fourness motif is often an integral part of the symbolism of the regulating and conciliating power of the Self. These mandalic figures not only seem to express order, but also appear to bring it about in the troubled psyche that is being imprinted with the transformative power of their imagery and resonating presence. Many cultures use similar images ritually for purposes of healing, for example, Navaho sand painting, Tibetan mandalas, Australian aboriginal art and so on.

The mandala shape is not the only living, dynamic transfiguring symbol of the Self. Cultural heroes can also serve as symbols of the Self: Christ, the Buddha, Krishna, Quetzalcoatl, Kali, the Virgin Mary, Pele of Hawaii, Isis, Kuan-Yin or any of the eternal God-images found in various cultures. Contemporary popular American symbols of the Self are Superman, Santa Claus and E.T., the latter of whom even resurrects from the dead. The creation of Mrs. Claus, not to mention Wonder Woman, in recent years is a happy contribution displaying the feminine aspect of the Self. Would there were more to balance out the masculine images.

The experiences of the Self in dreams and fantasies seem to produce a new, upgraded attitude regarding life's challenging situations. It does not leave us cold, but neither does it solve our problems for us. It simply facilitates and allows us to outgrow the problematical life issue at hand!

Jung described this phenomenon succinctly: "This outgrowing . . . revealed itself on further experience to be the raising of the level of consciousness. Some higher or wider interest arose on the person's horizon, and through this widening of his view, the insoluble problem lost its urgency. It was not solved logically in its own terms, but faded out before a new and stronger life tendency. It was not repressed and made unconscious, but merely appeared in a different light, and so became different itself. What on a lower level had led to the wildest conflicts and to emotions full of panic, viewed from the higher level of the personality now seemed like a storm in a valley seen from a high mountain top. This does not mean that the thunderstorm is robbed of its reality; it means that, instead of being in it, one is now above it" (*Collected Works*, vol. 13, par. 17).

Centering in the Self

When we get centered in the Self and begin overseeing things from its viewpoint, we coincidentally are drawn to the calm at the center of the storm, as it were, while all rages round us.

Centering in the Self takes place in a more permanent way only when our egos consciously discover and viscerally assimilate the significance and true meaning of the Self's images spontaneously surfacing from the depths. They appear more often than we think. When taken seriously and absorbed into consciousness on the levels of sensation, intuition, thinking and feeling, the experience of these images in dreams and fantasies will allow us to surmise and infer in a somewhat frightening way that the ego is not at all the pivotal center of the vast expanse of our psychic life, but rather only the center of an extremely limited waking consciousness. The feeling is akin to that of discovering one's house to be haunted—but by friendly ghosts or benign angelic presences! When we discover the Self—or, more accurately, when the Self discovers us— we feel as though we were born again to a greater, more multidimensional state of being and awareness. This state compellingly intimates a sort of death to our old egocentricity. It is a veritable mournful loss of who we thought we were. We may initially get very depressed over it, instead of experiencing astounding joy. In essence it is only the demise of a grand delusion produced by the distorted perception of who in fact we really are.

We are much greater than we initially perceive or have been taught to believe. If we will stop blocking our vision with incessant learned judgments and evaluations and "just look" very simply, very naively within, Zen-style, we will be able to see who we are in a much more focused way. Clear perception is achieved only by strictly suspending our much-cherished faculties of always wanting to judge and evaluate everything based on preconceived notions. The advice that follows is to be understood literally: When the two evaluative functions of thinking and feeling are slowed up or even suspended for a brief time, sensation and intuition, the perceptive functions, take over and provide us with incredibly penetrating insight.

When mental confusion, ennui and psychic sterility appear because we are living on the surface of our beings, or simply because of a stroke of "bad luck," only then do we usually begin searching for deeper meaning. Many times just to survive in life, to pay bills, to make ends meet, we are forced into a time-consuming, obnoxious involvement with work and the outer world, and we neglect all the enlivening psychic energies and treasures lying just below the surface of waking life. Under such fallow circumstances, the Self may, when we least expect it, rush up to our assistance and offer us an unwarranted gift of saving grace that can shake and overwhelm us to the marrow of our bones, in the strangest but ultimately most auspicious ways.

Thinkers locked into analyzing are suddenly besieged by convulsive emotional upheavals that intellectually elude them. Try to visualize Mr. Spock of *Star Trek* suddenly and inexplicably falling hysterically, head-over-heels in love. Intuitives normally attracted to the past or future may feel

oppressed and weighed down by the many concrete realities of
the present moment. Imagine your local psychic or clairvoyant
suddenly losing his or her ESP and having to get a job as a
waiter or waitress.

Feelers can become plagued by obtrusive thoughts that sour
the pleasant feeling environment that they habitually try to
create for themselves. An internationally famous opera star
may for no observable reason become plagued by thoughts that
her husband may be having an affair, though private detectives
inform her otherwise.

And sensates, with their two feet perennially on the ground,
may feel the rug being pulled out from under them by a flood
of negative intuitive possibilities and wild premonitions about
the future or irrational hunches and erroneous suppositions
about the past. Imagine your local Dairy Farmers Association
president inexplicably giving speeches on the prophecies of
Nostradamus at the regular monthly meetings.

These tongue-in-cheek examples of the first rumblings of
the Self are actually quite close to the mark. When people we
know seem to have made a leap in consciousness due to the
activity of the Self, it is as if they have unwillingly shifted
psychic gears totally and begun acting out of character. It is
similar to conversion experiences reported in spiritual literature, where from one day to the next people have a total
change of heart and mind.

Under all of these seemingly adverse conditions, our psyches
are essentially being plummeted into a renewal and a broaden-
ing by the Self in its decision to shake us to the core. It is like
a psychic earthquake produced by the lower layers readjusting
themselves under the stress of new requirements for adaptability to life's changing issues. The inferior function or a helping
function may have been totally neglected, and these forgotten
friends are now making their imposing presence felt in order
to provide us with a sense of wholeness. At the urging of the
Self, the neglected function provoked the apparent difficulty,

but it also ultimately contains the necessary psychic energy for a satisfying resolution of one-sided development.

"Salvation" comes to us as an upheaval in the form of our forgotten and neglected inferior function, rejected until now by the ego, and hitherto occasioning only minor mishaps in our daily lives.

In a more positive view, a piece of music may unsuspectingly awaken thinkers to the sheer thrill of Life in the midst of the dry abstractions and bloodless theories that had a stranglehold on them.

The feeling type who undervalues and even invalidates thinking approaches to life might suddenly be struck by an abstract truth that somehow thoroughly exposes and surprisingly clarifies the meaning of his or her personal existence. And though devastating to his or her cozy feelings about life, clear thinking opens the way to a broader and more comforting view of the dynamics of things. New thoughts appearing out of the blue enable the feeler to re-examine the forceful and tyrannical hold of constant feeling evaluations of likes and dislikes and of the many futile behaviors instigated by them.

Intuitives usually resist seeing and avoid focusing on the hard facts of the present moment in order to feverishly chase after life's elusive possibilities. Intuitives concentrate basically on the past (possible causes) and/or the future (possible outcomes) but rarely on what is in front of their noses. One day they might suddenly be constrained by an ugly set of circumstances to finally grasp a basic law of reality regarding causality, which teaches them that an action performed in the here-and-now is what generally produces definite consequences at some future date. They are thereby obliged to see the importance of the present moment in its intrinsic power to physically create the future. "What you sow *right now* is what you will reap later" is a concept that had hitherto eluded them entirely.

Sensate types habitually secure in immediate, concrete

three-dimensional reality are "miraculously" overcome by a
new perception in which the present moment is dethroned
from absolute sovereignty. At long last they get to see the
present as part of a chain of events coming from an indefinite
past and progressing to an indefinite future. Because of this
quasi-mystical connection to past and future, the present moment becomes relativized and is seen as being pregnant with
a vaster and more purposive meaning.

All of the above emancipating experiences, though upsetting, are actuated by the Self, the principle of wholeness, and
as such are described ultimately as divine experiences. All four
functions appear to be operative at the same time during a
fleeting divine experience. This supreme moment of grace, a
mandalic experience, a mysterious four-foldness, as Jung put
it, is generally perceived during one's encounter with the Self,
the sum total of our psyche.

When the forgotten fourth function lost in the unconscious
rises surprisingly to consciousness, this missing piece of the
psyche's circuitry of functions allows a great amount of energy
to begin coursing through the psyche. The raising of the inferior function is a veritable re-union, a kind of yogic relinking
and energizer. A new center of psychic command called the
"fourfold Self" comes into play, producing a sense of wholeness and well-being. This new center reveals itself to be emi-
nently more adequate and more valid than mere ego-
consciousness ever was. More specifically, we experience it as
a suprapersonal force that furtively, and lovingly, guides us in
creative ways according to some benign secret design known
only to itself. As a religious experience the transcendent Self
is termed "God" manifesting in us immanently. Divine immanence is an earthy, "feminine" experience, not an airy, transcendent, "masculine" experience. Its patterned coming and
manifestation into everyday consciousness is tremendously em-
powering, though jolting, and quickly passing and transient.
Again, we must remember that words utterly fail to describe
this phenomenal healing experience.

As mentioned, the sudden fashioning of the elements of the psyche into a unified whole is generally a short-lived ideal state for most of us rather than something that is lived continuously throughout each moment of every day. For most of us the uplifting experience remains a goal that we may only hope to reach on rare occasions for brief moments. It may come upon us unsolicited and go away just as quickly, leaving us with a persistent nostalgia.

The Self and the Archetypes

The Self is not only perceived as an integration of the four functions, and of the two attitudes of extraversion and introversion; it is also felt to be a kind of magical coming-together, a coalescing of all of the archetypes that give intense personal meaning to individual existence. For a brief instant all aspects of our being feel harmoniously and mysteriously orchestrated by a mighty force and in a way that completely transcends rational understanding. If love is the healer, the feeling it fosters is that we are loved, from deep within. The desire to discover one's truest nature and the total, uncondi- tional acceptance of one's uniqueness generally precede this intense meeting with the Self. The Self encompasses the entire gamut of archetypes. It gathers their forces into a paradoxical unity that can guide and mature us with the utmost ease if we can only learn to become receptive to its laserlike power.

When we single-mindedly ally our egos with the desires and activities of the Self, we are granted a new freedom to choose to walk along paths in life that were formerly barred to us. The story of the simple French peasant girl, Joan of Arc, illustrates what can happen when a higher power dictates a new, seemingly impossible course of action and lifestyle. One day in her garden, she heard "celestial voices" and was never the same again. A new destiny was imposed upon her from above, as it were. She had to follow the call. In a way, she no longer was allowed any personal choices in her new role as a political and historical catalyst. The Self's desires had become her own. Our personal desires and activities begin reflecting those of the Self, yet not as if these desires and activities came forth from a foreign entity. The Self makes us see that a life lived meaningfully cannot be based on the ready-made ego solutions that proliferate in our culture.

What the Self—our very own Higher Self—and the experience of it teach us to do is to have complete confidence in its guiding power. It is as if our whole destiny changes as our conscious character changes. With our newly found elevated consciousness, we become like a feather on the breath of God, to borrow a phrase from the medieval visionary Hildegard of Bingen. In so doing we become, as it were, co-masters of our destiny. To be co-master does not imply that the ego will take the lead over the Self, but rather that it will execute every urge and prompting of the Self without the slightest hesitation and with the greatest spontaneity. The basis for co-mastering our destiny is ironically "total surrender" to the Self as it makes its will manifest via dreams, inner visions and whisperings laden with meaning, emanating constantly from our unconscious depths. We eventually discover that the Self is a personality that we also are.

Events in life may be taken in either of two ways: as a blessing imparting compassion and empathy for those who suffer as we do, or as a curse that turns us into mental cripples. The choice is ours to make.

Some forms of psychic and physical suffering, if met with the right attitude, can be turned not only into what is euphemistically called a healing crisis but also into a leap forward toward wisdom-consciousness. For example, a male colleague suddenly became totally blind in both eyes, just after the end of long years of study. Both parents also suddenly died the same year. If it had happened to someone else, his fateful handicap could have been paralyzing in a host of ways and on many levels. But after the initial denial, anger, depression, prayers for a change of destiny and countless visits to all kinds of specialists, and finally surrendering all desire for control, he accepted the confounding workings of the Self as it manifested in him and throughout every aspect of his life.

One day in the silence of meditation, it came to him in a flash that in Nature whenever something is taken away, something else is given in its stead. His outer sight was taken, but a new inner spiritual sight began flourishing in him that was considerably more essential to his work as a psychotherapist than his physical eyesight could ever be. And so he pressed on in his life's work—and with colossal success. After his special gifts came to be known, people traveled for many miles to seek out his help.

Perhaps partly due to sense-deprivation, he developed penetrating intuitive insight into people's souls. Most people coming to therapy sooner or later complain of feeling powerless, alone or abandoned. Because of his experiences of the same emotions, he was able to give a genuine healing touch to the hearts of those who came to him for help. In this profound way, he is truly like a feather on the breath of God, finely attuned to every healing and balancing movement of the Self within him. He clearly demonstrates the old adage "Every true healer is a wounded healer."

If we do not cooperate intimately with the Self, with the Voice of Wisdom and the many forces that constitute it, it may very well coercively break into our lives, unbidden, under its shattering aspects instead of under its gentler, creative ones. No one can say when these forces will awaken from their slumber in the depths to enter and take charge of our lives. Therefore we must learn and become conversant with the symbolic language of the Self and its archetypal activities as described by the world's theologies, mythologies and religious lore. All of these disciplines reveal more about the hidden natures and psychic dynamics of those humans who formulated them than about the Absolute they are attempting to describe.

The only power that we can have over archetypal experiences comes about by educating ourselves about them and understanding how they use symbols and myths to communicate their life-giving energies to us and, through us, to the community at large. The story of Black Elk, the Lakota Sioux medicine man, shows how a jolting vision he received as a young boy was meant as a healing agent for his entire tribe when it was finally ritualized by the members of the tribe into a living mandalic ceremony. His autobiography, *Black Elk Speaks*, captures the beauty and mystery of this experience.

Ultimately, only by developing enough ego-strength through mindful living will we be able to accentuate the positive sides of the archetypes. If we do not work with them, they will work against us. A cooperative process can limit and neutralize the activities of their negative sides. Centering in the Self, *which is accessible always and everywhere*, is an art. Learning the Self's cryptic but highly significant language enables us to more easily accomplish this feat. Receptivity to the Self's guidance—through dreams, through intuitions, through magical synchronicities that blend outer and inner worlds in a transcendent moment—is the most sacred act a human being can perform and must be approached with genuine, heartfelt devotion, respect and awe.

As with all contents of the unconscious, the Self is often seen projected onto a minister, priest, rabbi, mullah, therapist or esteemed friend who shows us sincere empathy and unconditional acceptance of all the contradictions of our personalities. In common parlance, we call this "laying a trip on someone." Since the Self contains all possible opposites within itself with apparent ease, the friend or person upon whom the Self is projected generally is someone who feels comfortable with all the contradictions in his or her nature. Such a person, we hope, is able to help us feel the same way about our own contradictory natures.

Others can guide us only as far as they personally have progressed spiritually themselves. When we accept our dualistic nature, the strange union of opposites, the positive and negative sides of psychic life as symbolized by the Self, only then can we begin experiencing a new, deep-seated serenity despite all the tensions and stresses of our lives. These tensions and stresses are nothing other than the polarity that creates and animates the dynamic vitality of psychic life.

Chapter 7

Good and Evil: Befriending the Rejected

As one works with dreams and fantasies on the journey into the personal unconscious, repressed and suppressed entities are the first things encountered. Jung called them the shadow elements, and, as with all archetypes, they may be either positive or negative. Each "shadow" is a split-off entity that was once conscious for a brief time but, for one reason or another, was not deemed worthy of conscious acceptance and expression. The ego and the persona judged it to be out of sync with their goals and intentions.

We are all more or less acquainted with Dr. Jekyll (relatively positive) and Mr. Hyde (downright evil). And most of us know about Clark Kent and Superman, the former an ordinary, timid news reporter, the latter a superhuman, benevolent extraterrestrial hero and godling. Mr. Hyde is a negative shadow figure, and Superman a positive shadow figure. Both are generally hidden from the people who rub elbows with them.

The development of the shadow runs parallel to that of the ego. Whatever the ego does not wish to express for whatever inner- or outer-based reason is repressed into the personal unconscious. This repressed material may be of the nature of antisocial urges or even talents that we are too lazy or undisciplined to cultivate. Ironically the shadow often is usually apparent to everyone around us, but not to ourselves.

As with all other parts of the unconscious, the shadow is initially seen outside ourselves in projected form. The qualities that we hate most passionately in others and that get under our skin at every turn are the same qualities we despise most vigorously within ourselves. The same goes for those positive qualities that impress us most in others and that elicit admiration on our part. Something in or outside of ourselves prevents us from displaying our talents or even something like an above-average intelligence. Many highly intuitive people are forced by society to hide their innate extrasensory perceptive qualities since the insensitive dullards in their environment generally ridicule their psychic sensitivities out of envy or simple fear. In order to "fit in," superior individuals often have to hide or at least play down their extraordinary qualities. Being exceptional requires a daring spirit.

Rose Ann, an exceptional intuitive and clairvoyant, born in a small village in Ireland at the turn of the century, was severely persecuted as a child by her priestly uncles, who accused her of being a witch every time she predicted that a building would burn down, someone would die or some other unforeseen event would take place. In time she learned to keep her mouth shut and to pretend ignorance, though she felt much harm and damage could be averted if only she were allowed to tell about her intuitive insights without incurring the wrath of God in the form of her clerical uncles. To escape stultification, she migrated to America in search of the freedom to be who she was and to help humanity with what she felt were her God-given gifts. She became a "reverend" and died at a ripe old age, having dedicated her life, with all its fortes and imperfections, to the welfare of humanity. Many highly developed individuals have similar challenges to face.

Jung differentiated the *personal shadow* from the *collective shadow*. He observed that the personal shadow contained psychic characteristics of the individual person, which have gone unexpressed since the time of childhood or adolescence.

The collective shadow emanates from the collective unconscious and is a manifestation of the dark aspect of the Self that is capable of being projected onto minority groups within a particular culture or even onto whole nations. A collective shadow also represents a universal human dark side within all of us. The Nazi party in Germany displayed a very superior facade to the world at large, which covered a horrendous feeling of collective inferiority. Everyone around them was viewed as inferior—Jews, Slavs, Latins, Gypsies, the gays, Hungarians and on and on. The question is "Who was really feeling inferior?" Were the Nazis not in fact experiencing their own collectively unconscious self-disgust in projected form?

Genocidal wars are all based on the same principles of negative shadow projection: Turks annihilating Armenians, Stalin starving millions of Ukrainians, Chinese decimating the Tibetan race and culture, Russians forcing Russification in all the Soviet republics, European cultures destroying the native cultures of North and South America, Australia and South Africa. In Africa, minority tribes are slaughtered wholesale by majority tribes. In India collective shadow projections have given rise and form to caste systems thousands of years old— the higher the caste the fairer the complexion, the lower the darker. The countries of North and South America and Australia already have their own not-so-subtle forms of the caste system. These collective atrocities are inevitable whenever unconscious shadow material is not consciously owned and ethically integrated into the collective psyche.

Ethical behavior is sometimes taken seriously only when it is seen as producing a "profit" for the one being ethical. We must understand that virtue, a product of ethical thinking, is indeed its own reward. Hate and anger can cause stomach ulcers and heart conditions; deep-seated resentment can cause cancer. Practitioners of Chinese medicine have known for centuries that each sick body organ represents the disturbance of a specific emotion associated with that organ. A hate-free, anger-free, resentment-free psyche is a happy, and healthy, psyche. Who does not wish to be happy? Shadow projection only leads to hate, anger, resentment and, of course, to unhappiness and even despair. We must wake up to these facts.

Scapegoating others—projecting our inadequacies onto others and even killing them—does not really get rid of the problem of self-loathing; it only exacerbates these collective archetypal feelings of an irrational Scorpio-Pluto nature. On a more personal level, but also stemming from a collective projection, is the lamentable lot of women in traditional cultures. Since they are not expected to be intelligent or to even show any sign of intellectuality, they learn to suppress this side of themselves and, as a result, produce an intellectual shadow of a positive nature. This shadow of woman becomes sheer wasted energy in a world crying out for such an earthy, feminine type of intelligence. One could write volumes on this psychological carnage of women.

The Personal Shadow

Normally the personal shadow is encountered first and is seen as an alter ego or subpersonality that, if negative, creates a block to the creative aspects of our psyches. The negative shadow represents blocked-up, encapsulated psychic energy that becomes so because it is constantly being suppressed or repressed.

Whatever the ego resists will persist, in any case, and we literally energize these resisted qualities with our very resistance. While growing up, the ego is actually strengthened by resisting certain undesirable alter egos or morally ugly shadow forces. This is a necessary endeavor, as the young ego needs firming up, but later in life we find that the shadow merely turns into a cut-off quantity of psychic energy that can be and wants to be tapped, integrated and used. As life goes on, more and more shadow material collects, and a serious tension is created between the repressing ego and the autonomous shadow now battling more fiercely for recognition by the very thing repressing it.

Jung suggested that suppression of the shadow is as little a remedy as beheading would be for a headache. "If an inferiority is conscious, one always has a chance to correct it. Furthermore, it is constantly in contact with other interests, so that it is continually subjected to modifications. But if it is repressed and isolated from consciousness, it never gets corrected" (*Psychology and Religion: West and East, Collected Works*, vol. 11, par. 131).

Confronting our shadow is excruciatingly difficult as it strongly conflicts with *persona* ideals and demands. Consequently the task of confrontation generally meets with tremendous resistance by the ego and the persona. Many in therapy who suddenly come across their negative shadow in a dream simply drop out of therapy altogether. It is much easier to continue projecting our shadow material onto others in order to scapegoat and blame them for our sorrows and woes.

If we staunchly avoid letting the imp out of the bottle, the shadow-imp will exert a more forceful opposition on our repressive ego and persona. The ego and persona will in their turn have to exert more psychic energy to keep the imp corked up in the unconscious. All the energy spent in repression could better be used as taming energy, with an array of more practical and positive consequences.

We have had many reports of sexual improprieties committed by so-called religious and spiritual leaders. The particular form of Puritanism these people practice and teach others to practice forces them to put forth a more-than-angelic, asexual persona that acts as the cork in the bottle. The imp in the bottle is a simple instinctual creature with the ordinary needs and desires of all other beings of the animal kingdom. When this instinctual nature is denied, even with marital partners, and put in a restrictive straitjacket, it becomes transformed into a state of emotional or physical frigidity, and that is when the "wild beast" comes out. A succinct French expression sums it up: "Celui qui fait l'ange fait la bête" ("The person who tries to act like an angel [i.e., not having a physical body] eventually winds up acting like a beast"). The play on words is telling: "Bête" literally means "animal or beast" but is figuratively used as an adjective to mean "plain stupid." In other words, acting like something we are not is idiocy.

In my analytical practice, denial, repression and suppression seem to be fortes of those professionally involved in religion. They enter therapy when the "cork" can no longer contain the energized repressed material and when they begin suspecting that angels and humans are two separate species. More about this particular issue, which touches all "idealistic" cultures, is discussed later. The task is to learn how to keep our heads high in the sky but our feet planted firmly on the ground, an esoteric spiritual art that the principles of analytical psychology can help us to learn. We all must learn that sin and ignorant behaviors do not make us bad; rather they simply make us more human, and still capable of being loved by those who are not deluded by unrealistic forms of religious idealism that no human being can ever hope to live up to.

As long as the ego and persona continue resisting and repressing, they are in a state of identity with the shadow entities, since all unconscious forces contaminate ego consciousness without the ego ever being aware of the contamination. The first step in freeing ourselves from blind shadow impulses is to recognize that they exist. The second step is to act kindly but firmly in our attempt to imbue them with consciousness, while understanding the reasons why they become activated. It is when we dialogue with the shadow that we can separate the ego and persona from shadow contamination. Only after this has been achieved can we reasonably confront the other, multiple pairs of psychic opposites at deeper levels. Conversing, "having it out," with aspects of our unconscious minds is truly a transformatory act if engaged in with sincerity, empathy and humility.

Humility is simply the ability to acknowledge the truth about ourselves. It has nothing to do with invalidating or "sitting" on ourselves. Humility can disarm the fiercest of deceptive demons lodged in the dark shadow realm, because it is Truth itself. Most notorious gangsters and hoodlums have a "soft side." Humility gives us the calmness and patience to find out what that soft side is, and to catch hold of it. It is always fear that encourages a mugger to perform greater harm than he would do if he were instead met with simple acknowledgment and acceptance of his state of despair. Acknowledging a mugger's demands matter of factly calms him and may even disarm a potentially volatile and dangerous situation. The same holds true for a similar attitude directed toward our own shadow. Hate breeds hate. Hate directed at our shadow will only elicit an odious response from it in return, creating more unnecessary chaos and turmoil in our lives. We must learn "to take people by their heart," as it were, for we accomplish much more in this simple, feeling way. One catches more flies with honey than with vinegar, as they say, and this holds true for our pesty shadow sides.

It is like the case of a hardened criminal who can either be locked up in solitary confinement and forgotten about or forced to take active part in a psychological rehabilitation program truly intended to effect a change of heart in him. Sadly, we collectively behave toward our society's criminals (and minority groups who are not criminals) in the same way we behave as individuals toward our own negative shadow sides—with disdain, contempt and vengeful cruelty.

Lack of self-knowledge is our basic problem. If we know nothing objective about someone, if we do not perceive clearly and in a focused way, we usually tend to fear that person. And fear of that person will eventually lead to hating that person. The best defense against someone we fear and hate is immediate offense. We attack verbally or otherwise for no obvious reason. Our ignorance once again is seen as the originator of all kinds of irrational attitudes that in turn produce harmful behaviors, which in their turn create only pain and grief for others and ultimately for ourselves as well.

Only a troubled mind creates trouble for others. Peaceful minds create peaceful atmospheres around themselves. A troubled mind is one that is at odds with itself. It does not love itself in a healthy way because it deems that certain shadow aspects of itself cause it to be unlovable and hated. The cause is not the shadow per se but the attitude we harbor toward it. This negative attitude only antagonizes the shadow subpersonalities, which react to this loathing and lack of love in like manner. The ego then declares: "You see, I was right. These aspects of myself only act in hateful, unloving ways and deserve to be hated and unloved in return!" A vicious circle is thus created with this kind of false, self-defeating, absurd "logic."

The causes for this violent state of affairs are many. Perhaps our parents were always harping and hypercritical of us as children, or perhaps inherent archetypal conflicts and complexes opposed too many of our personal ideals and aspirations. Or it might be a combination of things. The point is that animosity breeds animosity; it does not rehabilitate. Shadow figures need rehabilitation, which is only accomplished with a willingness to befriend them with loving-kindness, patience and wisdom.

The principal ignorance to overcome concerns the bipolar nature of our human psyche. Only when we understand that all of Nature is bipolar, with positive and negative sides, will we be able to take our own human natures more in stride and even love them a bit more just as they are. Instead of trying to eradicate the negative, we ought to try to understand that Nature always has two distinct sides. When we accept this fact, we become less agitated and simply try to diffuse, not repress, our negative forces. Some highly evolved beings can spiritually transmute a negative emotion into a positive one by seeing through the negative emotion with the eye of transcendental wisdom, but for most of humanity diffusing negative forces seems to be the more realizeable means of avoiding suffering. Instead of assassinating a tyrannical ruler, we can symbolically hang him in effigy during a mass demonstration or campaign to vote him out of office. Instead of dropping bombs on an enemy nation, we can symbolically burn that country's flag or protest in front of its embassy or consulate. Acts that *diffuse* negativity and anger are engaged in all the time. Sublimation is the very nature of ritual acts. One is not throwing a whole pile of logs into the fire, but rather one log only, thereby acknowledging the existence of the fire, a mighty force of Nature.

The issue at hand is not to deny that negative feelings exist. If we lock the front door, they will exit from the back door, and we will not even be aware of their activity if they escape in this unconscious manner. We must bring consciousness into play. Ultimately all forms of negativity, such as hate and anger, stem from a feeling of not being loved. Love, the most complete form of consciousness, makes us feel at one with others. Not feeling this oneness of consciousness is painful, and painfulness can express itself as anger and hate or depression (anger turned toward oneself). Unconditional love is always the answer on the level of negative and hurt feelings; shadow figures and subpersonalities are no different from our egos or people in general in this regard. We all need the transformatory power of unconditional love to bring out the best in us. Venus, conditional love, and her brother Neptune, unconditional loving-kindness, are in us all. We only need to awaken them within ourselves with any means, traditional or otherwise, at our disposal.

The shadow differs from an unruly complex in that it was not a trauma that pushed it into the unconscious, as is the case with a complex. Our own persona ideals, influenced by family and cultural values, is what suppresses or represses the shadow material. Somehow or other we came to understand that the shadow element was categorically not worthy of love, and hence not worthy of expression either. Minority children in the newer cultures of the globe, where many ethnicities thrive side by side, may sadly try to erase ethnic traits that have been unofficially but clearly declared unworthy of love or expression by the majority. The erased ethnic qualities may include collective characteristics of typology that could be a wonderful contribution to the new mosaic culture at large. These suppressed typological characteristics get turned into shadowy subpersonalities that are lost on many levels to the child and to the new society as well. For the minority child this process is a loss of identity and creative energy; for the nation it represents a loss of balance and wholeness in terms of the one-sided way in which it forces the national character and consciousness to grow.

On a more personal level, a particular child may wish to hide a violent streak in his or her character due to parental pressures. The child represses or suppresses this vicious streak into the unconscious when the condemning adults are around, but it will burst forth compulsively when the first chance arises, when the restraining, suppressing adults are not present to control the child's shadow impulse. Threats and beatings will not rehabilitate the violent shadow personality; they will only drive it into hiding in the unconscious. It is like a lion tamer who has to be on guard at all times, despite years of work with a particular wild animal. Violence is an overassertion of power due to enormous and debilitating feelings of powerlessness that need to be compensated for. The child's feelings of powerlessness need to be skillfully and sympathetically addressed if any change is to take place in the area of violent behavior. In America models of behavior seen on children's and adult television programs foster violent reactions through sheer force of repetition to the exclusion of rational settlement of disputes and personal differences. Madison Avenue advertisers seem to be the only ones who understand that a fifteen-second commercial on television can manipulate millions of viewers to buy a certain product. Television producers and writers don't seem to realize or care that constant displays of violent actions have a powerful programming effect on both young and adult minds.

Our human behavior is in the main influenced by modeling behavior that we grow up with and see acted out around us every day. Not only individual parents but society in general must "parent" our children toward mature behavior. Mature parents seem to be fighting a losing battle against the immature, unevolved minds that create the popular media culture that unfortunately is "parenting" our children. Is it any wonder that the second-greatest killer of our youth is teenage suicide? What message do these needless deaths communicate to us?

In a dream or fantasy the shadow generally appears as a personality of the same gender as the ego and, when projected, is also ordinarily seen in a person of the same gender. Habitual conflicts with others of the same sex are often, but not always, due to the mechanism of shadow projection. That others are always to blame and we are never at fault is an indication that we are oblivious to our own shortcomings. This lack of awareness will keep us infantile and immature and will only worsen with time.

Failure to unearth positive shadow qualities is also an indication of stunted maturity. Naturally generous, optimistic, fun-loving people sometimes have the bad luck to have been born to stingy, grouchy, uncaring, depressive parents. The persona-ideal promulgated by these negative parents is anything but cheerful and positive, so the child is brainwashed into rejecting his or her inborn positive personality traits. The exceedingly bright and intelligent child may experience the same fate if he or she is born to parents who are low-brow, dull, slow or backward. Negative peer pressures or negative cultural programming may force the suppression of the more evolved spiritual qualities that many children are born with. Rejecting one's optimism and above-average intelligence, rejecting genteelness and sensitivity to the needs of others only leads to psychic misery. If not rectified, such attitudes may lead to psychic if not physical suicide. Repressions always lead to suffocation and psychic death until the light of consciousness is brought to bear on the repressed positive shadow qualities and until the frozen and paralyzed energies they represent are loosened up. Remember that shadow qualities, whether positive or negative, were once conscious and, due to pressure from one source or another, were repressed or suppressed to fester in the unconscious.

The Collective Shadow

When we ponder what might be the collective shadow of our contemporary high-tech, instant fix-it, instant gratification, eternal-youth culture, we can become weak-kneed. Publicly discussing the shadow side of America is not popular, as it is seen by shortsighted sentimentalists as un-American. Yet these same people criticize the Germans of the 1930s for not checking what was going on politically in their country. If as a nation we are to escape collective psychic suicide and death, we will have to confront our national shadow.

The American intuitive and healer Edgar Cayce suggested many years ago that our collective shadow side was self-righteousness, otherwise called hypocrisy. The expression "Our shit don't stink" expresses the same idea, implying that we are okay but others are not. The attitude implies that greed, corruption, irrationality and immorality, political and otherwise, exist only in other nations. We could easily imagine a positive shadow hidden in the American collective unconscious, perhaps the wise and compassionate heart of a typical American grandmother or grandfather. In practical terms, this would mean that the United States could become a special place to live in when our American elderly, who currently are by and large invalidated and neglected, are finally recognized for what they represent and have to offer. Perhaps a few lessons from Native Americans, Asians, and Africans, who are also invalidated citizens, would help bring respect and veneration of our elders in response to the practical knowledge they have gleaned from their many decades on the planet. America seems to be the sole country where the archetype of the Eternal Child (Mercury/Hermes: Gemini) dominates over all the others. Perhaps this is why our elders are often depicted in films and on television as doddering old fools. Patricide and matricide represent one of the shadow sides of the Eternal Child. Identification with any one archetype always implies an accentuation of its particular shadow side. None of us personally or collectively is beyond constructive and insightful psychological criticism. If we omit this element, the thing we are looking for most—happiness—will mysteriously elude us.

When our collective negative shadow is seen and experienced in projected form with one or another foreign country as the hook for it, what is it that we see there? Indeed, the entity attracting a projection does in fact have some qualities that make it eligible to be a hook for that particular projection. What is actually seen is an over-magnified *subjective* version of what might or might not be objectively "out there." For example, when a driver of a car wears dark-green sunglasses all the green lights he passes look subjectively much more intensely green and dark than they are objectively. The greenness of the traffic lights is exaggerated by the greenness of his sunglasses.

What qualities do we collectively project onto other nations who are perennially a "fly" in our national "ointment"? It is also important to note what these other countries project onto us, not so much to discover what their shadow might be (that is their task to resolve) as to discern what characteristics qualify us as a hook for their projections.

After World War II, for example, the defeated countries initially looked up to America as a modern, efficient, high-tech success story that they could emulate in their rebuilding process. Other nations like Cuba projected an imperialistic devil onto us as a nation. Even the projections of others onto us can help in our effort to become more conscious personally and collectively. In our desire to shirk off unconsciousness, the essential elements we need are practical compassion and practical empathy, whether the shadow nature be inner or outer. Biblical injunction brings this meaning into focus when it says, "Resist not evil," because the more we attack it, the more vicious it gets, and the less its transformation is accomplished.

We are unconscious through no fault of our own; it is a simple fact of Nature. Understanding this allows us to go even beyond tolerance. No one really likes being tolerated in any case, since being tolerated is synonymous with being patronized and looked down upon. We generally prefer to be understood and perhaps liked, if not loved unconditionally.

The world of anthropology teaches us that when Tribe A conquers and imposes its religion on Tribe B, the old gods of Tribe B become the devils of the newly imposed religion of Tribe A.

Religious sectarianism is an area rife with rampant shadow projections. Those who belong to large religious sects in our country see old or newly imported minority forms of religion as demonic.

Collective religious shadow projection appears to be growing fast in our multiethnic country where religions are arriving from all parts of the world. Remember that whatever we misunderstand we tend to fear; what we fear, we easily hate; and what we hate becomes an incredibly magnetic hook for our wildest and most hideous shadow projections. We most likely see in others of different religions our own fanaticism and our own repressed devils. To be sure, the newly imported religionists from Asia, Africa, the Caribbean and Mexico and the resurgent Native American forms are very probably also projecting all sorts of shadow material onto the majority religionists. In this instance, "Charity begins at home" could mean to love ourselves enough to clean out our own house (unconscious psyches) first of all the peace-destroying demons of ignorance that plague us and ultimately cause strife between ourselves and others.

Looking closely at the archetypal core of repressed evil, initially encountered in projected form, we will notice attached thereto an overwhelming power drive. The personification of power-hungry evil in our Western Christian culture is Satan or Lucifer, who was mythically the highest of the angels. The name "Lucifer" means "light bearer." He became filled with pride and conceit, and ambitiously attempted to usurp his Creator's power. At the command of God, Michael the Archangel drove Lucifer from heaven, making him fall into the bowels of the earth, whence he exerts his disruptive, hellish dominion over our world.

The Jewish Talmudic and Islamic versions have Lucifer falling from grace because he was jealous of Adam before whom God forced all the angels to bow. Since he refused to submit to Adam, he was cast out of heaven along with his cohorts, ever causing pain and strife for us humans in his prideful vengeance.

The Christian Lucifer is the story of an ego mistaking itself for God. A dilemma always occurs when the ego becomes inflated by identifying with the Self. The ego's main delusional tendency is to believe that it can dominate over the whole psyche, but the ego is merely a part and not the whole—a satellite, not the pivotal point. It is as if the Moon believed it was the source of its own light instead of understanding that its light derives from a central light-producing agent, the Sun. A distorted perception (an illusion) leads to a false belief (a delusion). The conscious ego becomes centered in itself and ceases to be aware that an unconscious exists, not to mention other multiple forces that exist in it as well.

The story of Satan is an allegorical description of our own Western psychological plight. We would do well to come to terms with our own demonic natures before crusading against our neighbors' devils.

The perennial homespun recipe, in lieu of an elaborate ritual of exorcism, for ridding oneself of Old Snatch, as he is sometimes called, is to poke fun at him and laugh heartily right in his face, and perhaps jump ten feet in the air at the same time and run at the speed of light in the opposite direction. A keen sense of humor seems to work in a similar way on devilishly grumpy human beings who take themselves deadly seriously and who cannot bear the thought of laughter. In point of fact, if we all learned to laugh at ourselves a bit more, our dark, hellish states of depression might just vanish.

The most tragic thing, psychologically speaking, about our Western mythic belief system concerning Satan, our unconscious archetypal demonic side, is that he is viewed as completely and irrevocably unredeemable. We even confine him to an eternal hell where he will reign supreme forever over lost human souls. Whatever happened to the concept of the absoluteness of Divine Compassion and its infinitely saving power? Are we really expected to find it easy or logical to conceive of an absolutely loving and infinitely merciful God who would allow a soul to suffer everlasting torment for breaking one of the Ten Commandments if that person dies before asking the Creator's pardon? If necessary, why can the creature not ask for pardon when dead in the spirit world? Can remorse not come after the fact?

Anyone with the scantest knowledge of depth psychology is acutely aware that in this mythic system God has become a hook for the projection of Satan, since any god who could be so petty and unbelievably cruel would be by definition no better, existentially speaking, than Satan himself. The theological counterargument is that the individual soul "chooses" hell, but who in his or her right mind would choose eternal torment? This logic is out of touch with the general movements of the human psyche, which often seeks what it falsely believes to be paths to happiness. Even the masochists among us "call it a day" after awhile.

Satan as a symbol of our own collective Western shadow

projected onto God is another tragic illustration of how our collective ego in its smallness has fashioned a god idol in its own puny, paltry and picayune image capable of inflicting infinite punishment for any finite act committed. Actually this demonic god-image does not issue forth from the spiritual teachings of Jesus, the West's cultural hero, nor does it express Jesus' theological and mythical role as redeemer and absolute victor over evil as revealed in the New Testament. Such an image is the outcome of warped human theologians who have turned evil into an absolute (a qualitative adjective reserved traditionally for the Godhead Itself). They absolutize evil by asserting that it is nonchanging and eternal. Theologically speaking, "absoluteness" is supposed to be a synonym for God, and not a synonym for a finite creature called Lucifer/Satan, astrally depicted by Saturn or Pluto or the ancient horned god Pan of pre-Christian Europe.

These very same theologians writhe and squirm when it is pointed out to them that it is they, not Jung, who have caused Satan to be part of the god-image in the West. Jung simply pointed out to them this sorry and monstrous god-image they mindlessly created by eternalizing evil, a factor that has racked the Western psyche for almost two millennia. Jung's definition of the Self that is active in the psyches of humans is an entity that transcends the purely mental qualities of what is commonly called "good" and "bad." Is this not what the mystics, Christian or otherwise, have been teaching throughout the ages?

Any god condemning a creature for human weakness (created by that god in the first place) to an eternity of torment is satanic, by any theological definition of the word and by any stretch of the imagination. That the Western psyche has never come to a healthy understanding of the nature of evil and its role in natural events is one of the symptoms of our collective Western neurosis. Our everyday attitudes ultimately stem from our society's god-image, such as it dualistically exists.

If the first commandment* of Moses were truly practiced, the mind would not hold even the most abstract ephemeral mental image of the divine, and the utterly inconceivable godhead would be experienced as being beyond the human categories of good and evil, the consequences of which would revolutionize life on this planet. Some religions try hard in this area, but all succumb eventually to the psyche's formal dictates of archetypally imaging even that which is absolutely transcendent of all finite shapes and forms. True mystics, persons able to go beyond form, in short, are very few in this world, and so is the universality that they teach.

For serious probing readers who are interested in the origins of this collective Western neurosis, looking up the following terms in an encyclopedia might be helpful: Gnosticism, Zoroastrianism, Mithraism, Manichaeism, Zervanism, Ahura-Mazda, Ahriman, Mandeans, Magi, Essene, Dionysus, Osiris, Seth, Isis. We are surprised to discover the ancient Sumerian, Egyptian, Persian and Indian origins of many modern-day Western neurotic attitudes that try to pass for Christ-inspired. For thousands of years people have traveled and traded and exchanged ideas from as far west as Rome and as far east as China, including all the countries and cultures in between. In earlier times there were no such things as plagiarism or copyright laws protecting written or oral works of thought. Countries periodically came under the military, political, cultural and religious domination of other nations, blending their differences as well as their gene pools.

We ought not be hoodwinked into believing that only Greece, Rome and the religion of Israel spawned the Western psyche. Those three cultures were generated by hosts of foreign

* "You shall have no gods except me. You shall not make yourself a carved image or any likeness of anything in heaven or on earth beneath or in the waters under the earth. You shall not bow down to them or serve them. For I, YHVH your God, am a jealous God and I punish the father's fault in the sons, the grandsons and the great grandsons of those who hate me; but I show kindness to thousands of those who love me and keep my commandments. . . ." (Genesis 20:1–6 of the Jerusalem Bible).

influences they would rather not credit. Syncretism (hybridiza-
tion on all levels) is all-pervasive and is ever at work, though
no orthodox sectarian would ever admit this. Actually the so-
called orthodox are ignorant of the real sources of their own
basically unorthodox attitudes, culled from non-Judaic and
non-Christic sources.* Our collective psychic problems go
back a long way.

I have taken this seeming detour into ancient history to
strongly stress that our human problems are collective, age-
old, perennial, archetypal and historical. Many of them are
blindly promulgated by various religious sectors unaware of the
deleterious influences that are extraneous, heretical and alien
to the original teachings of their founder. For example, one
single image, in this case that of Satan, can put millions of us
in a psychic quandary for millennia as we earnestly attempt to
resolve the problem of our propensities toward evil behavior
and its consequences.

One evening the movie *The Exorcist* was aired on television.
A foreign guest, a Tibetan monk, watched the entire film,
cringing and showing appropriate terror in all the right places.
I remarked to him that he had seemed frightened at times by
the horrific scenes, a fact he flatly denied. I pursued the matter
by remarking that he seemed to be making faces when particularly violent scenes were shown. His response was pointed. It
was not fear, he said, which made him wince, but rather
the attitude and wrong approach and methods of the priestly
exorcists themselves who were intent only on sending the
demon back to hell. This, he opined, was not at all the correct
attitude to take.

What was the proper attitude and correct approach and
method to deal with such a terribly upsetting situation? His
answer was succinct: The demon possessed the girl because of
his own personal ignorance and suffering. Troubled minds

* See *India and the Greek World*, Jean W. Sedlar, Rowman and Littlefield, Totowa,
N.J., 1980; and *Stolen Legacy*, George G. M. James, Julian Richardson Associates,
San Francisco, 1985.

always cause trouble for themselves and other people. Even trained Tibetan laymen, he said, can deal with such cases. An intense prayer of compassion spinning forth in blue light from the heart of the Tibetan exorcist monk or layman is directed toward the suffering and disturbed demon. This merciful prayer is for the demon's personal enlightenment, as he too is evolving toward spiritual realization and maturity, which he will reach one day in his future evolution. Is this not the same teaching of Jesus and others: to unconditionally love all of our enemies and those who hate and revile us?

Suppression, repression, self-loathing, anger, impatience, hate, condemnation, anathemas, as well as projection of the shadow, are not efficacious solutions, nor are rigid laws and false beliefs in a psychic reality (evil) that is permanent and unchangeable. The only permanent factor in life, if we try to perceive without preconceived bias, is impermanence. There is no absolute but the Absolute; all else is relative, finite, passing, changing and impermanent. If we see things from this angle, there is hope for our personal and collective victimization, caused by warped, official terrorizing beliefs concerning the nature of evil and apparently aimed at keeping the masses under control through fear instead of through spiritual understanding and insight.

Many readers may be wondering why there is so much emphasis on mythology in Jungian thought. Jung's answer is that mythology and psychology are one and the same. Consciousness is mytho-poetic and is best described in those terms. And if a mythology from another part of our global village is less neurotic, more philosophically astute and on the mark, and more relevant and meaningful in its insights, than the unhealthy, damaging dominant one of our own culture, why not use it for its therapeutic value, since we no longer have any excuse to be culture-bound, thanks to modern travel and satellite communications, and instant live, on-the-spot reporting. There is no longer any legitimate rationale for wearing "tribal blinders" that serve only to perpetuate our collective neuroses.

Within our own Western psycho-spiritual heritage there were indeed at least four psychologically adept thinkers who taught that God allowed evil because without evil to struggle against, there would be no challenge to test the human soul's mettle and to develop its moral fiber and powers. The first, Ireneaus, bishop of Lyons (born circa A.D. 130), was acknowledged as a saint. The second, Origen (born in Alexandria in A.D. 185), was condemned by a Church Council for stating that since the Devil was part of God's plan, he too would be saved at the end of time when all of creation would be drawn back into oneness with the Creator, since evil would no longer be necessary at the end of time. The third was Lactanius (died circa A.D. 330), the leading adviser of Emperor Constantine. The fourth was Pope Saint Clement (died circa A.D. 101), third successor to Saint Peter, who came to the same conclusions as Origen regarding the Devil's fate. It has been officially declared, however, that these ideas were only attributed to Pope Saint Clement and were not really his. How many of us have ever come across these names or any of their ideas in our Western history books?

The Shadow, Sin and Guilt

The shadow is the entity that we first encounter in our dream-work and our journey into the unconscious. No matter what its nature, it offers us an initial view of the repressed parts of our personalities. It has been said that, when transformed, the darkest shadow is eighty percent gold. The means for this alchemical transformation from lead to gold, as it were, will be discussed at length in chapter 12.

Jung's psychology is ethical (stemming from the feeling function of typology), and in this it differs somewhat from other schools of therapy. Ethics is firmly based on the understanding that one's own happiness can never be had at the expense of someone else's. In fact happiness achieved at the expense of another is not genuine, nor can it be long-lived.

Exploiting or taking advantage of others will merely turn them into enemies who will eventually want revenge or to set things aright by force, causing all sorts of mischief for us. Common sense dictates that the end does not justify the means.

Classically in our culture the negative shadow qualities were enumerated as the Seven Capital Sins, namely pride, envy, greed, lust, gluttony, anger and sloth. The antidote to these seven poisons was broken up into two pairs, one of seven and the other of nine. The group of seven, called Gifts of the Holy Spirit, are wisdom, understanding, prudence (supernatural common sense), fortitude, knowledge, piety and awe before the Absolute. The group of nine are called Fruits of the Holy Spirit, namely, charity, joy, peace, patience, kindness, goodness, faith, mildness and temperance. If we understand the Holy Spirit to mean the transcendent Self, then these healing states of consciousness, these Gifts and Fruits, are evoked by our strivings toward wholeness and by sensitizing our egos to the subtle movements of the transpersonal Self within, the very essence of wholeness, and they will generally keep us out of a lot of psychological trouble. They must be "prayed out" of ourselves.

Before we feel better concerning our negative shadow sides, we must expect to feel worse—downright depressed in fact. Surmounting the first barrier, <u>withdrawing projections and focusing on the darkness within</u>, is simply a depressing experience. Such a withdrawal is accompanied by a shattering of self-illusions and the feeling of having lived a false and hypocritical existence. In Jung's experience, Roman Catholics fared better at this initial stage than Protestants since from the age of seven Catholics ritually confess their sins to a priest, including misdemeanors on the levels of thought, word and deed. Sharing one's dark side, in what is called the Sacrament of Reconciliation, with another sympathetic human being is in itself a healing activity, albeit a humbling one. It is a tool, and the healing depends on how and with what attitude one uses it. And, no matter what our outer achievements, it reminds us that we are all still only human. Clinically as well, by revealing pathogenic secrets (for example, incestual desire, murder, perverse activity) to the nonjudgmental therapist the patient makes an emotional breakthrough toward healing.

Some pop psychologists proclaim that one should never feel guilty about anything, a bit of advice that is as shallow as it is lacking in common sense from a therapeutic standpoint. If an evil act has been willfully committed, the perpetrator will benefit psychologically by feeling qualms of conscience since sooner or later evil destroys itself along with the evildoer. Experience demonstrates this plainly. Legitimate feelings of guilt about willful selfishness act as a prime mover in allowing us to pull back shadow projections and to maturely and responsibly begin cleaning up our act. There can certainly be nothing wrong with that. However, compulsive guilt-dumping on oneself for no objective reason is symptomatic of neurosis and must be treated as such.

Actually, the more appropriate word for the experience of legitimate guilt is "compunction," a term that is thousands of years old but, strangely enough, forgotten in modern times. It means "to be touched, or affected by sorrow" for having betrayed a higher law. Compunction shakes us up to the point where a moral about-face (a *metanoia*) becomes a must, more than just an ordinary duty. It urgently focuses our whole consciousness on change, and we become single-minded in this endeavor. As the point of no-return, it is seen in the end as having been a prompting from the Self, a call to wholeness. People who take up the challenge to rehabilitate inner demons or to unearth rejected talents produce a betterment not only for themselves personally and individually but for the world at large, for all of us.

Animal biologist Rupert Sheldrake speaks of "morphic resonance," a theory that holds that, for instance, if a rat of a certain species in a Tokyo laboratory learns a new trick, this accomplishment increases the possibility for a rat of the same species in faraway New York to learn the same trick with greater ease.

The moral of this biological theory, if it is true and if a corollary can be said to exist in the realm of human psychology, would confirm the age-old idea that when one human individual effects a deep change in himself or herself, a change is simultaneously effected somehow or other in all other human beings as well. This is a healthy sort of creative power over the world that few of us could have ever imagined we possessed.

Apropos of self-development, the popular term "yoga" is not just *hatha yoga*, or physical exercises, as is commonly believed; it includes a whole range of mental, emotional and spiritual exercises. Yogis engage in their practices to speed up the evolutionary process of self-realization that results in the awakening of dormant spiritual powers. The first thing studied on this path toward the acquisition of latent potentials is not any of the power-producing yoga techniques at all. The very first subject taught by the master to the student of yoga is ethics, and for a very practical reason. Ethics teaches the student how to use the powers of the soul safely, for the good of all, so that our egos will not become inflated and intoxicated with power and turn the acquired powers into forces destructive of others and ultimately also of the "realized" yogi. (How many of our nuclear scientists or politicians have studied ethics in preparation for their high-powered jobs?)

We could say that these marvelous yogic powers—telepathy, clairvoyance, clairaudience and so on—are really the positive shadow qualities latent in us all. We deny their existence because our extraverted-sensate-thinking culture demands that we do so. This is really a pity.

Einstein is quoted as having said that we humans use only about ten percent of our brain's capacity. Very few of us seem to believe his statement and consequently do nothing about awakening that other sleeping ninety percent. Perhaps we need more real-life models such as Einstein himself or Mother

Teresa, Mother Hale of Harlem, the Dalai Lama, Elisabeth Kübler-Ross, Martin Luther King, DaVinci, Michelangelo, Galileo, Father Damian of Molokai, who dedicated his life to helping the lepers of Hawaii, all the untold lay volunteers who work in cancer, AIDS and geriatric wards of hospitals or with the homeless of our inner cities. These models—instead of fantasy television, movie and Disneyland heroes and heroines—might be better alternatives in helping us harness the dormant powers of our minds and souls. Fewer hours of collective fantasizing and vicarious living in front of our television sets, and more time spent relating to the potent forces of the mythic movies of our own minds, starring the entire cast of meaning-giving archetypes, might move us more speedily in the direction we all say we wish to go, namely, to happiness and contentment and self-development.

Chapter 8

The Opposite Sex— Inside and Out

We are never simply attracted to the opposite sex at large. We are generally attracted only to certain individuals, to persons we usually call "our type." But what constitutes our type? Let us step back a few paces to get a better look.

We initially experience aspects of our unconscious outside of ourselves in projected form. A man seeks certain feminine qualities in his girlfriend or wife and a woman looks for particular masculine qualities in her boyfriend or husband. Jung observed that these sought-after masculine and feminine qualities, besides being outside ourselves, are also intrinsic facets of our unconscious minds. There is a biological basis for this assertion, which will be discussed below.

Logos and Eros

Expressed in various ways by all the masculine deities of mythology—Mars, Mercury, solar Apollo, Jupiter and Uranus, to name but a few—the generic masculine quality Jung called the *Logos* principle. *Logos* is a Greek word meaning "word," "verb," "science," "reason," "discernment" and "abstraction," and it gives rise to such adjectives as "penetrating," "imposing" and "assertive." The English word "logic," a derivation, implies a focused consciousness capable of objectively and clearly differentiating one thing from another, lucidly cutting through ignorance like a sword.

The Logos father principle creates a distinctive focused awareness in us as it struggles continuously to release itself from the fusional, dark consciousness of the maternal womb, the realm of the unconscious. In the unconscious, each thing is fused with the next, everything is continuously coalescing, becoming blended and "contaminated," as it were, with all other unconscious entities. The Logos father principle, on the other hand, throws a celestial solar light on things in the dark, just as the sun does in the darkness of space, enabling us to see distinct forms and shapes in all of their separateness, individuality and differentiation. In this aspect it is phallic, penetrating, combative of and mastering the forces of darkness, unfocused unconsciousness and mental slumber.

The quality that typifies all the goddesses Jung called the Eros principle. Eros (Cupid) was the son of Aphrodite (Venus), goddess of love, beauty and harmony. He is an extension of his mother, the goddess of love. As a mythic personage he is the active masculine agent of a wholly feminine principle. Eros represents feminine earthy relatedness to all people, creatures and things. This relatedness is spontaneous, personal, feeling and instinctive. The gestating child in the enveloping security of the mother's dark but nurturing womb is our first experience of this feminine principle. Suckling at the mother's breast in the loving warmth of the mother's arms is a further experience of the feminine principle of relatedness. It produces in later life such erotic (the adjective that derives from "Eros") things as the phenomenon of food sharing, the ritual of communion and solidarity among those at table. It is understood that one does not share food with one's enemies, for whom no Eros exists; food is partaken only with those for whom one feels a certain bonding, which is a primitive "feminine" instinct originally awakened by suckling in infancy.

As was already stated, the Eros principle is the dark unfocused and confusional unconsciousness of the maternal womb, of Mother Nature in all her lunar and tidal instinctuality, ever waxing and waning, knitting and weaving together all forms of earthly beings, giving birth to them and reabsorbing them in death. Everything in Mother Nature's realm is coextensive with everything else in the cosmos and interlinked in slumber on a physical and psychological "webbing" ever created by her. Even to see this basic truth takes an Eros-consciousness, since this interconnectedness is the undifferentiated, unifying, ever-bonding oneness of the Eros mother principle. To recognize it outside ourselves, we first must notice and understand it inside ourselves.

Individuals, male or female, who are entirely in the grips of the Logos principle, displaying no developed Eros whatsoever, are often involved in unrelated, authoritarian, cruel and relentless power plays, with an emphasis on "law and order"— qualities that typify one-sided, austere and dour patriarchal societies.

Whenever the earthy feminine principle, the Great Mother goddess, is rejected and not honored and respected for what she represents, she takes her revenge on oppressive patriarchalism by appearing negatively and destructively. She is a major archetypal force to be contended with, whether we like the idea of a feminine deity or not. She has been called Mammon for her negative aspects by patriarchalists who refuse to see her positive sacred side and thereby foster negative displays from her.

"Mother" in Latin is *mater*, from which we get the Latin word *materia*, or "matter" in English. If we do not allow her to express through us the Eros principle of instinctual friendliness, bonding and oneness with all creatures and plants and the Earth herself, she manifests in our psyches with a vengeance as compulsive and enslaving *materia*lism and addictive consumerism, which really is a display of how much Logospower we can wield. When we do not cultivate a healthy Erosrelatedness with the things of the feminine material world, relations with her turn sour, and the things of the Earth become prey to the power-mongering, greed, manipulation and control of a one-sidedly developed Logos principle. The present catastrophic state of our Earth's ecology is the direct result of the imbalance of the feminine Eros and masculine Logos principles, specifically in the collective psyche of the Western nations, based on the Judaeo-Christian heritage that insinuates that "Father, sky, spirit, Logos" is good and that "Mother, earth, flesh, Eros" is bad. This mentality also implies that it is all right to subjugate the feminine Earth along with all women, her representatives. Of all the theologies of our planet, YAHWEH, the Judaeo-Christian God image, is the only bachelor god in existence, implying that the divine can only be masculine. Where does that leave the feminine? We must understand that theology tells more about the psychology of theologians than it can ever hope to do in describing the Indescribable Absolute. If a culture's god-image is imbalanced, everything in that culture will be imbalanced. Western culture now endangers the very existence of the planet because of its basic disregard of the vitally important and life-sustaining feminine Eros principle.

We foolishly fail to realize that we cannot escape archetypes, and we especially cannot do so by pretending they do not exist. The feminine Eros principle is here to stay, so we might just as well give her free rein to better our relationships with loved ones, significant others, children, our own bodies and the Earth herself. The Great Goddess is none other than our own bodies, so then why are we poisoning her, polluting her and causing her to suffer all kinds of illnesses? One-sided involvement with the Logos principle keeps us out of touch and unrelated even with our own bodies, not to mention the bodies of our children, whom we mindlessly expose to all kinds of poisons, toxins and filth. How fully awake and aware can we be if we operate solely on the Logos principle to the exclusion of feminine Eros, which keeps us connected to objective earthy reality, to causes and effects?

On the other hand, however, those psyches that solely express the Eros principle to the exclusion of Logos are experienced as boiling over in vulnerability and hypersensitivity, with no ego-boundaries. They display subjective feelings of confusion and chaos, and the most maudlin sort of sentimentality; they exhibit a complete lack of discipline, so that psychic anarchy reigns supreme. The imbalance can produce a magical, superstitious, suspicious, scheming and shifty mindset and mentality. The "good-hearted slob," naiveté and nurturance personified, can be yet another expression of Eros untempered with Logos. Compassion must always be wedded to wisdom if there is to be psychic well-being and balance.

To recapitulate, overemphasized Logos produces an unrelated kill-joy personality, one-upmanship, competitiveness and the desire to have power over others. Overaccentuated Eros produces foggy thinking, co-dependency, lack of self-identity and vague ego boundaries, as well as extreme passivity in the face of life's challenges.

Psychic equilibrium comes about only when the firming up of the Logos principle and the softening touch of Eros are constantly at play with each other. The masculine and feminine principles desperately need each other; when they cooperate, they show their best faces. The meeting ground for them is the human psyche, irrespective of one's personal gender and sexual orientation. They are also active on the biological level.

Psyche and Soma

Modern studies in genetics and neuroendocrinology tend to substantiate Jung's intuitive perceptions of typical and archetypal masculine and feminine differences between the sexes. If *psyche* is an expression of *soma* (body) and vice versa, then the hormonal makeup of individual male and female bodies, according to recent studies, could be considered to be an influential factor in the expression of Logos and Eros qualities. High levels of testosterone make individuals, whether male or female, aggressively and typically masculine, expressing more of the Logos principle. High levels of estrogen produce more typically feminine behaviors expressive of the Eros principle. There are also other suggestive factors to consider. In the course of their bodily evolution males have become adapted to more physically demanding and competitive activities than women, resulting in the biological basis of the division of labor. Such factors were formerly seen as merely culturally determined.

A woman releases one egg per lunar cycle, roughly four hundred in a lifetime, while a man produces one hundred million sperm in one ejaculation. Is it any wonder then that women tend more willingly toward creating a bonded, monogamous family unit while men tend more readily toward unrelated polygamy in their masculine capacity to fertilize billions of ova in a short time frame?

Modern chromosomal studies indicate that babies are already psycho-sexually differentiated at birth. Testosterone, the male hormone, or the absence thereof, appears to be the decisive factor in the formation and organization of the central nervous system, which determines masculine and feminine behavioral patterns. Any nurse with experience in a maternity ward can detect distinct masculine and feminine behaviors even among the newborn. In no way is one sex more intelligent than the other, but there are important differences in the way male and female psyches generally express themselves; this is determined in part by biology.

Many argue that children are brainwashed by adults into stereotypical masculine and feminine cultural roles. The same people never wonder, however, why these stereotypical behaviors have been adopted by almost all of the myriad cultures and peoples of Earth. Why would people universally encourage Venusian and lunar nurturing in their daughters and Martial aggressiveness and solar heroism in their sons if there were no biological or archetypal factors involved?

Those readers who remain unconvinced or who wish further details may find much research information in *Males and Females*, by Corinne Hutt (Penguin, 1972) and *Brain Sex*, by Ann Moir (Michael Joseph Ltd., London, 1984), which discuss these issues from the viewpoint of biology. According to geneticist Moir, the amount of masculine or feminine hormones present in the mother's body during the early weeks of gestation determines whether the embryo's brain, regardless of sex, will operate more on traditionally masculine or feminine lines. According to her research, there can be men who function psychically in ways classically attributable to women, and there are women who can function psychically in ways that men traditionally are noted for, all due to the amounts of various hormones present in the mother's body. Moir is saying that there are men who can perform "women's jobs" very well and women who can perform "men's jobs" very well, regardless of sexual orientation.

Be that as it may, the biological basis for masculine and feminine characteristics has been raised because Jung's observations of the archetypal nature of psychosexual differences have been dismissed by some people on the grounds that Jung failed to produce extraverted-sensate evidence to prove their validity. He indeed did not produce this type of biological evidence but rather proof of a practical, intuitive, clinical nature. Intuition, it will be remembered, is the perceptive function of consciousness that can read "between the lines." Jung died in 1961 before the science of genetics came into full bloom. Behaviors, we now have reason to assume, are partly influenced by society, culture and parents, to be sure, but what these outer factors modify, suppress or exaggerate are genetic predispositions that are already biologically encoded in the embryo.

Consequently both the masculine Logos and the feminine Eros appear to have a solid foundation in biological and genetic factors. Both are considered archetypes, along with all the other patterning instincts of the psyche. Both principles are active in each sex but in entirely different ways.

Before Jung declared his thinking about dreams, for instance, he based his findings on the empirical evidence of 63,000 dreams of men and women examined by him in thorough Swiss fashion. He observed that the most revealing images, among the many welling up from the unconscious minds of men and women, were those describing the dynamics between the two sexes. Just as with the autonomous complexes, the archetypal features of the opposite sex are often experienced as mysterious, fascinating and possessing a tremendous magnetic power of attraction.

Jung observed that in the psyches of the men he analyzed, each held an image of a woman who did not exist in time or space. It was the image of an "eternal woman," lodged deeply in the man's unconscious as an archetype of the primordial feminine, seemingly inherited from remotest times and somehow engraved in humanity's memory bank, filled as it is with the numberless impressions of human womanhood since the time of Eve. Jung found that since this archetypal image of woman is thoroughly unconscious, it is always seen outside of the man in projected form, on the person of his beloved. This sort of unconscious projection may very well explain the whys and wherefores of sexual attraction and repulsion.

Jung believed that within every man is an unconscious woman and in every woman is an unconscious man.

The projection of the image of the opposite sex onto a man or woman is the dynamic for heterosexual mating and bonding and all-alluring romance. Survival of the species as well as individual rapture and ecstasy are also effected by projection of the unconscious image of the opposite sex. Heartache and heartbreak must unfortunately be added to the list of results of the projection of feminine or masculine elements onto the wrong people. "Love," otherwise known as projection of the contrasexual soul image, can indeed be blind.

Anima and Animus

The unconscious feminine soul image in a man Jung called the *anima*, the Latin word for soul, which is a feminine noun in that language. The masculine soul image in a woman he called the *animus* (the *-us* is a masculine noun ending in Latin). Among other things, the unconscious anima in a man is the dynamic of the Eros principle in him, and the unconscious animus in a woman represents the dynamic of the Logos principle in her.

As with all archetypes, the contrasexual archetypes of anima and animus are actualized through the early personal experiences of their projection onto mother and father, respectively, or onto any other important and significant females and males in the child's immediate environment.

We say, axiomatically, that a girl marries her father and a boy marries his mother. Mother indeed "colors" a boy's anima and father a girl's animus, just as mother shapes her daughter's feminine ego and father his son's masculine ego.

In the case of a boy developing his masculine ego-consciousness, his feminine side is by and large left undeveloped and undifferentiated along with the inferior function of consciousness, both remaining in the depths of his unconscious. The same goes for a girl concerning her masculine side, which, in conjunction with her inferior function remains, on the whole, undeveloped and ignored. Sooner or later those compensatory elements buried in the unconscious will have to be elevated into consciousness, accompanying the movement toward wholeness instigated by the Self, a process Jung has called individuation.

As was stated earlier, that word comes from the Latin *individuus*, meaning "undivided," "not fragmented" or "whole." Individuation actually begins from the moment of conception and stretches over an entire lifetime. There is no specific time or age for it. It intimately involves "marrying" the qualities of

the two sexes within ourselves. This process generally begins
well after marriage, but nothing in psychic life can be pin-
pointed to a specific schedule.

Perhaps because of their biology, women tend more to project their animus and their emotions and fantasies onto a single
concrete male, although he usually takes multiple forms in her
dreams and fantasies. Her psyche tends, perhaps partly because
of biology, to be more monogamous than that of a man. Her
animus, personifying her masculine unconscious, represents
her masculine polygamous instincts. He generally appears in
dreams as a most diversified series of figures. The multiple
men seen in her dreams and fantasies compensate for her
monogamous feminine ego-consciousness attitudes pertaining
to bonding. In real life, however, she generally tends to focus
on a single male partner.

Human and nonhuman males tend to be relatively more
promiscuous than females, which implies that, without an
integration of the bonding-prone anima, the aggressive masculine principle, left to itself, generally pushes men compulsively
into multiple relationships and uncommitted sexual encounters. A man's anima allows him to express relatedness and
commitment to a significant other. Men generally believe that
because they have made physical love with a female partner,
they have made tremendous strides in expressing the full gamut
of Eros; nothing, of course, could be further from the truth.
Truly integrated and developed Eros implies anchoring, emotional relating, bonding, sharing, commitment and even remembering anniversaries. When women do not bring a
developed Logos into their marriage, they lose themselves in
their husbands in a sort of "participation mystique," to use
the French phrase. They remain always "wife" vis-à-vis their
husbands, never becoming "woman," "friend," "confidante,"
"seductress." Without Logos their individuality gets lost in the
shuffle. Very few males or females ever attempt to consciously
integrate the contrasexual in themselves, simply because they

do not know it is there. The dire consequences of this inaction—broken relationships—are seen tragically all around us.

All men have breasts and nipples, and if they do not biologically produce actual liquid nourishment for infants, on the psychological level this present though undeveloped feminine factor ought to inspire a nurturing attitude whereby fathers may "father" their children with the spiritual truths of the Logos principle.

The undeveloped phallic part of a woman's genitals (i.e., the clitoris), though not sperm-producing, on the psychological level ought to inspire a "masculine" attitude in her whereby she may inseminate the Eros values of relatedness and friendly connectedness into the consciousness of her children as well as of that of her husband.

The animus and anima are not three-dimensional entities. They respectively represent a "god" and "goddess" who inhabit a more ethereal realm than that of our ego world. They can make us do things that our egos can never hope to do.

The role of the animus is to awaken a woman out of the heaviness and inertia of Mother Earth consciousness, catapulting her into a growing and more secure Martial and solar self-confidence. The "woman" part of her should not disappear. There are many goddesses of myth, such as Vesta (Hestia), Minerva (Pallas Athena), Diana the Huntress (Artemis), Ceres (Demeter, Isis), Juno (Hera), the Amazons and the Muses who can act as models of independence and who can show her the way. These goddesses are alive and well in a woman's psyche and are waiting to be acknowledged and to jump into action. Besides these mythic figures, the modern woman needs models and examples of them in real life, starting at an early age, in order to actualize the goddess qualities that are innate within her. If the models are not present in her family or clan members, she must consciously seek them out among friends, teachers or characters in films or novels. Passivity in this regard leads only to more unconscious living.

What the assimilated and made-conscious animus imparts to a woman is of the nature of Logos—differentiated knowledge, crystal-clear understanding and a profound spiritual meaning to life. Without the animus's positive help, brought about by assiduous work with her dreams and a passionate attempt to understand them, a woman might spout all sorts of learned collective ideas and opinions culled from hearsay, which only arouse animosity in truly thoughtful people and which in the end never really satisfy her personal longing to know the truth for herself. Such a process actually deprives her of real spiritual and intellectual development, which is precisely what traditional patriarchal societies want in order to control and exploit her.

As for men, the more they are dominated by a rigid macho persona, the more their anima remains unevolved in the darkness of the unconscious. Because the anima remains unintegrated in a healthy way into consciousness, she can plunge them, when they least expect it, into compulsive effeminacy, deadly moodiness, extreme irritability and all-consuming hysteria (this latter concept being derived from the word for "uterus" in Greek). The unresolved anima does not give any warnings or reasons for her behavior, but many times it has to do with a feeling of being unlovable or unloved. An undeveloped anima in a man produces an Eros principle that is totally out of whack, relationally speaking, and an uncultivated animus in a woman expresses the discriminating Logos principle of a Neanderthal man. An undeveloped anima and animus can lock horns when both the man's and woman's egos are tired, under attack by a complex or just plain wounded for one reason or another.

When a man forgets his ego and deals with his wife from his anima level, in order to defend herself against her husband's powerful "goddess," she has to dig up her powerful "god." But both "god" and "goddess" are unconscious entities, so literally all hell (i.e., the underworld of the unconscious) breaks loose. To avoid this type of disaster, every man and woman should

learn about the contrasexual elements in each one's unconscious, men needing to acknowledge that it is okay to have a
woman inside and women needing to acknowledge the same
about the inner man. Then both men and women need to
work on lifting those contrasexual qualities into the light of
ego consciousness, incarnating and expressing them in everyday life. A healthy sort of religious or spiritual practice could
help in this endeavor by involving communal encouragement.

A boy will naturally suppress, to a point, the mother-anima
image in himself as he strives to develop his masculinity, and
the same holds true for girls regarding their father-animus
image. Both boys and girls as little children, however, traditionally remain in the realm of mother and grandmother while
the men are away most of the day at their masculine endeavors.
This happens even if the infants and toddlers go to day-care
centers where most models may be other children or a teenage
caretaker.

Human psychology, one could say, is based at least fifty
percent on the profound psychological principle of "monkey
see, monkey do," otherwise known as "modeling." The little
boy's dilemma, if he is in a traditional family situation, is to
disidentify with Mommy. At a certain age he must begin to
identify with Daddy, whom he might see briefly in the morn-
ings and evenings and on weekends, while Mommy or another
female figure is present most of the time. He may or may not
successfully achieve this detachment from mother's realm, for
a variety of reasons. If he does not, he remains what is called
a mamma's boy.

The important thing is that he be consciously helped by
both mother (to whom he must die) and father (to whom he
must be born). (Yes, fathers too must "give birth" to their
children, especially their boys.) So-called primitive societies
perform all kinds of initiatory rituals and rites of passage to
facilitate painful transitions from one stage of life to another.
The best that Western culture has produced in this regard is
the Boy Scouts and perhaps the now-effete puberty rites of

Confirmation and Bar-Mitzvah, since Judaeo-Christian arche-typal forms, as all archetypal forms in religious history, have lost their power and need newer expressions. This is a fact of Nature.

One hopeful sign in this direction is a recent upsurge of middle school (junior high school) graduation ceremonies—complete with scrolled diplomas, orchestras and the general hoopla—creating a special rite of passage to encourage early teenagers to pursue the next level of studies and the next level of psychological and pubertal development. It seems, however, a rather enfeebled attempt at effecting rites of passage for our youngsters, who have taken matters into their own hands using acts of "heroic" vandalism or teenage pregnancy as initiatory signs of their rising to a new level of maturation. All genuine rites of passage involve an enacted dying to what was, involv-ing some truly grueling and painful experience—something akin to Marine boot camp. The actual forms of the initiation must come from the more intuitive members of a particular community, as each community has it own special needs. If the positive archetypes of initiation are not tapped, then the negative sides will manifest unbidden, as they have in societies where a sense of the religious or spiritual has been crushed by left-brained hyperrationalism.

The demands of high school can constitute a sort of initia-tory rite of passage into adulthood, as can those of college, but our culture still sorely lacks something more profound and basic—the sacred aspects of the mysteries of death and rebirth, which would make the process of education a truly profound emotional experience. American teenagers, alas, are physi-cally killing themselves instead of ritually doing so. Spirituality of some kind could indeed provide the necessary ritual.

Young girls in traditional societies, where mother works in the home or in the nearby fields, have an easier time regarding modeling. Young females in industrial societies may or may not have a corporate or working mother on whom to model. Indeed a mother or father might be missing entirely because of divorce, separation or death, with ensuing consequences regarding actualization or nonactualization of the conscious masculine or feminine ego and the unconscious animus or anima. When no one is available to act as a model, actualization of the archetypes is stultified and psychic growth becomes impeded. (Readers desiring a more detailed discussion of the myriad intricacies of child development from a Jungian perspective may want to consult *The Inner World of Childhood*, by Frances G. Wickes, or *Children as Individuals*, by Michael Fordham.)

If the father or an older uncle or grandfather is missing from the everyday environment, the boy child will have only his mother's masculine animus to take as a model. This creates a dilemma in psychic growth since the mother's animus is unconscious; if the boy's three-dimensional masculine ego tries to identify with it, it may become very ephemeral, wispy and unsuited for functioning that would be expected of him in everyday encounters. On the other hand, his anima would be influenced very much by his mother's feminine ego, creating an imbalance in him; that is, his anima would be too charged with Mother energy and his masculine ego would be "undercharged." Each case is individual—the human psyche is too subtle an entity to submit to rigidly fixed rules.

The boy, after successfully "dying" to his mother (who on her side must consciously release and "die" to him) and her realm in order to develop his masculine ego, will have to reconnect at mid-life with those same feminine images of Mother, the Virgin, the Witch, the Whore, the Lover, the Spiritual Guide—all the manifold varieties of woman from the beginning of time—and with undeveloped feminine elements lodged his unconscious, where they will have been collecting psychic energy through the years. He may be frightened by what these aspects signify, but he ought to comprehend that they will only manifest negatively if not allowed positive expression.

If unwilling to comply with the demands for recognition by

the inner woman, he will connect with an outer woman and
project the more magical aspects of the anima on her. This
state will create an immature and unevolved relationship so
that she, not he, may live out all his bewitching feminine
sides. He may even run off with his twenty-two-year-old secre-
tary or start an affair with a neighbor's wife. This is a heavy
burden for a wife or any woman to carry; the dynamics of the
situation keep her man infantile, immature and a bore to
live with, devoid of the imagination and fascinating mystical
aplomb that only his anima can provide him from within. He
may even display aspects of the Puer Aeternus, the archetype
of the Eternal Child (Latin *puer* = boy, whence the English
word "puerile"), someone cute but who has never grown up.

In contrast to one-sided machismo (a Spanish word meaning
"exaggerated maleness") is the example of the gloriously psychologically androgynous, grinning, semitoothless figure of
Mahatma Gandhi—a definite "ringer" for the Wise Old Man,
symbol of the Self and psychic wholeness. He mobilized huge
political forces through his charisma and marvelous Venusian
strategies of passive aggression.

On the other hand, there are men who—because of their
genetic predisposition or lack of classical male modeling—
may experience an intense overidentification with their anima. This type of male will seek his own undeveloped masculinity in another man. This inaccessible, unconscious Logos
principle may be projected onto another man who possesses a
stereotypical, crude form of masculinity and whose image is
thus irresistibly appealing in its Dionysian and sexually aggressive, magnetic vigor. He in turn is looking for more refined
qualities, which he lacks in himself. The allure of this type
of romantic image is proportionate to the intensity of the
identification by the man with his anima. In the homoerotic
relationship that ensues, the earthy masculinity of the hook
for his projection rubs off, as it were, onto the ego of the
anima-identified male. His ethereal, more spiritualized masculinity is absorbed by the partner, in a process akin to the

age-old principles of sympathetic magic. Actually, the same dynamic is operative in a man-to-woman relationship; however, in the case of heterosexuality the man's ego masculinity awakens the female partner's animus traits, and she his anima qualities.

For a woman overidentified with her animus, the same dynamics are at work in the opposite direction. She may live out of her discarnate Logos animus principle and attempt to connect with the more refined qualities of the Goddess in a relationship with a woman upon whom the Goddess has been projected. Ideally, individuals, no matter what their sexual orientation, ought eventually to develop psychological androgyny (masculine-feminine balance) to be complete, whole human beings. This is effected when the anima or animus is "married" to the man or woman's ego-consciousness. It is called a sacred marriage, since it takes place entirely within the psyche of the individual man or woman.

Interestingly, for the homosexual the loved one of the same sex is the carrier of the projection of the Self, whereas for the heterosexual the loved one is the carrier of the projection of the anima or animus. This is a complicated and subtle issue and requires in-depth treatment to do it any justice. A more complete view of this topic is provided by the extremely insightful book *Jung, Jungians, and Homosexuality*, by Robert R. Hopcke.

When the second half of life has been reached, no one—thanks to Mother Nature's rhythms—can resist the pressing onslaught from the unconscious, which urges acknowledgment of itself. The many neglected aspects are always observed to spring up at this time in an attempt to bring about wholeness and individuation. Although simply a repeatedly observable facet and stage in human nature, it can be an exciting time in a person's life. It need not be a mid-life crisis, as so many wrongly expect it to be; it becomes so only if we fiercely resist the changes Mother Nature wishes to bring about. A function of the animus or anima is to serve as a bridge or link between the ego-consciousness and the inner world, in the same way that the persona is the mediatory function between the ego and the outer world. It brings the contents of the collective unconscious within reach of ego-awareness.

At the juncture of mid-life, if this internal movement toward wholeness is willingly and wholeheartedly complied with, a certain rush of success can be experienced. Having made her animus conscious, the woman will now also stop trying to "score points off others," especially men. Owning up to her masculine side allows her to assume the authority of a positive Saturn/Kronos/Jehovah, which gives new direction to her life. She drops the old neurotic game of struggling for supremacy in her married and career life. She no longer argues to overcome and dominate her "adversary" but rather strives to discover the truth within her that nurtures the potentials of creative thought. She ceases relegating the responsibilities of "achievement" to her husband or significant other and seeks an active position in society all on her own. She too can now incarnate those unconscious masculine images and aspects of the Hero, the Scholar, the Spiritual Guide, the Tribal Chieftain, the President of the Republic. The negative animus, which in the past limited her personal freedom as a woman, through a sense of inferiority, can now empower her through the above-mentioned masculine images, which she finally understands to have been hidden aspects and abilities of her own psyche.

She must not, however, allow this new-won lucid, differentiated consciousness and capability for crisp abstract thought, which can be valuable assets in her professional life, to develop into cold, ruthless, destructive elements in her personal relationships. When she retains her Eros life as a woman, she can safely express her newfound masculine qualities in their proper spheres of professional achievement and career competitiveness. Keeping the Eros and Logos energies balanced can only help her to keep her life in balance; the demands of relationship and the demands of professional authority ought to be equally respected in their mutual domains.

On the inner level, the integrated animus can act for her as the Priest, the Sage, the Interpreter of inner images and Clarifier of spiritual Logos truth, all of whom initiate her into the secret life of the eternal symbols of the unconscious; they are carriers of the spiritual values from the depths of the collective unconscious into the reaches of her own soul. It is the animus that leads her to transpersonal relationships she never believed existed until now. It is the animus who brings about "the marriage of heaven and earth" within her, enabling her to bring forth the Divine Child who is her very own Self.

On the other hand, the man who at mid-life answers the call to wholeness by making his anima and his feminine soul more conscious will find that petty erotic adventures no longer hold the fascination they did when he was younger. His Eros and Venusian-anima elements, now integral parts of his ego-awareness, are no longer as compulsive as they were when they were only the unconscious forces of youth. He no longer projects his emotional anima conflicts and failures onto his wife or mother or women friends, whom he self-righteously blamed during all the years when his anima, the woman inside him, was still suppressed, denied and unconscious. The emotional problems of his life are now seen as having been caused not by all the outer women in his life but rather by the ignored woman within. He formerly had thought that these outer women had to change, instead of realizing that his own inner woman had to be recognized and brought into the light of day. Had he done so, his inner woman would have ceased inflicting her confusional, bewildering, irascible, moody, despair-provoking defenses against him because of his unenlightened and adamant rejections of her.

When befriended, the anima can lead the man into the mysterious realms of the collective unconscious, much as Beatrice led Dante to the higher world in the *Paradiso*. When she begins doing this for him, he comes to an understanding of why, when still unacknowledged, she thrust herself upon him with such irrational, yet irresistible, power and force. He also begins understanding why he foolishly interpreted this attention-getting tactic as being so threatening to his masculine ego-identity. He had failed to see that he was dealing with an eternal "goddess," the embodiment of vital life forces that give meaning to every single aspect of his life.

When stubbornly resisted by the masculine ego, the anima goddess perennially appears as the mermaid or siren who lures her man with an otherworldly voice into the depths of the ocean of the collective unconscious to drown and destroy him with confusion and madness. Seen in the light of Jungian psychology, madness (clinically named "psychosis") is the psyche's way of forcing wholeness and new life from the deeper strata onto a hyperrigid, one-sided, meaninglessly superficial, ego-centered individual. Madness, as all other forms of pain, signals in a neutral way that something has gone amiss and is trying confusedly to rectify things. It may also be a simple escape and attempt to take refuge from unbearable outer circumstances.

When unresisted, the anima-siren will share with a man her embodiment of the tempting instinctual wisdom of earthy, oceanic Mother Nature, who has her roots in the collective unconscious. With this gift of herself, she can bring him out of the masculine clouds of his rationalistic stratosphere into a broader instinctual understanding of life as it really is, as well as into an intuitive comprehension of the mysterious workings of his earthly human nature. When acknowledged, honored and paid heed, she reveals to a man the nonrational (not irrational), wispy secrets of the human soul. This world newly opened to him makes him feel reborn due to the sudden onrush of creativity he now feels and in the past sorely needed and missed.

The sign of his having achieved androgyny is the joyous spontaneity and warm friendliness now enlivening all of his relationships. Having become more mellow and more at home with his feelings, he can finally escape the dreadful loneliness

of the purely masculine Logos principle. This Logos principle
had cut him off from others by impelling him to blindly lord
it over them, an impulse that is now seen as a defense mechanism that kept people at a safe distance.

The Role of the Inferior Function

For both males and females, when the contrasexual is finally
assimilated, through much painful discipline and serious professional work with dreams and fantasies, the anima or animus
is seen to be permeated by the inferior function. In short, the
soul-image manifests the function that had been the least
developed over the years, and the anima/animus images will
clearly reveal their connection with it.

Put simply, an abstract-thinking professorial type will observe his anima expressing primitive emotionality with a strong
bent toward Venusian seductiveness. An intuitive, sensitive
poet type will encounter within himself an overly sensate
Mother Earth anima. A feeling violinist will encounter an
Einstein-type animus lurking in the darkness of her unconscious. And a lusty, two-feet-on-the-ground Hausfrau sensate
type will eventually meet up with an extravagantly intuitive
Merlin the Magician animus figure. The unconscious truly
compensates for whatever is lacking in consciousness, and its
treasures bring us extreme joy, if not also a satisfied mind.

If we want to catch a glimpse of a particular man's anima,
we need only look at his wife or close lady-friend, and vice
versa for a woman. We always try to unite with the type of
the inner man or inner woman through the people we project
upon in the outer world, namely our spouses or lovers. However, only when a man takes back the anima projection from
his wife, and a woman does the same in retrieving her animus
projection from her husband, can husbands and wives finally
begin to love their spouses as those persons objectively are.
Until that happens, it can be said that they were only in love

with their subjective projections, aspects of themselves. True love begins only when all projections are consciously taken back to oneself, inasmuch as that is possible

In the case of "love at first sight," we can be one hundred percent certain that the parties concerned are suffering from a massive projection of the anima or animus. The only remedy for this type of lovesickness is an old-fashioned, long-drawn-out courtship that will perhaps enable the lovers in time to differentiate the projected soul-image from the hook that had fused with it. In the long run, people are not soul-images or archetypes and will fiercely rebel if they are pressed into behaving like archetypal gods and goddesses. Ultimately, idealizing a love partner in this way is an unrealistic attitude that only leads to deep frustration and eventual massive disappointment for both partners.

When we accord to our own inner life its due recognition of the "magic" it makes us feel, projections tend to get withdrawn with the help of time, and we begin having at our disposal all the energy that was bound up in habitually projecting our unconscious parts. Allowing fragmentation of ourselves by projection is pointless. Although the feeling of being "in love" is heavenly, we do it at the expense of self-knowledge, inner poise, wholeness and individuation, a heavy price to pay.

When projections are withdrawn, we notice that love relationships no longer smother us because we achieve an inner freedom by objectively knowing who we are and who our loved ones are. We stop losing ourselves in our partners, with all the neurotic co-dependency that this implies. When we withdraw projections we become capable of a more objective, authentic love and possibly of a more conscious devotion and loyalty because we can finally see who we are really dealing with.

One partner may achieve withdrawal of projections, but the other may not. The problem that remains for the partner still projecting is that he or she is still loving an aspect of his or her self projected onto the partner, and not the partner as he or she objectively is. The projected-upon partner may be uneasy and insecure if he or she is aware of the dynamics at play. Fear comes about formulated as the following question: Will he still love me when he finally begins seeing who I really am? No one can answer this question or address the fear until the projection is withdrawn. The same process more or less exists in all romantic relationships, whether heterosexual or homosexual.

In a committed, long-term relationship, we are forced, like it or not, to pull back projections and to own up to the opposite sex within ourselves. In "open" or nonmonogamous relationships, anima or animus keeps getting projected onto mistresses and lovers in a never-ending, vicious cycle with little chance for self-integration because the thrust is ever toward the outer world. We extraverted Americans have great difficulty seeing this simple truth, though the pain of the divorce courts seems to be bearing down upon us, at last producing faint glimmers of lucidity regarding interpersonal relationships and family life.

When we are whole within ourselves, there is finally something solid to offer our love partners. We can give unreservedly of our individuated selves without there being any fear about losing our individuality.

As was stated earlier, the principle of "monkey see, monkey do" is half the lesson in psychology. If one's parents were psychologically evolved and mature, as a rule the child by mere osmosis will fare better in psychic development. Most of us, however, had parents who were very human, and sometimes their influence was so devastatingly painful that we would rather forget that we ever had parents at all. If this is the case, we may feel that we would do better to start from scratch. This is not an unrealistic idea; it can be achieved by understanding that we can indeed rebirth ourselves by bringing together the masculine and feminine, the conscious and unconscious elements in ourselves, which will produce a new state of consciousness. We are virtually reborn when this inner "sacred marriage" takes place. The process is speeded up if we educate ourselves about the realities of depth psychology and begin applying Jung's principles.

If a man and woman have intercourse, under favorable conditions a child is born nine months later. Likewise, when our ego engages in "intimate relations" with the opposite sex deep within ourselves, an "alchemical" transformation takes place. A "child," or whole new state of consciousness, is born that transcends the old opposites of ego and anima/animus. We can completely rebirth ourselves and indeed start from zero, as it were, by engaging in the task of making conscious what is unconscious the moment the need is felt. It is all individual. This is essentially what psychic "alchemy" is all about: a simple process that is actually a lifelong struggle that we can accomplish, God willing and with proper guidance. We are more likely to succeed if we actively learn on the levels of both head and heart. "Book learning" and psychological education are only a small part of it; another is the pursuit of spiritual practices wherein sincere devotion for Father and Mother God is encouraged to flourish in our hearts. Right-brained religious practices with all their symbols are what connect us to the vitalizing realm of the Divine, our highest Self, and beyond into the blissful transcendental realm of dreamless sleep where we are at one with universal Consciousness and Spirit, our fullest potential.

Now more than ever with all the cultural changes taking place, not only in the West but worldwide, and with the traditional roles of women and men altering, no one of sound mind can return to the worn-out, sexist assignments of past eras, which so negatively affected our collective psycho-spiritual development. Neither sex can disregard the task of making the contrasexual more fully conscious since, if there was ever a time or era that encouraged development of the anima and animus, it is this Age of Aquarius, the archetype of psychic androgyny and individuation that is upon us and that will reign supreme, if not quietly, for the next two millennia or so.

Chapter 9

A Matter of Spirit

By working and interacting with dream images and figures on a regular basis, the contrasexual anima or animus eventually becomes more assimilated into consciousness, due to a determined, receptive, cooperative ego. Furthermore, the unconscious will continue trying to produce in us a much saner and more whole androgynous psyche, via the genuine power it possesses to bring about certain very lofty psychic goals. It will coax us toward a manifestation of our greatest potentials despite leaden inertia, possible misgivings and various inner and outer distractions of all kinds. We are somehow "doomed" to reach the stars, as it were, both above and deep down within.

The truest natures of a man and woman, of all of us, are personified by the Wise Old Man and the Great Mother, who appear only after the personal unconscious has been brought into the light and is operative as an active partner in day-to-day living. Both the Wise Old Man and the Great Mother are symbols of the Self that have remained until now in the deeper strata of the collective unconscious. They are very specific images of the Self, blueprints of a superior consciousness that we may share in.

Spirit and Matter

The Wise Old Man personifies incarnated, manifested, *materialized* spirit and the Great Mother represents *spiritualized* matter that is thoroughly imbued, permeated and saturated with spirit. These images represent, respectively, how men and women first experience the Self on a very concrete, personal, existential level. Each gender has its own special experience with regard to this. This does not imply that the Self is not active from infancy or childhood; it only means that the opportunity has finally come to deal with this reality in a more complete, conscious way.

Historically in most cultures matter and spirit have been classified as two separate categories. An inexorable split in the human psyche has been created as a consequence of viewing reality in this way. Matter is seen, for the most part, in such categories as Mother, Earth, flesh, incarnation, realism, sensuousness, intuition, impulse, emotionality, Eros, mercy and the personal. Spirit is envisaged as Father, sky, space, invisibility, transcendence, abstraction, discipline, rationality, the principles of law and order, Logos, justice and the impersonal or transpersonal.

Ultimately, according to the contemporary new physics and the Eastern sages of antiquity, what we call matter and spirit are merely two aspects of the same reality, the same consciousness. This is numerologically symbolized by zero (0), the inconceivable emptiness out of which comes the fullness of all Creation. Biblically stated, the truth regarding the immanence of Spirit in matter has been expressed as follows: "For in Him [God] we live and move and have our being" (Acts 17:28). Despite this profound teaching, we have perennially looked for the Absolute up in the sky somewhere, or in a futuristic afterlife, as if the Divine as revealed or intuited were not ubiquitous here and now, as if the Divine were something to have instead of something to be.

In their appearances in dreams and fantasies, the archetypal images of the Wise Old Man and the Great Mother may range from the crudest forms to refined and sublime ones. The ideal male (the Wise Old Man) may be depicted as a phallic symbol, a medicine man (a shaman), a prophet, a high priest, a genuine guru or spiritual master, an Arthurian Merlin, a Divine Fool or a Mahatma Gandhi type. The ideal female (the Great Mother) may emerge from the unconscious portrayed as a dark cave, a fertility goddess, a medium or sibyl, a medicine woman (a shamaness), a Pallas Athena wisdom-goddess type, an Isis or someone like Mother Teresa of Calcutta.

The danger that comes in the wake of these bigger-than-life images lies in the tendency of the ego to unconsciously identify with them. If this happens—and it usually does—an inflation of the ego ensues since the part (the ego) mistakenly believes itself to be the whole (the Self), with all the dire consequences that this hubris and pride portend. We need only look at some of the Roman emperors, or contemporary medical doctors, or psychotic patients whose egos literally believe they are God incarnate. In the case of the first two, power can be intoxicating and go straight to their heads. In the case of psychotics, in whom the ego has become very fragile, identifying with divine power actually gives a necessary psychological boost to the ego.

The identification with the archetype of the divine is consciously broken by the simple but effortful act of seeing the archetype and ego for the separate entities that they are. Differentiation of the ego from the Self is achieved through relentless dream-work, which sooner or later makes the ego more than aware that it is only a satellite of the pivotal consciousness called the Self. Healthy humility—simple recognition of the way things are—allows the blind identification to dissolve and give way to a sane, rejuvenating, cooperative union of the ego with the Self, the archetype of supreme power. It is coincidentally at this same interval that a man actually frees himself from being an extension of his earthly father and that a woman finally cuts the psychological umbilical cord that binds her to overdependency on her natural mother.

For example, a husband and wife, both psychotherapists themselves, were in analysis for many years. Both were extremely attached to their parents and very much attached to their mutual therapists. After a spiritual quest, including a return to the traditional religious practices of their youth and a pilgrimage to a miraculous shrine in a foreign country, both became intensely attached to their "divine heavenly parents." They became detached from their earthly parents to the point of wanting to settle on the opposite side of the country away from their families, and both left their psychotherapists, who had become extensions of their earthly parents. They were able to cut the psychological umbilical cord to both biological and therapeutic parents only after their pilgrimage had provided them with such soul-stirring and deeply emotional experiences of a divine power, both outside and inside them, that they felt loved and nurtured on an immediate and intimate heart level. Their lives were never the same again. The Divine was experienced by them as real; it was distinct from them, but they were able to share in its Nature, the fruit of which is called psychological maturity. Such experiences may appear to be meaningless or irrelevant to persons unawakened to the latent powerful realities of the unconscious. To those who have not had a religious experience, no real explanation is possible; to those who have, no explanation is necessary.

Generally speaking, after a man disidentifies with the Wise Old Man and a woman disidentifies with the Great Mother, the opportunity of becoming a distinct individual, of becoming individuated, is soon offered. One ceases being one's father's son or mother's daughter and surrenders to the tremendous, joyous freedom that being a child of God can bring. As the moon reflects the solar light, so too does the ego now more fully reflect its Higher Self, whose image it intimates to everyone around. This state of spiritual childhood, like a child, needs intensive nurturing and tender loving care to grow and flourish.

Jung noted that for a man God is a masculine experience and that for a woman God is a feminine experience. In short, for a man the Self will be a masculine image and for a woman the Self will appear as a feminine image, because ultimately most of what one can experience of the Divine on the level of psyche is basically what is divine in oneself. Let us not forget that the gods and goddesses are images of what we all may become.

The Self is both Father *and* Mother; Dame Julian of Norwich's book *Divine Revelations* ought to be consulted for further exploration of the eternal maternal aspects of the Divine that have been consciously neglected and ignored by the powers that be in Christendom. In Judaism, the *Shekkinah* (Yahweh's consort and manifested feminine energies) of the occult Kabbalah has quietly saved the day within this tradition, but warnings of impending insanity are proclaimed by some religious leaders if one even dares to think of studying this portion of Judaic esoterica.

Heart and Mind

The psychological dilemma created by splitting matter from spirit is reflected on a lower, more popular level in Western humanity's perennial conflict between heart (Eros) and mind (Logos). This split occurred mainly because many Westerners falsely and unequivocally equate mind and intellect with spirit. Consequently it is not really a conflict between matter and spirit as such but rather a problematical offshoot of the artificially left-brain-created split between soul and spirit.

For some students of Wisdom, spirit is what animates the soul, and soul is what animates the body. "Soul" is equatable with the Greek *psyche* and the Latin *anima*, both of which mean "soul." The Latin *spiritus*, Greek *pnevma* and Hebrew *ruach* all literally mean "breath" but imply an inconceivable

Spirit or Divine Transcendence, all qualities. The archetypal image of Spiritual Transcendence is in each of us and represents the principle unifying all of us on earth and the whole universe. Spirit can be called the soul of our soul. No adjective may ever actually qualify it adequately, however, since it is entirely metaphysical. All we can talk about are the ways its energy reverberates in our psyches.

The rift between head and heart manifested itself sporadically in the West from classical times, but it appeared in a more virulent form during the Renaissance in the fifteenth century. The contagion spread mainly among the nations of northwestern Europe, moving the consciousness of these populations further and further from a positive relation with the world of instinct and the realm of the unconscious. This psychic imbalance became firmly entrenched in most of the West during the eighteenth-century Age of Enlightenment and evolved to the present psychic stance and views of rigid hyper-rationalism that ludicrously and arrogantly calls itself scientific, a term intending to make us believe in its infallible all-knowingness. This shortsighted mentality ridicules and negates all opinions except its own, which are solely based on extraverted sensation and thinking and left-brain dominance. The unconscious nonrational sides consequently strike back with a vengeance. They do so in exceedingly ugly ways in the forms of amorality, violence of every category, chaotic relationships, and drug and alcohol abuse among all ages and social groups. This need not be so, if we could only begin expressing the full range of our psychic potential and human typology. It all really comes back to learning about the values of the ways in which our psyches operate and putting them into motion.

Regarding the plague of alcoholism, Jung is reported to have personally told one of the founders of Alcoholics Anonymous that "the alcoholic is really looking for 'spirit' in a bottle instead of in the true world of spirit which is within his or her own being." Jung was saying that there is a more direct route than the detouring fruit of the vine, something the alcoholic may not be aware of and needs help discovering. We know that alcohol helps remove a psychological wall that blocks the drinker from having access to his or her own deeper feelings and instinctual life. Alcohol, however, offers only a temporary solution and remedy that do not transform the deficient psychic situation on a permanent basis. Alcohol eliminates symptoms for a brief time; the spiritual disease, however, remains untreated. Only spiritual practice can remedy spiritual ills (which Alcoholics Anonymous is more than aware of in its use of the Twelve Step Program) and so can a deep understanding of Dionysus, the archetypal god of wine and ecstasy.

Actually, various gods are at play in the Western psychological drama that began in the Age of Enlightenment, which saw the rise of Western nation states, of left-brained, puritanical forms of Christianity, as well as the overrationalisms and supremacy of the new religion called modern science, wherein the left cerebral hemisphere has been deified to the neglect and denigration of the other ninety percent of the aspects of human psychic life.

Dionysus and Apollo

One of the archetypal divine protagonists is Dionysus, lord of wine, ecstasy and untamed natural instinct, who rules over the irrational aspects of human nature. In ancient Egypt he was known as Osiris, in India as Shiva and in Rome as Bacchus. In astral symbolism he is the Scorpio/Pluto archetype of the mysteries of procreation and total transformation in the repeated cycle of suffering, death and resurrection. (Remember that every archetype has two distinct sides, and Dionysus is no exception to the rule.)

It is he who offers humanity the ecstatic pleasures of wine, women and song. Feminine eroticism is his domain par excellence. On a grander scale, he represents all the primordial instinctual life force that is in perpetual opposition to everything that is petrified or dead in us and that tends to remain that way through habit, fear, ignorance or inertia. Dionysus will use any means at his godly disposal to crush the forces that resist life, including the punishments of neurosis, madness and destructive violence expressed as nastiness, quarrelsomeness, sadomasochism, rape, incest, human sacrifice and terrorism—all horrid Dionysian categories. When least expected, he will rush up convulsively from the deepest emotional and instinctual level of the genitalia, where sexual energies gather until they no longer are containable. If this energy is frustrated, Dionysus will release his full, devastating, volcanic fury. Seen in this way, there is something to be said for the slogan "Make love, not war"; it is perhaps more profound than we initially thought.

The word "orgy" derives from the ancient Greek word *orgia*, the name for the ecstatic ritual worship of the god Dionysus. In Dionysian ecstasy (*ex-stasis* = "to stand outside of oneself"), powerful emotions can no longer be contained by the body or mind and, as a result, force one to be transported to another realm that is beyond three-dimensional reason. Ecstasy is positive and therapeutic. We all need ecstatic experiences in life. If many Western forms of religion have failed, it is because in the main they have ceased being Dionysian, mythic and rapturous. They no longer foster "enthusiasm" (a word derived from *en-theos*, which is a state of being "en-godded").

For example, the traditional Catholic Mass of Western Europe was divided into two parts, the Liturgy of the Word and the Celebration of the Sacred Mysteries. During the first, left-brain part, a portion of the New Testament Gospel and an Epistle of Saint Paul were read aloud in the native tongue of the participants. The priest then gave a more or less intellectual commentary on the day's historical readings, also in the vernacular of the country. With the left brain now satisfied, the Celebration of the Sacred Mysteries began, which dealt with issues pertaining to the right brain, namely myth and mysticism, symbological gestures and rituals involving alchemical transubstantiation of ordinary bread and wine into extraordinary substances, the body and blood of Christ. This part was conducted in a nonordinary language, most often Latin. The mysteries brought God out of masculine Father-sky-spirit transcendence and into feminine Mother-Earth-flesh immanence. Remember that the newborn's first outer experience of mother is suckling at the mother's breast. To the newborn mother is food and food is mother. The first part of the Mass, the Liturgy of the Word, exemplified what Jung calls the Logos principle, i.e., analysis of sacred texts, but the other half, the Celebration of the Sacred Mysteries, was a pure expression of the Feminine Eros principle, including a communion service in which everyone became one in partaking of the Lord's flesh and blood, which was meant to be an ecstatic experience.

After the Vatican II Council of the early 1960s, the feminine, Eros, second part of the traditional Mass was reduced to masculine, Logos, left-brain dominance and sheer unadulterated boredom, all to the strains of twanging guitars that one could hear on the radio any time of the day or night. The Council considered this to be bringing the Church into the twentieth century. In fact, it was an invalidation of the sacred that only the symbolic and mythic and right-brained can offer. In short, the Church self-destructed when the patriarchs imposed dry Apollonian reforms and suppressed all the rapturous, enthusiastic, ecstatic Dionysian elements of the celebration of the Sacred Mysteries. The God-image since Vatican II has officially reverted back to a purely patriarchal one, despite efforts of a few balanced priests who courageously tried to reinstate respect for the feminine Eros God images. These few voices, however, have been silenced by church authorities, like those who imprisoned Galileo for stating that the sun, rather than Earth, was the center of our solar system, and those who, in another time, burned Joan of Arc at the stake because she was doing what women were not supposed to be doing.

Among European nations, only the Eastern Orthodox churches of Russia, Greece, the Ukraine, Armenia, Romania

and Serbia maintain a healthy balance of masculine and feminine principles, since Eastern Europe never succumbed to the
pathological left-brain-inspired eighteenth-century Age of
"Enlightenment," along with the rigid one-sidedness of
Cartesian thinking, which still dominates Western Europe as
strongly as it ever did, ravaging the collective Celtic psyche
that it infected. One wonders if it ever dawned on these
patriarchs that as soon as they abandoned Latin as a sacred
language, thousands of young Westerners began espousing ecstatic Eastern religions, chanting ancient Sanskrit hymns in
practically all the cities of the Western world. If one cannot
get psychic balance at home, nowadays one can simply import
it, thanks to air travel and advanced communication systems.
Dionysus is alive and well and dresses in Asian clothes.

On an existential level Dionysus is orgasm, which allows
humanity to transcend ego-consciousness to suddenly become
aware of a greater aspect of consciousness through ecstasy.
Sexual ecstasy, accompanied by deeply charged romantic emotions, offers us more than an intimation of the Divine Self.
Puritans will have difficulty even considering this concept,
since they worship a god-image diametrically opposed to that
of Dionysus.

When two people come together in ecstatic union, they
instinctively transcend their bodies and minds and exit into a
spiritual dimension, the "abode of the gods." Sex is sacred in
most religions that see things from this point of view. The act
takes us beyond itself in much the same way that the take-off
fire generated within missiles at a rocket launching site propels
the rocket up and away from the gravity of Earth to the weight-
lessness of space and the unearthly dimensions of other worlds.
Dionysus is a god of extremes, propelling us between far-apart
polarities. Dionysian energy causes a rocket to fire within us.

When we understand the importance and role of Dionysus,
it comes as no surprise that The Song of Songs of the Old
Testament, the Hindu Gita Govinda, which describes the dalli-
ance of the Divine couple Krishna and Radha and other mysti-

cal literatures of the world employ explicit sexual language and imagery to describe the experiences of the mystics in their highest and most intense spiritual union, or, better put, reunion with the Absolute. This is not meant to imply that the archetype of spirit or even spiritual realities are "caused" by sexual experience or by a sublimation of sexuality. "Spirit" is a principle in its own right. Orgasm merely quiets the body and mind to allow consciousness to transcend the ego-mind and corporal distractions, leaving it free in ecstasy to roam among other dimensions of psychic reality, among them those of the world of spirit. This is precisely why sex is considered to be a sacred act. Severe physical suffering may also accomplish the same results, as can any other experience that is capable of breaking the mesmerizing and enthralling hold that three-dimensional ego-mind and body consciousness have over us.

In French orgasm is *la petite mort*, "the little death." In English "climax" implies an ending in the same sense. Dionysus irrationally "kills" and puts an end to the everyday, humdrum, slumberous identification of earthbound consciousness in order to allow the sexual partners to experience something spiritual that is tremendously bigger and more transcendent than themselves, but which is accessible within them. It frees them from the bondage of constant, relentless cerebrality, which restricts consciousness to a stifling and deadening three dimensions. Most people imagine that what they are looking for in sexual experience is intense physical pleasure, when in fact humanity appears to be unconsciously yearning for both the warmth of human love and the experience of sexually induced ecstasy, the opening up to transcendence, to a divine experience of the multidimensional consciousness of Spirit. The goal and the means to it are two different things. In sum, to get to spirit with the help of Dionysus one goes thoroughly into matter via sexual experiences, to get catapulted, as it were, to matter's polar opposite, the Spirit. This is the nature of Dionysus; he is a god of extreme polar opposites contained within himself, and he allows us to experience each side of his far-reaching polarities in his very original way. Each archetype is bipolar, and sex (matter) and ecstasy (spirit) are the bipolarities of one and the same archetype, personified as Dionysus.

Those ignorant of the raison d'être of Dionysus (Scorpio/ Pluto in astral symbolism) in the cosmic plan try to suppress him by overemphasizing the aspects of the rational god Apollo (Leo), the sun's brilliance and beauty, hyperfocused solar consciousness, who is the very antithesis of irrational and emotional Dionysus. It deserves repeating: Whatever we misunderstand we fear and whatever we fear we attack or try to flee. In the case of Dionysus, some segments of humanity use the polar opposite force of Apollo to launch an all-out attack that in the end only produces a silly backfiring and seesaw effect, resolving nothing.

In our psyches Apollo represents reason, knowledge, aesthetics, discipline, a detached dispassionate nature, loftiness, objective intellectual clarity, science, mathematics, medicine, music, poetry and the arts—all those subjects and agendas we spend thousands of dollars on each year to learn about in academia. He can manifest as a glimmer that can illumine or a glare that can blind. Apollo always moved about accompanied by a retinue of nine muses (his glorious solar rays personified), much like a brilliant and good-looking young college professor promenading on campus encircled by a host of fawning young students. The muses were Urania (astronomy), Clio (history), Melpomene (tragedy), Thalia (comedy), Terpsichore (dance and choral song), Calliope (epic poetry), Erato (love poetry), Euterpe (lyric poetry), Polyhymnia (sacred poetry). They represent the various talents present in all of humanity.

Although he was socially popular, Apollo was least at home in the realm of romance, having no real success with women, much like the modern film character James Bond, who is dashing, heroic and brilliant, with many women chasing him, but who is basically a "cold fish," aloof and emotionally inac-

cessible. In fact, Apollo's distant, imperial personality ultimately put women off despite his riveting handsomeness,
which was in contrast to the revolting effeminacy of his trans-
vestite half-brother Dionysus, who mercilessly and strangely
magnetized all manner of women to himself. (Ninety percent
of Dionysus's devotees were women since they probably felt
that his effeminate nature allowed him to be sympathetic and
more understanding of their own feminine natures and needs.)
Apollo's motto "Know thyself" also contrasted with Dionysus's counsel "Be thyself." Apollo's accent on cold, rational
knowledge was the diametrical opposite of the intuitive wisdom of Nature that Dionysus gloriously incarnated.

The practical ancient Greeks realized that a balance between the two was necessary when they dedicated their famous
temple at Delphi to both Apollo and Dionysus. Apollo, the
right use of reason, ceded Delphi to his half-brother during
the winter months when the sky became cloudy and the sun's
rays shone brightly farther south than Greece. According to
the historian Plutarch, both deities received continual homage
and honors at Delphi throughout the year from pious, balance-
minded devotees, who did not pit one god against the other
but rather paid homage equally to both, at Delphi and within
their own psyches.

The one-sided, Apollonian, puritanical work-ethic culture
of contemporary Western nations has been the cause of im-
mense inner conflict on and off for much of the past two
thousand years, not only, as some imagine, since the reign
of Queen Victoria, who reportedly was not very Victorian
herself.

Dionysus, the splendid, indescribable thrill of just being
alive, has been shortchanged with ever-mounting attempts at
total suppression since after the fall of the Roman Empire. As
a result, much psychic Dionysian energy, natural élan and
instinctual meaningfulness of life are forced to go underground
into the collective unconscious, where they fester and gather
momentum. They explode onto the surface from time to time,

manifesting as crusades, aggressive international imperialism, world wars, genocides, widespread abuse of people in general, and drug, alcohol and sexual abuse; the greater the suppression, the greater the explosion of negativity.

This archetypal overview is not meant to favor Dionysian qualities over Apollonian ones. What needs to be publicly invalidated from the rooftops is one-sided Apollonianism as well as one-sided Dionysianism, since what we need is psychic balance between the two. All the "gods," all the archetypes within us, have their psychic roles to play. We need to constantly remind ourselves that whatever is blindly suppressed, repressed or resisted will persist in the unconscious in any case and eventually will erupt in gruesome and destructive ways and forms. We control the negative sides of archetypes not by suppressing them but rather by actively accentuating and living out their positive sides. We cannot escape them altogether, no matter how hard we may try.

The questions remain: What do well-meaning Apollonians do with their emotions besides suppressing them? How do they undo contractive, Saturnine emotional constipation? Why have we gotten ourselves into this mess to begin with? One way to deal with bottled-up feelings is to stop telling ourselves what we should or should not feel. Let us learn to feel precisely what we feel without "should-ing" on ourselves. Let us initially look at the spontaneous expression of feelings as they well up in us while suspending silly, rationalistic judgments about them. This witnessing exercise can be done any time of the day or night. The problem is that habitual "should-ers" tend to lie to themselves even when they begin to feel what they feel. For starters, courage and honesty concerning the activities of Dionysus within themselves are what Apollonians need to shamelessly cultivate.

An easy way to become aware of one's feelings is to sit down alone at a table with drawing paper and crayons, watercolors or pastels, and allow yourself to doodle with the colors without paying any attention to the dictates of aesthetics. Helpful too is writing down a dream in the morning and trying to paint or draw its feeling-tone, or simply discussing the dream at the breakfast table with loved ones. One ought not to try to analyze feelings but rather to acknowledge them and let them out in one of these ways. The type of music we choose to listen to at any given moment is also revealing and can give a great clue for those completely out of touch with their feelings, as the choice reflects unconscious feeling-tones.

The ethical task at hand is to educate ourselves about the positive values of the Dionysus archetype since it has been the one under attack for so long. We already know too much about Apollo. The positive qualities of Dionysus are *joie de vivre*, rapture, spontaneity, instinctual human meaningfulness and laissez-faire; the negative are ennui, angst, emotional limbo and neurotic malaise. Dionysus enables us to die to the past, to stop worrying about the future and to live in the present moment. Nothing is more immediate, more attention-getting and more therapeutic than intense rapture, ecstasy and the therapeutic state of trance he inspires. People simply do not know how to enjoy life. The positive side of Dionysus allows us to do just that, spontaneously and without ado.

Dionysus was worshiped with song, music and dance, and it was said that it was the god himself who sang, made music and danced in and through his devotees. He is the intoxicating healing power of these three activities that allows the heart to open up to untold dimensions. The therapeutic Dionysian effect is lost, however, if we passively watch others on a television set singing, making music and dancing. That is akin to watching an aerobics show for the purpose of losing weight while swilling beer and munching on pizza.

Jelaluddin Rumi, the thirteenth-century Persian spiritual master, living in what is now Turkey, introduced the three Dionysian practices of song, music and dance into the order of Whirling Dervishes he founded, to the great consternation of the orthodox-minded. He stated categorically that "whoever knows the power of the dance dwells in God."

His whirling dervishes themselves declared that "when your body is spinning, there is a completely still point in the center. When you dance, all the stars, the planets and the endless universes dance around that still point. The heavens respond; and invisible kingdoms join in the dance."*

The human body and emotions ought not be forgotten or neglected, but in the realms of religious experience they generally are. They too can be instruments of spiritual practice, along with the refinements and finesse of the Apollonian muses, since it is Dionysus alone who allows us to pray with our hearts and bodies and "guts," and not only with the elegant artistry of our heads.

Orpheus the Savior

The Greek mythological savior who comes to our aid as a model and who operates and effects a harmonious union within ourselves between Dionysian and Apollonian elements is the demigod Orpheus, who is himself the archetype of transcendent balance, beyond light and dark, the perfect synthesis of Dionysian and Apollonian forces. If Dionysus is the irrational and Apollo the rational, then Orpheus represents the nonrational in each of us, a quality that synthesizes the best of the previous two and expresses psychic wholeness. If Apollo is masculine and Dionysus feminine, then Orpheus is neuter, a neutralizing force of the former two, producing transcendence from these pairs of opposites that have most of us pulled in opposite directions as if on a cross.

The historical Orpheus lived around 1150 B.C. He had inherited his mother Calliope's vocal talents to the extent that when he sang and played his lyre, everyone would fall into ecstasy and swoon away, including the most savage beasts, who would settle quietly at his feet. His divine voice even

---

* *The Gods of Greece*, by Arianna Stassinopoulos and Roloff Beny, Harry N. Abrams, New York, 1983, p. 104.

made the trees sway to and fro, and allegedly also tamed the
ferocity and wildness of high-strung Dionysus and the searing
fire of Apollo. He made everyone aware that sounds can almost
be seen and touched, that they can release hidden energies
that heal all our woes. He awakened everyone to the fact that
the images of lyrics can in some strange way be heard and felt
and that they can relieve our inner turmoil and soothe our
psychic anguish by the enchanted visions of reconciling symbols they evoke in our souls. In contrast to standoffish Apollo
and lecherous Dionysus, neither of whom showed true relatedness in love, romance came easily to Orpheus. His musical
magic reduced to ashes the thousand and one invisible barriers
separating all creatures from the light and bliss in their own
heart-centers as they fell hopelessly in love with him. He
inspired the more recent tale of the Pied Piper of Hamlin,
a watered-down version of the ancient god. Psychologically
speaking, beautiful music can heal our souls and make them
whole again.

According to Homer, Orpheus sailed with Jason and the
Argonauts, and during their adventure his bewitching lyre
brought strength back to the weary rowing limbs and bodies
of the sailors and uplifted them when their spirits flagged. He
calmed many a would-be quarrel with his peaceful music, and
he even saved the power-driven one-sided Logos sailors by the
spell of his lyre from the thralldom of maddening sirens' voices
trying to lure them to their psychic deaths under the waves of
the collective unconscious.

In twentieth-century Western culture, Elvis Presley somewhat incarnated the archetypal powers of an Orpheus. It is
even rumored that he never died and is somehow eternal, like
an archetypal deity. He gave teenagers an acceptable form of
expression for the Dionysian qualities produced by the sudden
onset of puberty. The Beatles, too, possessed the same numinous Orphic power to evoke healthy forms of ecstasy, offering
a message in their lyrics that often expressed the poetical spirit
of Apollo and the thrilling liveliness of Dionysus. The Orphic

"middle way" operates while respecting the positive sides of both Dionysus and Apollo. Orpheus allows us, psychically speaking, "to have our cake and eat it too." It was within his capacity to tame the dark side of Dionysus, the upperworld counterpart of underworld Pluto/Hades, as the following myth recounts.

Once upon a time, Orpheus was married to Eurydice, whom he loved with a passion and who one day was fatally bitten by a poisonous viper. Heartbroken, Orpheus descended to the Underworld to fetch back his departed wife. He succeeded in charming with music and song Hades and his spouse Persephone, Lord and Lady of the World of Shades, who granted him his wish. No one under his voice's spell could resist his charm. Orpheus "drew iron tears down Hades cheek, and made Hell grant what Love did seek" (Ovid). The royals imposed one condition, that at no point on the ascent from death to life should Orpheus look back at his beloved Eurydice, a condition to which he gave full-hearted consent. As he left the realm of dark Hades and stepped out blissfully into the daylight, he mindlessly turned around as Eurydice was still in the dimly lit cavern. It was too soon. He reached for her with all his might, but she missed his hand and faded back into the gruesome darkness, muttering one faint "Farewell," lost forever to her benumbed, shattered and forlorn husband. Like the rising sun, he went forth alone into the morning. His journey was like that of a man fallen asleep who communes with his anima in a dream in his own depths, only to lose her entirely upon awakening the next morning.

Although the story ends tragically, Orpheus models for us the power of relatedness, diplomacy, charismatic soulfulness, charm, courage and the heroism of blind loyalty and undying love. He had power over the Lord and Lady of Death, over certain irresistible, barbaric archetypal behaviors and specifically over hell's darkest instincts and inexorably blind forces of ferocity, all associated with Dionysus, until that fateful last moment when he turned around to look. He lost his wife, but he somehow managed to return to the Land of the Living, as very few have ever done. It was a resurrection of sorts, akin to modern-day near-death experiences. His exceptional exploit proved that love conquers all—except, sadly, the definiteness of death. The myth can be understood on many symbolic levels, just as a dream can.

Orpheus was really a skilled healer—a wounded one, as all healers are—whose power lies in his therapeutic use of sound. His personal warmth produced psychic harmonies within his listeners. His voice and music were the expressions of his own inner balance of head and heart. These elements can heal us too if we can ever learn to express them in our lives as Orpheus did in his. He is an archetype of transcendence of both life and death. In our own souls, Orpheus is a dormant archetype that awaits awakening.

In his capacity as a genuine synthesis of Dionysus and Apollo, he tempers both negative extremes of earthy, hysterical Scorpionic Dionysus and heavenly, poised Leonine Apollo. He combines their positive powers into sheer nonrational, charismatic magic that destroys hellish negativity, melancholy and gloom, while moving us to tears of empathy, eliciting and evoking our deepest love. He makes us want to move mountains for him despite our hellish depressions, as did Hades and Persephone, because of the musical healing that he makes resonate in our souls. If we are to heal ourselves individually and collectively, these Orphic qualities need serious consideration, meditating upon and cultivation. To fathom his secrets takes determined effort on our part, but the rewards are many. He is not so far off. He is just a dream away—literally. In India the ancient intuitive seers called him "AUM," the divine sound creating and sustaining the universes and echoing throughout them all, and in our psyches as well. The "A" sound represents waking consciousness; the "U" sound represents the dream state; and the "M" sound stands for the dreamless sleep state. The echo of "AUM" is none other than the fourfold Self. As a symbol of the Self, Orpheus is divine music that heals. To hear his music within us, we must become very still.

Historically, Orpheus was a reformer of the grotesque Dionysian cult, which was cannibalistic, full of indiscriminate copulation cut off from romantic sentiment and gruesome practices of emasculation of men and mutilation of women's sexual organs. Archetypally Orpheus incarnated all that is best of the intense, natural mysticism of Dionysus. He allied and tempered it with Apollonian theological refinement. Orpheus appeared as a divine bringer of culture. He represents the introduction of a whole new element in Greek religious life, namely an all-consuming craving for the mysterious deification of one's own personal life. This brings us back full circle to the meaningful theme of the Wise Old Man and the Great Mother, the archetypes encountered at the crucial point in the Jungian journey of individuation, and the psychic reunification of matter and spirit. The Wise Old Man and the Great Mother can only be correlates of the Orphic process as it takes place in a man or a woman at this pivotal stage of psychic unfolding.

Qualitatively, Orpheus, despite the tragedy in his life, is indeed a synthesis of the feminized masculine principle of the Wise Old Man and the masculinized feminine principle of the Great Mother. He models for us the same equipoise of psychic androgyny as the Wise Old Man and the Great Mother. Just as they do, he strikes an ever-resounding, responsive chord deep within us, through his unique pathos. One might ask, how did he come to manifest such qualities? Gods, demigods and archetypes just are the way they are; that is all we can say. These givens of Nature are hidden forces within us, and they all can be invoked into waking consciousness if we know their names. "To name is to invoke the presence of" is an age-old axiom of magic. We need only call Orpheus forth and engage him in friendly but respectful dialogue, a powerful exercise that enables him to work his healing on us. Imagination, too, is reality; if it is not, then we human beings also are not.

Highly endowed Orpheus met a tragic end and, like Dionysus, was murdered by being torn to shreds. His preserved head produced wondrous oracles in a temple on the isle of Lesvos, and his spirit lives on in his legacy: the healthy balance that his refined teachings brought about in the spiritual practices of the Mediterranean. His refreshing influence of psychic harmony has never really left us and is felt sporadically even today in the many spiritual traditions that celebrate the balance of head and heart, where joyous singing, hand clapping, even dancing are encouraged: the Protestant Pentacostals, some Baptist groups and the relatively recent charismatic movement in the Catholic Church, not to mention ecstatic practices of Hasidic Jews and Sufi-Muslims. It has also miraculously survived among Native American, African and Australian tribal groups.

On a developmental level, the movement from Dionysus through Apollo to Orpheus is the ordinary rite of passage from the chaos of puberty and adolescence to early adulthood to a more balanced psychic maturity. When the Dionysian forces of uncontrollable instinct have alchemically merged with the Apollonian demands of early adulthood, the union of the two archetypes in effect produce a happy marriage between masculine spirit and feminine earth. With Dionysian suffering come wisdom and mastery over emotional excess and affective chaos since there are limits to the pain we can inflict upon ourselves in the name of instinctual permissiveness. We mature and, despite our revolutionary anti-establishment instincts, as the years wear on and as we are exposed to higher cultural thought by dint of society's pressures, we begin singing a new song that harmonizes with those of others around us. It may be a love song or even a poetic hymn, but it emanates from a heart that is finally at peace with itself and the world. Whatever its ultimate source, this solid declaration of the

triumph of messianic Orpheus comes forth out of our depths
and into our lives as an inspired voice proclaiming the truth
about our divine destiny. Orpheus embodies the raison d'être
of the practice of depth psychology and the inner journey, and
is the very heart of the "alchemical" transformational work
that the inner journey entails.

On a completely inner level, the sacred Mysteries founded
and inspired by Orpheus taught that the feminine and masculine principles personified respectively by Scorpionic Dionysus
and Leonine/Solar Apollo were really the two sides of one
single divine archetypal reality.

Orpheus, whose name presumably derives from that of a
fish, was often pictured as a fisherman holding a rod, and with
a fish at his feet. * With all of this symbolism he can only
represent the archetype of Pisces/Neptune. (*Pisces* in Latin
means "fish.") Pisces and Neptune, Lord of the Sea, symbolize
the cosmic ocean (the collective unconscious) that contains
all possible archetypal imagery completely blended and merged
with each other. In the unconscious realms all differentiation
has been eradicated by the uncanny ability Pisces/Neptune has
to literally absorb the most contradictory things and fuse them
into incredibly harmonious and beautiful symbolic images that
heal. As such, Pisces/Neptune/Orpheus represents transcendence of opposites.

Pisces/Neptune, besides being unconditional love and the
higher octave of Venus-Eros on the feeling level, is the archetype of the symbol-making capacity of the unconscious. This
symbol-making capacity, which Jung called the transcendent
function, allows consciousness to transcend and rise above
inner tensions and to regain peace, balance and unity via
psychic symbols that harmoniously bring together ostensibly
irreconcilable opposites. The therapeutic value of symbol formation is a difficult concept to grasp for people who do not

---

* See Walter Wili's article, "The Orphic Mysteries and the Greek Spirit," in *The
Mysteries* (*Papers from the Eranos Yearbooks*), edited by Joseph Campbell, Princeton
University Press, Princeton, N.J., 1955, p. 67.

keep track of the outpourings of inner realities. Appreciation of the symbol-making activities of the unconscious comes only after deep introspection and working with dreams, as we will see later. Orpheus obviously incarnated this principle in miraculously accomplishing the seemingly impossible synthesis of Dionysian and Apollonian qualities within himself. He is the Piscean symbol of their synthesis.

The same theological evolution took place with the Greek god Dionysus as it did with Osiris, his more ancient, Egyptian counterpart. Osiris was originally lord of the dark underworld and only later became associated with the Sun through his son Horus, conceived in Isis after much theological soul-searching on the part of the Egyptian priesthood. Osiris and Dionysus personified the same archetypal qualities, which were called by different names. But it took many centuries for the fully developed right-brained theology of Egypt pertaining to this archetype to finally reach and penetrate the left-brained Greek world through the historical efforts of Orpheus. Ancient Greeks could not accept foreign ideas and concepts until they were thoroughly hellenized and cleansed of their foreignness.

The Orphic god-image synthesized feminine Dionysian and masculine Apollonian traits in perfect harmony in a way that only a Piscean/Neptune symbol-making power could conjure up.

Deity is experienced by the soul as a union of opposites and is hence transcendentally androgynous, equally feminine and masculine but neither at the same time. Such was the nature of Orpheus.

Even in the Book of Genesis, the creation of woman from Adam's rib implied a state of androgyny in the original man, who was created in God's (presupposed hermaphroditic) image. Orpheus is the redemptive return of this "original man," and brings salvation.

In the Orphic view of things, the division of primordial androgyny into the opposing polarities of feminine and masculine, of Dionysus and Apollo—whose mutual tension sustains the visible phenomenal world—is just an outer appearance. Basically they are merely the two aspects of the same reality.

The myth of Orpheus and psychic androgyny describes the process each of us has to pass through. As was stated earlier, the gods and goddesses are images and models incarnating the highest potentials we are capable of. None of us can escape the integration of our own matter and spirit aspects.

When the female and male of a species are reunited, the result is an experience of bliss. Bliss is the principal description of the reality of divine transcendental androgynous union; as such it is permanent and absolute. It is not only something we may experience but the very nature of who we humans ultimately are. Bliss is also the very nature of Phanes. Phanes is parallel to the historically earlier god Horus of Egypt, the son and synthesis of Osiris and Isis, the masculine sky and feminine earth, being the superlative radiance of the sun at high noon. Phanes is the name given by Orpheus to the new god-image composed of the perfect union of irreconcilable opposites, Dionysus and Apollo. The new symbolic image of the Self, Phanes transcends both since he contains the coalesced opposites within himself. Legendary Orpheus's own being incarnated and radiated the healing rays of Phanes to the world via his voice and music, much as an Enrico Caruso or a Maria Callas did in modern times.

In order to create the phenomenal world, androgynous Phanes, not the sun exactly but rather Solar Radiance, divided itself, and the two polarities of female and male appeared. (This is a repetition for Greek consumption of the Egyptian creation myth that recounted that everything, all planets and life on them, were originally projected out of the divine sun.) Dualistic creation, however, is experienced by us as painful and diabolical due to its lack of wholeness. (*Diabolos* in Greek means "thrown or cast into twoness"; it represents our own painful, psychically fragmented human state.)

The much-desired reunion of the two, existentially experienced, is effected by live, dynamic, psychic symbols appearing in the soul in dreams and fantasies. These symbols are sometimes seen projected onto the heavenly bodies. (*Sym-bolon* in Greek means "thrown together or brought into oneness.") The divine symbol to be evoked within oneself, according to Orpheus, is Phanes, the divine radiance and fullness of consciousness, the unity out of which all that lives in our solar system issued forth. The return to original Oneness, Light Absolute, is sheer delight, and it is the symbolic activity of this specific archetype that brings about this blissful merger in us. We each individualize this fundamental Unity, which seemingly is independent of time and space as we normally know them. When we consciously individualize this Oneness in our lives, all of its creative power begins producing "miracles" for us and those around us.

The Orphic psycho-spiritual goal for humanity is, therefore, the return to our original solar Oneness, which is a union of opposites experienced as psychic androgyny. The goal is not 93 million miles away, as is the sun, but as close as our own contact and cooperative participation with the healing realities of the collective unconscious. The goal is brought about through the dynamic production of symbols by the transcendent function within each of us, active always and everywhere.

On a biological level our personal evolution into godliness is effected by equal and simultaneous functioning of the feminine right and masculine left hemispheres of the brain mutually communicating and cooperating without the slightest hindrance. This action produces a woman or man of Solar Light. We must become, poetically speaking and according to this Orphic imagery, a star-woman or star-man, stars being suns, producers of their own light. It is useless to see the light—we must become the light.

The Orphic ritual of initiation resembled Orpheus's journey to the Underworld and journeys of shamans and shamanesses the world over, as well as that of Dante and countless others, who first go to the Underworld and then to the Upper World within themselves to reconnect with and be energized by the powers of both realms. This ritually induced ecstatic process permits one to "die" to one's old self in order to be reborn to one's truer, fuller nature. In the Upper World, the Empyrean, one becomes acquainted, as Orpheus did, with the celestial archetypal deities and the music and dance of the planetary spheres. Such acquired and experiential knowledge in turn allows us to teach these same mysteries to those souls still fragmented in their Earthly existence but who are ripe for initiation into wholeness, which can be brought about by making conscious the three worlds within us all.

In the Orpheus legend, myth combines with ancient astral symbolism, which we must try to understand on the level of depth psychology, to become yet another example of how we project dynamics of the unconscious upon the heavenly bodies. It states that Orpheus is paradoxically both "this" and "that" at the same time, but also neither.

Each of us is really a miniature solar system, a concept that is now seriously being discussed in what is called the new physics. Quantum physics has discovered that, at the atomic level, matter has a dual aspect. Light may manifest as particles or as waves, depending on a variety of conditions. In Christian and Hindu theology, the Absolute is One and yet under certain conditions can be seen as Father, Son and Holy Spirit or as Brahma the Creator, Vishnu the Preserver and Shiva the Destroyer. Truth is always paradoxical, likewise the truth of Orpheus. There is no space to give a full, detailed explanation of all the subtleties of this new science, but the suggested reading list at the back of the book contains recommended books as well as titles on ways to meditate. The chapter on dreams outlines a specifically Jungian and psychological approach to integrate all that has just been delineated about physics and androgyny. Let us not so much look up as look inward to observe what Orpheus is trying to relate to us. It is yet one more factor that urges us to turn to the healing, symbol-making capacity of our own psyches for resolutions to all of life's quandaries.

The effort of the inquiry must be ours. "Ask, and you shall receive; seek, and you shall find; knock, and it shall be opened unto you. For everyone who asks, receives; and the one who seeks, finds and to the one who knocks, it shall be opened" (Luke 11:9, 10). In all of our suffering, hope never need be lost if we know what to do and are steadfast and determined to do what must be done to uncover the mystery of who we are.

Some readers may be surprised to learn that Eastern Orthodox Christianity holds the idea that it was not only the Israelites who yearned for a messiah but also their Greek and Near Eastern ancestors, who produced all of this mythology pertaining to the legendary savior named Orpheus. Indeed it was Augustine of Hippo (A.D. 354–430) who opined that Christianity was only another name for the "eternal religion" as practiced in the Mediterranean from the most ancient times.

Christian mythology finds many parallels in Egyptian mythology, such as the story of Osiris, who died and was resurrected each spring; the eating of cakes in the form of Osiris and drinking a sacred beverage, both of which were called the body and blood of Osiris; the sacred baptismal rites coming out of ancient Sumer, home of Abraham; and so forth. *

Building Bridges

On a collective outer level, in the contemporary obsession with dominating the material universe around us, we are internationally becoming evermore estranged and alienated from a healthy relationship to the material universe at large and

* See *The Story of Christian Origins*, by Martin A. Larson, Village Press, Tahlequah, Oklahoma, 1977.

especially from a positive relationship with Nature. This includes our physical bodies, which are none other than the Goddess herself, whom we are poisoning at every turn. This news is being shouted at us from every quarter, but instead of joining a movement to save the planet, many just shrug their shoulders and think, "What's the use?!"

Indeed, although we cannot change other people or society, we can change ourselves, and when we change ourselves, something in the society in which we live also changes. We can change society on the "cellular" level, as it were. If we find ourselves disconnected with the rest of creation and living out of harmony with the forces of Life, which are mainly instinctual, the way back to union with this vitalizing feminine divine force is through allowing ourselves a little more ecstasy and love, both Eros-bridges to the solar centers of our own beings and paradoxically also to the world around us. Dionysian ecstasy and Orphic love can be very contagious—and healing, striking a chord deep within, whose sound will surely reverberate throughout the world. If these images seem mystical and poetic, they are meant to be; when speaking about this profoundest level of consciousness, only poetic mystical imagery is appropriate.

In a letter dated August 31, 1945, to an unnamed addressee, Jung proclaimed his views about his intense spiritual interests with regard to analytical psychology: "You are quite right: the main interest of my work is not concerned with the treatment of neurosis, but rather with the approach to the numinous [the *glowing divine awareness within our psyches*]. But the fact is that the approach to the numinous [i.e., the sacred] is the real therapy, and inasmuch as you attain to the numinous experience, you are released from the curse of pathology [*psychic suffering*]. Even the very disease takes on a numinous character" (*Letters*, vol. 1). Jung is intimating that there is no animal or creature, no plant life, nothing in the whole hierarchy of Nature with which we are not intimately spiritually interlinked. The effect of our Orphic and Dionysian pursuits will

be felt specifically because of our unity with all things. Archetypes do not die or disappear. Dionysus and Orpheus have not
abandoned us; it is we who have abandoned them, but this
cannot be for long.

Dionysus and Orpheus have been gathering energy in the
collective unconscious, and the signs of their return are everywhere. They are breaking down the barriers between people;
governments hostile to religious experience are giving way.
The two "deities" are asking us to participate in and share the
joys of creation, as the overemphasis on Apollo has been too
boring and too searing for words. I remember sitting in a large
room at a courthouse for more than a week waiting to be called
for jury duty. For some reason, ninety percent of the candidates
that week were men. The thought flashed in my mind one
day, as I sat in that room, how utterly boring, dull and dry
the atmosphere was without a balance of women present. It
must be the same feeling in an all-boy or all-girl boarding
school where some parents send their children for a "well-
rounded" education.

It is indeed a tyrannically scorching Apollonian mentality
that is laying waste to the realities of Mother Nature, of whom
we are all an integral part. Let us welcome Dionysus and
Orpheus consciously in our own lives in their attempt to free
up the suppressed instinctive powers that keep us in contact
with the health-giving vegetable, animal and the subtler supernatural worlds found within our own bodies and minds. Our
collective salvation is deep within our own natures. Let us not
hesitate to reach for it. It is as easy as turning on a television
set, only what we need to look at are our portable internal
broadcasts going on twenty-four hours a day.

Eroticism in the broadest sense of the term is the bond of
attraction that unites two opposite and complementary poles.
Remember that the god Eros shoots his arrows of love through
our hearts and not through our genitals. Be that as it may,
the "eros" of sexuality that most people only talk about is
procreative of emotional bonding if romance is involved or of

physical children. The "eros" of symbol-making on the psycho-spiritual level, which Jung observed in the realm of depth psychology, is procreative of the Orphic spiritual child, one's personally lived experience of inner and outer Nature as a sacred entity. It comes about through the aegis of the Piscean/Orphic symbol-producing transcendent function. When we are thus healed by it, so is everything and everyone around us in the same way that any sound produced by a voice or musical instrument will resonate outwardly from its source, influencing all that it encounters with the positive harmonies that make up its being.

Synchronicity

With regard to this mysterious ability to change our environment, Jung liked to recount a true story originally told to him by his sinologist friend Richard Wilhelm.

Jung's friend was stationed in a small provincial village in China, which was in the throes of famine due to a long drought. The people were suffering tremendously and continuously put forth prayers and rituals with no positive consequences. The only thing left was for the elders to go in search of a famous rainmaker who lived in another province. Wilhelm had never heard of such a profession and was eager to see what would happen. Several days later the rainmaker arrived in a horse-drawn cart. He was a short, wizened, quite ordinary-looking old man. Wilhelm overheard him ask for a private hut to stay in, somewhere away from the village, where he was to be completely undisturbed. He asked for enough food for at least three or four days. On the morning of the fourth day the villagers awakened to a heavy downpour of rain, after which it even snowed a bit, a rare phenomenon for that time of year.

Jung's friend was positively bewildered and ran to speak with the old rainmaker, who had left the hut and was preparing to depart for his home province. "Did you make it rain?" asked Wilhelm. The old gentleman denied that he had. Wilhelm insisted that there had been a terrible drought until the rain-maker's arrival, after which it began to pour and even snow. The old man then explained that in the region he came from, everything was as it should be; it rains at the appropriate time and is sunny when sunshine is needed, since the people living there are harmonious in themselves. But, he remarked, this was not what he found in this village. The people here were out of harmony with the Tao (divine connectedness) and even out of sync with themselves. He said that when he first arrived here, he had at once become contaminated with the low consciousness of the villagers who had brought him here, so that he absolutely had to remain completely alone until the harmony between him and the Tao was reestablished. Then it naturally had to rain!

Assuredly the wizened old man was a shaman who knew the secrets of Nature. Then again, there is an Orphic shaman in all of us who have access, if desired, to the very same sources of power and archetypal deities that he had. The moral of this story is not only about the power our intimate connectedness with Nature and Her divine forces can have but basically about how the spiritual life of one individual is so immensely important and so influential concerning the practical, every-day life of our community and environment. The Western psyche will find such a story hard, if not impossible, to fathom due to its noncausal explanation, but this is precisely the problem of our Western-accentuated, left-brained hyperra-tionalism, which takes everything literally and does not under-stand that life is basically symbolical, and which most certainly does not live in the interconnectness of all of Nature. There is nothing to "believe," if we simply would allow our right cerebral hemisphere equal time with our left.

The miraculous manifestation of rain in the story is termed by Jung as a synchronistic event. Jung coined the word "syn-chronicity" to describe a meaningful link between two events that cannot be explained by the concept of cause and effect. In the case of the Chinese rainmaker who did not make or cause rain to fall, his explanation was based on the spiritual practices he probably performed in his hut for those three days. He probably just sat down and concentrated all of his focus on just plain doing nothing. This put him back into the original state of perfect harmonious consciousness, which is at the center of our beings. Jung called this still center the Self; the Chinese traditionally call it the Tao.

When we tranquillize the ego-consciousness by the practice of just focusing on our breathing to the exclusion of everything else, including the entertaining of thoughts, we allow the Self or the Tao to permeate the outer layers of our being. When inner harmony is allowed to return, it is reflected back to us in the outer world. We often hear people say, "The world is friendly to those who are friendly," an idea that has nothing to do with causality but rather with reflections. Jung developed the concept of synchronicity in his later years; it cannot be grasped by one's intellect alone but rather by using the function of intuition, which perceives realities that the five senses simply do not register.

For example, when Gabrielle came to consult with me for the first time, she sat opposite me and I sat in a chair with my back to a large window that spanned the whole wall except for a door to an outer balcony. She immediately began telling me how her husband had forced her, because of their poor financial circumstances, to abort what would have been their fourth child. She loved children very much and had always wanted to have a large family. Her husband was adamant, so to please him she had an abortion. She began sobbing uncontrollably as she revealed how she prayed every day for the soul of that aborted child.

Just as she said this, we heard a loud thud against the window behind me; startled, we spontaneously got up and went out the door onto the balcony, where we saw a lifeless sparrow that had flown into the window, blinded by the glare of the sun, thus killing itself. We both walked back inside and took our seats. She was very quiet now. When she finally spoke, she said a similar incident had happened another time when she had recounted the story of her abortion to another therapist whom she had seen only once. This is what Jung would call a meaningful coincidence or a synchronistic event. Birds have perennially symbolized the human soul in many cultures of the world. The event did not make Gabrielle feel any better; in fact, it made her feel worse.

Jung enumerated three categories of synchronistic events. The first type involves a correspondence of meaning between an inner thought or feeling and an outer event, such as Gabrielle's story of praying for the soul of her aborted child.

A second type of synchronicity describes how a person may have an inner vision or dream of an event happening far away and later proven as historical fact. The German philosopher Immanuel Kant recounted in a letter how he was present at a social gathering in Germany when the equally famous Swedish clairvoyant and spiritual philosopher Swedenborg had a vision of a raging fire taking place in Stockholm, hundreds of miles away. He even stated that his own house had been spared. The fire was later verified to have taken place at the exact time Swedenborg was telling his vision to the people at the gathering.

A third type of synchronicity involves a person who may have precognitive dreams, visions or a simple premonition of some kind that in fact occurs as foreseen at a later date. President Lincoln reportedly had dreams shortly before his assassination in which he saw his body lying in state with mourners filing by.

Synchronistic events are nothing to be "believed in." Jung is not preaching a new religion but is acknowledging the function of intuition as being as valid as sensation, feeling or thinking. The best way to understand the concept of synchronicity is to have a personal experience of an uncanny type of meaningful coincidence, such as those described here. Synchronicity always deals with a thought, vision, dream or premonition that is noncausally connected to some outer event.

204 O
JUNG TO LIVE BY

As I was walking down the street one day to catch a train, the image of Myrna, a student of mine from three years before, lodged itself in my head. It was like looking at her face on a television screen. There was no reason to be thinking of her at all, since I hadn't seen her in three years. As I was walking briskly and reached the corner, a woman turning the corner from the other direction bumped into me and I into her. It was Myrna. The image of her in my consciousness and the actual encounter with her a few minutes later were noncausally connected in some fashion: a synchronistic event. Those of us who are by nature prone to introspection tend to encounter more synchronistic events than those who are unaware of what their consciousness is receiving. Synchronistic events truly make us feel interconnected and interrelated with the world at large, the transcendent Self being the invisible connection that unites us all.

We must allow the vibrant life of the transpersonal Self to flow through us. We must ultimately go beyond pleasure and pain, love and hate, wisdom and ignorance, health and sickness, good and bad, since in Nature we observe that everything eventually turns into its opposite (day becomes night, winter turns into summer, youth evolves into old age, blossoms transform into fruit that ripens and then rots), and our lives become a terrifying see-saw. Everything is in flux. In ordinary consciousness, pleasure gives way to pain and pain fades to pleasure, love turns into hate and hate may evolve into love, and so on. Ecstasy allows us to experience all the pairs of opposites of which we are humanly capable and hence to transcend them all through the process of standing outside of ourselves. In so doing we ascend to a new transpersonal space, a divine state of consciousness of the Self beyond even the highest wisdom and compassion, a state that is inconceivably greater than anything that can be defined. In ecstasy we find ourselves standing outside all dualities and enjoying the bliss of universal, infinite Oneness with all that is, an experience of soul that has perennially been called God. This is undoubtedly the state the rainmaker experienced. The dreamless sleep is the direction we must travel to reach this Shangri-la of magical, awesome harmony. When we discover that the state of dreamlessness is always concurrent with dreaming and waking-consciousness, we will have finally "returned home" on a permanent basis.

Chapter 10

To Thine Own Self Be True

Individuation is the process that leads to ultimate meaningfulness in life after our egos have come to terms with the various facets of our unconscious.

In *Archetypes and the Collective Unconscious*, Jung stated that we never totally integrate and assimilate the unconscious into the sphere of our ego-consciousness. On the other hand, it would be disastrous to try to suppress the unconscious because its energy is life itself and life would powerfully attack us if we ever foolishly tried to keep it down, as neurotic patients try to do.

Psychic wholeness cannot come about when there is a conflict of interest between the conscious and unconscious or when one of them begins attacking the other. Both must have their place in the spotlight, since they are the two halves of one team, as it were. The conscious sphere with its logical and reasonable concerns must be acknowledged, and the seemingly less-organized life of the unconscious ought to be allowed to express itself as much as the one-sided ego can put up with. Both parts of our psyches will agree on some things but disagree on others. This normal state of affairs is due to the friction caused by the two "rubbing against each other" so that an indestructible fire is engendered, which we call an individual consciousness. Jung called this encounter between the two halves the individuation process.

A Balancing of Opposites

Jung's psychology states that among all the pairs of opposites within the human psyche, an intrinsic law of compensation appears to exist that expresses itself in the psychic capacity to correct any undue imbalance between the conscious and unconscious. This law of compensation creates a reconciliation of opposites within us, the tension of which produces a more refined psychic energy and more nuanced life. When all the aspects of consciousness and unconsciousness come together, we are slowly made aware of an entity called the Self that is synergistically greater than the sum of the psyche's parts.

The Self, since it is a composite of all the elements that constitute psyche, appears to have an intentionality all of its own, irrespective of the ideas and wishes of our ego. In *Psychological Types* Jung succinctly delineates this subordinate relationship: "Inasmuch as the ego is only the center of my field of consciousness, it is not identical with the totality of my psyche, being a complex among other complexes. Hence I discriminate between the ego and the Self, since the ego is only the subject of my consciousness, while the Self is the subject of my totality, hence it also includes the unconscious psyche. In this sense, the Self would be an ideal factor which embraces and includes the ego. In unconscious fantasy the Self often appears as a superordinate or ideal personality" (par. 706).

In *Psychology and Religion* Jung continued to elucidate and refine this relational concept. He stated that the term "Self" was an appropriate one for the unconscious entity that expressed itself in mini-form, as it were, as the ego-consciousness of the waking state. The ego is really like a puppet in the hands of the puppeteer, or Self. The ego is acted upon by the Self, which is much bigger than it, since it is the sum total of psychic life. Like the unconscious, the Self is an innate given out of which emerges the ego, a mini-version of itself. The Self is in a way a large unconscious blueprint of what the ego should be like in the three-dimensional world. The ego gets the distinct impression that it is merely a reflection of something much bigger in the depths of the unconscious.

In *Two Essays*, Jung uses language that his detractors have cited to brand him a "mystic": "Intellectually the Self is no more than a psychological concept, a construct that serves to express an unknowable essence which we cannot grasp as such, since by definition it transcends our powers of comprehension. It might equally be called the 'God within us.' The beginnings of our whole psychic life seem to be inextricably rooted in this point, and all our highest and ultimate purposes seem to be striving towards it" (par. 399).

Jung is attempting to describe universal human psycho-spiritual experience, a concept or image of deity that has allowed the most positive and sublime qualities of the human soul to blossom in individuals—a concept, too, over which humanity sadly has committed countless, unbelievable atrocities.

In understanding the depths of the human psyche, it is not wise or fruitful to rigidly stick to an extraverted thinking-sensate approach (the so-called scientific approach), as this yardstick is by the definitions of typology only one way among many of apprehending reality. Since the eighteenth-century Age of Enlightenment, extraverted thinking-sensation has tried to dominate the Western psyche in a tyrannical fashion in an attempt to know its own psychic truth.

Descartes, the French philosopher, with all his hypercere-brality, typifies this lopsided, arrogant, deluded mentality; he even held "experiments" during which he pierced knitting needles through the bodies of animals, sermonizing to his students that, although the tortured animals cried out in painful anguish, they could not possibly be suffering any real pain since, according to him, they did not have souls.

Statistics compiled by People for the Ethical Treatment of Animals predicted that in 1991, "six to eight million animals will die every month in our nation's commercial, military, and federally funded university laboratories. That totals nearly 100 million animal lives [destroyed in experimentation] that are scientifically unnecessary, medically unreliable, and always undeniably evil."

The obscenely off-target Cartesian mentality, totally lacking in the faculties of intuition and feeling and common sense, produces such statistics today in many secular Western countries, where animals are sacrificed on the altars of almighty science, the fanatical religion of the modern age. It is a kind of patriarchal, narcissistic cerebralism totally disconnected from the Feminine Earth, animals, Nature and even of a sense of one's own bodily incarnation. Only such a pseudo-scientific mentality could work such havoc and devastation on all things earthly and, by extension, on women in particular. All hope is not lost, however. Regarding this, Jung states: ". . . Sooner or later nuclear physics and the psychology of the unconscious will draw closer together as both of them, independently of one another and from opposite directions, push forward into transcendental territory, the one with the concept of the atom, the other with that of the archetype" (*Aion, Collected Works*, vol. 2, par. 412).

Fritjof Capra, in *The Tao of Physics*, and Gary Zukav, in *Dancing Wu-Li Masters*, describe the astounding similarities in the discoveries of late-twentieth-century physics and the intuitional, spiritual teachings of the ancient Hindu and Buddhist scriptures. These ground-breaking books (both available in paperback) are eye-openers for those extraverted sensate-thinking personalities who are becoming more aware that their so-called scientific viewpoints are myopic, ridiculously uneducated, one-sided, globally death-producing and utterly antiquated. They are especially enlightening for those who do not know where to turn for a respectable and more complete and updated picture of Reality not based on now-inadequate Newtonian concepts.

The new physics teaches us that energy is never destroyed, it simply changes form eternally. The very molecules of energy of which our body, minds and souls are composed have always existed in one form or another. In fact, it is myopic to speak of individual energies cut off from each other, as ultimately there is only one energy manifesting in multiple ways and forms. British physicist Stephen Hawking is striving to express and prove this mathematically. This Oneness that the physicists are discussing is what we traditionally have called the manifestation of God. When we intuit that universal energy or consciousness is individualizing as each of us, awesome healing power will flow through our lives.

Right Brain vs. Left Brain

On a more mundane level, most of Jung's discoveries and observations are "compatible with the neurological formulations which have achieved currency since his death," according to Dr. Anthony Stevens in his book *Archetypes*, which integrates psychiatry with psychology, ethnology and biology. He comments: "Throughout his life Jung stood as the champion of 'intuitive,' 'receptive' modes of apprehension, insisting that they were no less valid than the rational and abstract. He maintained that the rationalism of modern life, with its depreciation of everything non-rational, had 'precipitated the function of the irrational into the unconscious' " (p. 254).

When the irrational elements—Dionysus, for example—are forced into the unconscious, they can only be experienced negatively, in the form of rampant compulsions and addictions of all kinds that translate as years of inconceivable crucifixion and living death for many wretched souls.

Stevens informs us that the personal unconscious, visual imagery and primary thinking in the right hemisphere of the brain would suggest that this side of the brain should be predominant in the activities of dreaming, fantasizing and active imagination. "EEG records have demonstrated greater activity in the right hemisphere than in the left both during dream sleep and during sexual fantasy just prior to orgasm (Bakan, 1976). Wilder Penfield was able to induce dreams and visual hallucinations in patients having brain surgery under local anaesthetic by stimulating areas of the right cerebral cortex but not the left. . . . The intellectual bias of the left hemisphere and its somewhat condescending attitude to the activities of the right goes some way to explain the dismissive views commonly expressed in our culture concerning the value of dreams and fantasies" (op. cit., p. 257).

Indeed how could a fixated, left-brained individual ever suspect that such an entity as the Self might exist if this fixation does not even allow for simple acknowledgment and validation of the capacities of right-hemispherical functioning?

Stevens elaborates not only on the right and left hemispheres but also on the four distinct brains: "It must not be forgotten that in all primates the phylogenetically [pertaining to the genealogical history of time and space, and its own motor functions] much older parts of the brain still exist and still possess their full functional integrity. Yet for the greater part of this century psychologists have done their best to overlook this fact, devoting themselves tirelessly to the study of cognitive and perceptual processes while leaving emotion and instinct to the biologists. There are signs that this bias has begun to change—largely through the work of Paul MacLean, the American neuroscientist, who has conceived of the brain not as a unity, but as *three brains in one*, each with a phylogenetic history, each differing in kind from the others despite the myriad interconnections linking them together, each with 'its own special intelligence, its own special memory, its own sense of time and space, and its own motor functions' (MacLean, 1976). Henry and his colleague Stephens, argue that the dominant hemisphere represents a fourth and phylogenetically most recent system which is peculiar with our species" (op. cit., pp. 163–164).

According to MacLean, as paraphrased from Stevens's *Archetypes*, the brain possibly could have evolved in four stages:

The Reptilian Brain: The brain stem, which is the most primitive part of the brain, contains nuclei controlling processes vital to the sustenance of life, such as the cardiovascular and respiratory systems and the reticular activity system maintaining the alertness of consciousness. The reptilian brain is without emotions, nor does it possess any cognitive appreciation of past or future events. Behavioral responses are instinctual and automatic.

The Paleo-mammalian Brain: Known as the midbrain, this is

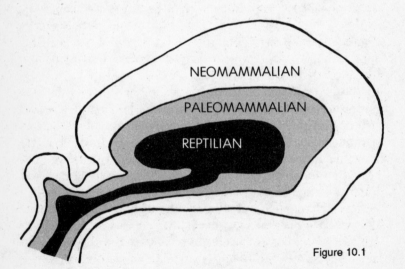

Figure 10.1

composed of the limbic system, the hypothalamus and the pituitary gland, which controls all other endocrine glands. These latter two control hormone levels and the balance of hunger and satiety, sexual desire and gratification, thirst and fluid retention, sleep and wakefulness. Fear and anger both emerge in the limbic system along with the instinct to fight or flee. There is less rigidly instinctual behavior and more conscious awareness. The complex midbrain controls many basic responses and attitudes to the environment.

The Neo-mammalian Brain: Also known as the neocortex, this section is responsible for cognition and sophisticated perceptual processes. It is in direct contrast to instinctive and affective behavior.

The Human Brain: This section is where cerebral lateralization has occurred, with the development of the left-dominant hemisphere operating in the levels of temporal, rational, sequential, empirical and analytical thinking, along with the use of language and speech typical of Western thought; and the right-dominant hemisphere, operating on nonverbal, visuospatial, simultaneous, symbolic, intuitional, global-overview and synthesizing levels, typical of Eastern thought.

The table on p. 214 breaks down the qualities typical of each hemisphere.

Stevens agrees that the right hemisphere has more to do with the processing of archetypal components. He states: "Jung's concepts of archetype, collective unconscious and symbol are more closely associated with the use of the imagery, *gestalt* [form] and visuospatial characteristics of right hemisphere functioning. The metapsychological foundations built by Carl Jung are proving to be soundly conceived. There is a rapidly growing body of evidence linking our mammalian inheritance of basic brain stem functions with man's unique religious, social and cultural achievements. Society has scarcely begun to consider the implications of these discoveries" (op. cit., pp. 266–267).

Dichotomies of Brain Hemisphere Attributes*

Left Brain	Right Brain
Intellect	Intuition
Convergent	Divergent
Intellectual	Sensuous
Deductive	Imaginative
Rational	Metaphoric
Vertical	Horizontal
Discrete	Continuous
Abstract	Concrete
Realistic	Impulsive
Directed	Free
Differential	Existential
Sequential	Multiple
Historical	Timeless
Explicit	Tacit
Objective	Subjective
Successive	Simultaneous

* From Springer, Sally, and Georg Deutsch, *Left Brain, Right Brain*, W. H. Freeman and Co., San Francisco, 1981, p. 186.

The Self and the Ego

The implications may be that Jung, with his concept of the Self, facilitated a more in-depth and inclusive understanding of the mechanisms and dynamics of psychic operations. By showing that there is something greater than the ego always at work, Jung observed that the Self pulls and tugs and aims the ego in the right direction, as well as creating situations that may awaken the individual to new awarenesses.

Jung historically attempted to broaden the rigidly deterministic biases of Freud, who explained all psychological disturbances as basically caused only by the traumas of childhood. Jung agreed that this was true only part of the time, since in his observations the development of maturity could be arrested by such a simple thing as an inordinate fear of progressing into a new stage of individuation without any historical basis causing this particular fear. Jung observed that an individual could even regress because of this innate archetypal fear to an earlier stage of development and become fixated there. Resistance to change can be quite powerful, and there is no conclusive proof that the sole cause of psychic resistances is a trauma. Archetypes are of various natures, some daring, others very timid, some futuristic, others harping on the past. They too play their role in creating our reactions to life, and archetypes, as we have learned, are innate in the human psyche, transmitted via genetics. They can be activated by culture or simply activate themselves. Parents who have many children can testify to the uniqueness of each child from birth, despite socio-cultural programming.

It is the Self, the archetype of transcendence, that can give the ego a psychic push since everything in the unconscious seeks outward manifestation. The Self coaxes the ego consciousness to become broader and fuller by assimilating the contradictory contents of the Self and by experiencing the entirety of its psychic life. It is by the light of the Self that all psychic elements are gradually manifested, "For there is nothing hid except to be made manifest, nor is anything secret except to come to light" (Mark 4:21).

The Self instigates individuation. It attempts in many ways to align the ego with all the potentials of the psyche, with all that we may ever possibly become. All the inherent psychic bipolar qualities are what compose the Self, so in a strange way the Self is mobilizing its own forces as it wakes itself up. On a gross biological level, the Self manifests as all those organic cerebral components mentioned above that clamor for integration and conscious orchestration but whose very nature is beyond words and rational thinking. To describe this process, only right-brain approaches such as metaphors, poetry, myth, analogies, allegories and symbols seem to do it any justice. *

This path of Self-realization, recognized by many in its completed form in such diverse spiritual figures as the Christ, Moses, Mohammed, the Buddha, Confucius and Krishna, is perhaps for most of us more a process than a goal achievable in one lifetime. In Jung's experience, for most of us there is no instantaneous access or painless road to knowledge of the Self. Although each of us is as unique as our thumbprint, becoming that uniqueness paradoxically implies relating to the Self, which is an unpredictable universal mystery in each and every one of us. In a way, individuation is a burgeoning experience of the macrocosm that is to be found within the microcosm, of the universal which is truly replicated in the individual. This finds its parallel in the studies of holography in the new physics. Individuation can be said to be a simple awakening to this psychic fact through the agency of the imponderable grace of the Self, and living responsibly with that power-generating awareness.

The Problem of Pain

The experience of the Self in its capacity to bring together seemingly irreconcilable opposites does not necessarily leave us pain-free. Pain and suffering are a healthy, guiltless part of

---

* Some useful definitions: (1) Metaphor (in Latin, metaphora = "transfer"): a figure of speech in which a term or phrase is applied to something to which it is not literally applicable in order to suggest a resemblance of some kind as in "the strong arm of the law," "a mighty fortress is our God," "The light of the spirit," etc.; (2) Analogy: a resemblance or similarity in some particulars between things otherwise unalike; a ground of comparison or inference that if two things agree or can compare with each other is some respects, they will very likely agree in others, such as in tracing the analogy between "the heart and a machine," "a river and the flow of one's thoughts"; "the gentleness of a breeze and the fury of the wind"; (3) Allegory: a figurative treatment of one subject under the guise of another; a presentation of an abstract or spiritual idea via an image, picture, or through a concrete personification of some kind, such as the parables of the New Testament or a symbolic narrative as found in Aesop's fables, wherein various animals personify human virtues or vices.

living life on this planet, although some shrill voices of New Age thought would have us believe otherwise. There is no struggle-free enlightenment. Psycho-spiritual disciplines that are undertaken with great resolve, dedication and single-mindedness are what produce the liberating self-knowledge for which we all yearn.

Suffering is not an illness or a reflection of bad karma, as some would explain it. It is a natural part of a life full of challenges that allows us to flex our psychic muscles. It is also the other side of the coin of what we term happiness. Only when we strive to avoid suffering at all costs—through human weakness, lack of courage or simplistic understanding—do troublesome complexes and psychic or somatic illnesses proliferate. Pain is merely a neutral signal that directs our attention to a specific issue.

Apropos of the strong human resistance to experiencing difficulties and tensions, Jung states in *Psychology and Religion* that "suppression amounts to a conscious moral choice, but repression is a rather immoral 'penchant' for getting rid of disagreeable decisions. Suppression may cause worry, conflict and suffering, but it never causes a neurosis. *Neurosis is always a substitute for legitimate suffering* [my italics]" (p. 75).

Neurosis feels like a meaningless, frustrating stalemate. In contrast, enduring the tension of opposites that the Self may impose on us as a challenge to growth always carries with it a sense of genuine suffering that promises some future spiritual breakthroughs to personal fulfillment. This somehow is infinitely more bearable because it is meaningful suffering. It is generally of an ethical nature, and once the pull in opposite directions has been endured (for example, "Should I kill the man who has run off with my wife or not? Should I kill my wife or not? Should I kill myself or not?"), we seem to rise above their pull, above the opposites of murder or utter despair. We move up to an inner place of wisdom that breathes in renewed freedom and balance (for example, "She was a millstone around my neck all those years in any case. Did I

really need that? Good riddance to her and good luck to her
new lover. He's going to need it!").

The suffering that such a state of affairs can bring about is
ultimately purifying. After we have achieved the hard-won
awareness that Fate has been extremely good to us despite our
initial doubts, it slowly dawns on us that we are spiritual
beings. This healing insight is an intuitive perception of some
suprahuman someone or something "up there" who is watching over us. "Up there" is really in the "heart," another term
for the unconscious, where the Self resides. It is also an inspir-
ing awareness of our own godliness, based on the logic that
cats produce kittens, dogs produce puppies, cows produce
calves, and God produces godlings, namely ourselves. Our
only problem is that we have forgotten who our real parent is.

In *The Relations between the Ego and the Unconscious*, Jung
wrote: "But the more we become conscious of ourselves
through self-knowledge, and act accordingly, the more the
layer of the personal unconscious that is superimposed on the
collective unconscious will be diminished. In this way there
arises a consciousness which is no longer imprisoned in the
petty world of the ego, but participates freely in the wider
world of objective interests. This widened consciousness is no
longer that touchy, egotistical bundle of personal wishes, fears,
hopes, and ambitions which has always to be compensated or
corrected by unconscious countertendencies; instead, it is a
function of relationships to the world of objects [i.e., *outer
objective reality*], bringing the individual into absolute, binding,
and indissoluble communion with the world at large" (*Collected Works*, vol. 7, par. 275). "Snapping out of it" is how
the vernacular would put it. It is a maturation into a larger,
more liberating reality, a kind of spiritual birthday in which
we are born into an entirely new state of being.

In truth, as we transcend the former narrow confines of ego,
our individuality is not lost but rather expands out to infinity.
This is really the moment when we are reabsorbed into our
truest nature, which is continuous rapture and imperturbable

bliss. Many before us have achieved it, and many will do so after we are gone.

Religious old-timers used to say, "There's no salvation without the cross." They were talking about an inner psychic cross that pulled one in opposite directions. When we simply sit tight, using all of our strength, not budging an inch, stilling our minds by deep and slow breathing while refusing to act out any irrationality but also not fighting with the impulses of murder or suicide, we spiral up to a higher overview, a new, more objective perspective of ourselves and others and of what is happening. This is salvation. This is individuation. What appeared to be an insoluble, enfouling catastrophe and emotional morass we simply outgrow—with the help of patience, and a willingness to calmly put up with a particularly trying circumstance using a tried-and-true technique.

It is useless to describe this type of excruciating but liberating experience to anyone who has not been through something similar. Somehow or other we experience a kind of divine grace from the depths just by sitting tight. That process allows us to operate out of our higher Self, instead of operating out of the pettiness of the peevish little ego. Apropos of this, Jung observed: "The Self is a quantity that is supraordinate to the conscious ego. It embraces not only the conscious but also the unconscious psyche, and is therefore, so to speak, a personality which we *also* are" (op. cit., par. 274). If the Self can stand the tension of opposites that compose it, then so can we, since it is who we also are, as Jung states, if only we would try to grasp the magnitude of this reality.

A Reflection of God

In spiritual terms, we can say that we are not God but neither are we different from God. We are a reflection of God, "made in God's image," but the part can never fully understand the whole. It can only experience the whole. To do this, the ego must learn to still the discursive mind and rambling emotions, the two functions of evaluation. "Be still and know that I am God" (Psalm 46:10). Finding our inner quietness will literally awaken us to the awesomeness of our lives.

When we allow ourselves to experience the "whole" and center ourselves in it without judging and dissecting, Jung writes: ". . . there develops a personality who, so to speak, suffers only in the lower storey of himself, but in the upper storey . . . is singularly detached from painful as well as joyful events" (*The Secret of the Golden Flower, Collected Works*, vol. 13, p. 67). This is serenity and equanimity, two terms that have seemingly fallen out of use in modern times. They are still accessible to us, and the consolations that they bring can be felt by those who know how to look for them single-mindedly. "If Thine eye be single, Thou shalt be filled with light" (Luke 11:34). The Buddha taught in this regard that even a greedy man who thinks only about money all day long all of his life will one day reach Nirvana, the ultimate spiritual liberation, the very moment he turns his fixated thought from money to attaining Enlightenment, so powerful will his single-mindedness be. Lawrence LeShan's short and simple book *How to Meditate* is indispensable in learning to be single-minded.

If you wish to meditate immediately, simply choose a quiet place to sit down comfortably with your back straight and head held high. Eyes should be half-closed. The center of your body awareness should be allowed to shift from your head and to settle down in your lower abdomen. Simply count your breaths from one to ten, beginning again at one repeatedly. Consider the mind to be like a television screen. If a thought enters from the left or right, let it simply fade away in whichever direction it wishes to go. Give no importance or have no attachment to any thoughts or mental images, but simply count one on the in-breath, two on the out-breath, three on the in-breath, and so on up to ten. Then begin all over again. Focus only on the breaths. This simple exercise will awaken the "eternal witness" in you regarding the workings of the inner world.

There is no extraverted-sensate, scientific proof of transcendental experience except the proof of one's own living experience, which considers the need for scientific evidence to be completely irrelevant, confirming what Blaise Pascal has said, "The heart has reasons that reason knows not of." The ultimate in psychic experience is "the kingdom of heaven" that is within, which, when experienced, leaves no room for doubts. This treasure is not won without effort. The effortful adventure, called the individuation process, will unfold itself in its own time, whether we want it to or not.

The Divine has an infinite supply of imagination. Individuation is consciously incarnating the uniqueness of that divine thought with which each of us was created, which is embedded at the very core of our being. We need only to look deep enough and in the right place to see it. Looking at it spurs it into action and unfoldment, as if we charged it with the energy of our concentrated attention.

We will never be able to work along with this process of individuation without the knowledge of specific techniques and skills, however. A book may only teach in generalities and cannot do what a well-trained counselor can. Therefore, despite the knowledge of specific techniques and skills written about in the following chapters or in recommended books, it would be beneficial to engage in serious inner work with a qualified therapist, if possible. Also, many Jungian study groups have sprung up in cities and towns across North America and elsewhere. Called Centerpoint or Friends of Jung in the United States, they can be located in the telephone directory.

One need not be neurotic or psychotic to begin a Jungian journey. Anyone seeking individuation or simply suffering from aimlessness or meaninglessness can begin the process. It is for the young, the middle-aged and the elderly. The Jungian prospective method is focused on what we may be, what we are heading toward, and not only on effecting a "cure" by minutely unearthing possible causative traumas of the past. Events of the past are not neglected by the Jungian therapist, but they are counterbalanced by arousing positive forces in the unconscious that will carry the blocked person toward the prospective creative goals of individuation.

Jung offered ways and means to effect psychic transformation that are akin to the spiritual practices of many cultures and time periods in their use of collective, traditional symbols used in many ancient rites and rituals of initiation. Jung's prescriptions for evoking an individuation process, however, are based on the natural Self-propelled movement of the human psyche in its capacity to produce original, spontaneous, organic, transformative, energy-carrying symbols, without imposing anything on the individual from an outer traditional collective system. All of this occurs automatically, based on the belief that the Self within knows exactly what the individual needs, spiritually speaking, for the purposes of individuation and that the Self generously offers whatever is necessary via the dream-life, fantasies and soul-productions of each individual.

Jung was by no means against the practice of traditional collective religions by an individual. In fact, many analysands reconnect with the spiritual traditions they were raised in, only on a totally new footing, or perhaps with other newly chosen collective spiritual disciplines. In analytical psychology there are no fixed rules.

Jung accents an intense, face-to-face inner encounter with the Self, focusing on the unique manner that the Self wishes to use to communicate its healing power to those who are seeking wholeness. There can be no substitute for this intimately personal pilgrimage.

Chapter 11

Perchance to Dream

Only a serious personal engagement in Jungian inner work can be considered a real lesson about the meaning of dreams. Reading about dream understanding leaves one at best only on the level of theory. Our own dreams themselves are too close to us, in the same way that the nose on our face is too close to us for us to see it without the help of a mirror. In analysis, the therapist acts as the necessary mirror, allowing for some perspective on our dreams. Recording a dream in a diary and leaving it alone for a period of a few days or a few weeks may also help to get some perspective on it, as reminiscing about our past often gives us new insights into what really happened.

As Jung said, the dream itself is its own best interpretation, so all we need is assistance in seeing the dream more clearly and more objectively. The analyst can fulfill this role in various ways, but we can do much on our own to determine what our dreaming is all about, since the dreamer ultimately has the last word about the meaning of a dream.

There are no fixed rules for understanding a dream. Interpretation is actually something that is not advisable. Remember the proverb "Translators are traitors." What we wish to do is to understand our dreams in their own "foreign language" of symbols.

In lieu of a personal analysis with an analyzed graduate of a Jungian Institute, some helpful guidelines in dream understanding can be offered to the reader in an introductory book of this kind. Nothing can compare with bouncing our dreams off a knowledgeable person; such a process may help us to assimilate the wisdom of our dreams. This help may come from a variety of sources, including an intuitive spouse or a person who has worked with their own dreams over a long period of time.

What we see in our dreams, generally speaking, are our psychic contents and their dynamics, as delineated in the previous chapters. To recapitulate, the four states of consciousness are the waking state, the dream state, the state of dreamless sleep, and the composite union of the previous three, which Jung has termed the Self. This chapter will focus on the dream state, which includes daydreams, as well as regular dreams during sleep. In a normal eight-hour sleeping experience, we spend roughly only two and a half hours intermittently dreaming. Six and a half hours may be utterly dreamless. The ancient seers and writers of the Hindu *Mandukya Upanishad* say that dreamless sleep is when we "go home" to our truest and innermost selves and no longer need the language of images.

The imagery of dreams can specifically concern personal psychic aspects such as the ego, the persona, the shadow, the anima and animus. Some imagery of a general nature includes complexes and archetypes, complexes being the basic contents of one's personal unconscious and archetypal images being those emanating from the collective unconscious. Archetypes themselves are invisible metaphysical postulates, which the psyche does not directly perceive. What the psyche does perceive are archetypal images, which is what analytical psychology focuses on.

The Self, although the ordering principle of the psyche, cannot be defined with words. It often appears visually, however, in symbolic form that is awe-inspiring and full of a sense of fascinating sacredness. In its numinous, awesome imagery the Self is indistinguishable from the perennial and age-old symbols of what all cultures traditionally term God, with all the feelings and emotions commonly associated therewith. Its image is that of a union of all psychic bipolarities canceling each other out: an unportrayable, inconceivable, divine transcendence. On a human level, the symbol of the Self charges the whole psyche with an inscrutably electrical but serenely heightened state of consciousness.

Symbols in Dreams

By "symbol" Jung means "an intuitive idea that cannot yet be formulated in any other or better way" (*Collected Works*, vol. 15, par. 105). The symbols of dreams are the forms in which archetypal psychic energies manifest and become discernible to our everyday minds. A symbol is, therefore, the very essence of psychic energy in a meaningful, imaged form that is generally beyond the ken of everyday categories and terminology.

The word "symbol" derives from the Greek *symbolon*, which means "thrown together." The mermaid is a perfect and clear example of a symbol, something that is not seen in everyday life and that is purely a thrown-together product of the human psyche. The image of a creature half-fish and half-woman presents two known entities brought together to produce an unknown third entity that is entirely new and fascinating. This third entity is a symbol that presents a visible meaning behind which is hidden an invisible, more profound meaning. A fish is a primitive denizen of a deep ocean such as we possess in our unconscious. The mermaid may symbolize the hidden archaic feminine energies in the depths of a man's psyche that are in the process of becoming human and that have not been fully integrated into a man's consciousness, as it still possesses an element of primitiveness, i.e., the fishtail.

Explaining the mermaid symbol in words betrays the emotional impact of the symbol, as words are definitive and leave nothing for the imagination to play with. Symbols, on the other hand, carry the ego-mind beyond its definitive and limited third dimension to the undreamed-of dimensions of the human soul. They supply humanity with meaning and meaningfulness that make life something worth living. Symbols in this sense are nonrational carriers of meaning and meaningfulness from the hidden realm of the unconscious to the ordinary realm of consciousness.

Jung differentiates between symbols and signs. He accuses Freud of not understanding the true meaning of the symbol, which does not point to something else beyond itself as does a sign, but which itself expresses and represents its own meaningful essence.

For example, for Freud a pencil in a dream meant a penis. Jung believed that Freud interpreted a pencil as a sign, something that points beyond itself to something else. Jung asked Freud whether if one dreamed of a penis could it mean that one was really dreaming about a pencil? According to Jung, Freud's obsession with repressed sexuality made him reduce most symbols into signs of a uniquely sexual nature.

A road sign says "New York—50 Miles" and therefore points beyond itself to some other place. A police badge worn on a man's shirt indicates that the man wearing this sign is a policeman. On the other hand, a symbol is "the best possible description or formulation of a relatively unknown fact" (*Collected Works*, vol. 6, par. 814). Symbols are pregnant with meaning. A cross or a Star of David or a national flag is a symbolic picture laden with meaning. Dream symbols are not explanatory signs but rather images of unconscious contents, energies and realities which on the whole transcend conscious categorization. They are expressions of psychic dimensions that cannot be portrayed in any other or better way in their attempt to communicate with the three-dimensional ego. We human beings are multidimensional and cannot describe or explain our human experiences with a three-dimensional yardstick of words that simply does not measure up to who we fully and truly are.

According to Jung, the more conventional a person's mentality and the more extraverted-sensate a person's typology, the more will that person be hindered in understanding symbols and in experiencing their deep meaning. He or she will view symbols as signs and reduce the broader, multidimensional, unknown meaning of the symbol to that of the limited three-dimensional known meaning of a sign. In short, minds that take everything literally miss out on the nuances, shadings and subtler realities of psychic life. They do not understand the figurative language of their own psyches. This approach is typical of left-brained rationalists, who by and large have a secret fear of the ultimately inexplicable, untranslatable nature of human life on this planet. They wish to make all aspects of human life understandable and therefore controllable. They have no appreciation of the nonrational, which describes the very nature of symbols. When symbols manifest, they resonate meaningfully in their nonrational way in all four functions of consciousness simultaneously—thinking, feeling, intuition and sensation.

Signs are unambiguous and unipolar. Symbols are ambiguous and bipolar. For instance, Freud sees the issue of incest as just and only that. He fails to see that dreams dealing with this topic could very well possibly be symbolic expressions of a universal yearning of humankind to return to the paradisiacal state of the mother's womb (i.e., the unconscious), a state free of responsibility and human concerns that requires no difficult decision making. A return to the maternal womb can also be positive if it symbolizes a need and desire for spiritual rebirthing, or a total starting-over. An incest dream could symbolize the ego finally penetrating its own matrix, i.e., its own personal unconscious, and connecting with all the hidden contents thereof in order to re-energize itself for purposes of transformation and renewal. Then again, it could simply reveal an incestuous psyche. The possibilities are many. Symbols are polyvalent, possessing many values or meaningful implications.

A symbol (something compounded) is usually composed of a *thesis* (woman, for instance) and an *antithesis* (a fish, which is "opposite" to woman) whose combination produces a *synthesis*, a symbol (mermaid) with a meaning that is beyond that of a simple woman or a simple fish. We could say that when left brain and right brain combine, their product is a symbol, a psychic reality transcending a solely left-brain concept or a solely right-brain concept.

A symbol mediates between all those "incompatible" elements of the conscious and unconscious, between what is known and what is unknown. As Jung says, "The symbol is neither abstract nor concrete, neither rational nor irrational, neither real nor unreal. It is always both" (*Psychology and Alchemy, Collected Works,* vol. 12, pp. 270–271). Symbols are paradoxical, as indeed Truth is in general, not to mention human consciousness.

The symbol-making capacity of the psyche, this ability to synthesize pairs of opposites into a symbol, Jung calls the *transcendent function.* By "transcendent" Jung does not imply anything metaphysical; rather he wishes to show that the symbol-making capacity facilitates a transition, a transcending from an old, possibly negative attitude to a new and different one. We can indeed rise above conflictual tendencies when the Orphic transcendent function is activated and produces resolving symbols. Put simply, a symbol representing a new state of consciousness can push out an old symbol that represented an outworn state of mind. This is what is meant by psychic renewal, a process that is directly affected by the almost magical powers of the symbol-making capacities of the unconscious.

Dreams as a whole act as bridges between the lower and upper worlds, between the unconscious and conscious minds. Consequently, symbols, as synthesizers of conflictual dynamisms, can act as healing transformers of psychic energy. They bring together in themselves what we thought were only irreconcilable opposites. They can consequently be restorers of wholeness and equanimity (psychic balance).

Symbols are never consciously devised, since they emanate from the realm of Pisces/Neptune, the collective unconscious. By their very nature they relieve the tension of opposites within the psyche by opening up new paths into which previously blocked psychic energy can flow. In this way they are capable of breaking a deadlock of psychic conflict. Intrapsychic factors and archetypal forces in the dreamer reveal themselves as symbols and, if made conscious, if understood nonrationally, speed up the process of healing and individuation.

The divine symbols of the world's mythologies are ultimately the projected intrapsychic realities of the human psyche. When they are assimilated into our waking state and taken back from their projected state, they will "divinize" and "deify" the individual psyche. Theologically speaking, for example, according to the teachings of the Eastern Orthodox Church, deification is the end product of spiritual practice, as it is also with most Asian religions. This may come as a surprise to some Westerners who are unaware of the original and most ancient teachings of the Orthodox version of their own religious heritage. *

A real danger exists, however, for a weak or undeveloped ego that might be completely sucked into an overidentification with the divine Self. This overidentification with God produces an inflated ego, which manifests symptomatically as exaggerated arrogance accompanied by a lack of footing in the everyday world.

The ideal, of course, would be to have one's head "among

---

* See *The Orthodox Way*, by Kallistos Ware for a more complete description.

the stars" and one's feet cemented in the Earth, but everyday life unfortunately usually reveals a different picture.

Psychosis is a distinct possible outcome if the ego overidentifies with the Self rather than simply experiencing a cooperative union with its presence. "We are not God but neither are we different from God" is a paradoxical expression that is very hard for most people to grasp and thus to experience sanely, because they usually either want to be God or to be utterly different from God. Paradox can be very off-putting, especially to the minds of literalists, those who take things only at face value. Experiencing paradox or the paradoxical truths of our soul is like being stretched out on a cross, an instrument of torture, being pulled in opposite directions. Paradoxical truth stymies the mind. The tension of opposites composing the Self is indeed a veritable cross to bear. When borne patiently, however, and with understanding, it can lead to total psychic rebirthing: a "deification" of sorts.

What's in a Dream?

Generally what we initially experience in our dreams are the activities of our complexes. The core of a complex is an archetype clustered over with images associated with memories and episodes of our personal history and pertaining to that particular complex.

In the first half of life dreams generally concern themselves with the ego and its strengthening via development of the main inborn attitude and the functions of the individual's typology, as well as development of the persona and the shadow. We deal with these issues to establish ourselves in a suitable niche in society.

In the second half of life, the dream interest shifts to the realm of the archetypal forces hidden below the levels of the personal psyche, in the more impersonal strata of the collective unconscious.

In analysis, dreams usually take us back to our early years, when shadow elements were split off from the ego-ideal and pushed into the unconscious. The shadow generally appears as an alter ego of the same sex as the dreamer. When, through dreamwork, we make conscious these shadow qualities seen in our dream, we project less onto others of the same sex and have less dislike and envy toward these others simply because they are no longer "hooks" for projected shadow qualities that we now see as aspects of our own mind. For example, an elderly woman dreamed that everywhere she went she was followed by a harsh, carping woman whose words poisoned every situation that her dream ego found herself in. In waking life the elderly woman was a diabetic who totally neglected her illness, and she was a victim of her own increasing irritability, moodiness and harshness, the result of her worsening condition. From childhood, she had been deaf in one ear, a state that was more than symbolic psychologically. Through the years, her husband and children tried in vain to make her see that, despite her sweet and caring personality with strangers outside the home setting, she was an obstinate shrew with family members. Now that she was widowed and emotionally abandoned by her fed-up children, her unconscious repeatedly tried informing her of the reason for her present solitude.

Relations with others of the same sex become smoother as a consequence of the withdrawal of these shadow projections if and only if the dreamer owns up to them. Figures of the opposite sex to the dreamer generally represent the anima or animus qualities. Likewise, when we allow these contrasexual qualities to surface and make them conscious, we set in motion a process that creates androgynous wholeness. Relations with the opposite sex in the outer world then become, ideally speaking, more realistic and genuine, with no false expectations. The integration of the contrasexual soul image allows the individual greater freedom of behavior and outlook, as the accustomed restricted way of psychic functioning is now modified by the complementary viewpoint of the opposite sex within oneself.

In traditional cultures where "men are men and women are women," when integration of the repressed anima or animus takes place, men stop being maudlin or stiff and begin expressing a greater spontaneity and healthier, more mature sentiments; when women assimilate their animus, they stop aggressively scoring points with other people, especially men, and begin expressing personally thought-out opinions and a more focused outlook on life. When they are unintegrated into consciousness, both anima and animus tend to remain undeveloped and express themselves in unrefined ways. When acknowledged by ego-consciousness and raised into everyday consciousness by attempts to assimilate their energies via dream images of them, the anima and animus learn to exist in a more cooperative mode of existence with our egos, who have made room for them, so to speak.

In relationship to the shadow, we can say that the anima or animus is generally less fully integratable than are the shadow elements that appear in dreams. The shadow was conscious before it was repressed or suppressed, making it easier to bring up. The anima and animus, on the other hand, are unconscious until they are discovered in dreams and fantasy or observed as projections. Lifting them up is an entirely new venture and therefore not an easy one.

Many older people have failed to cultivate a sense of personal identity that goes beyond biological parenting, which may produce dreams of depression, meaninglessness and generalized malaise once the children have grown up and are living on their own. This syndrome implies that there has been too much of an identification with one's parental persona to the detriment of other important facets of one's psyche. After the last child has left, a husband and wife may stare at each other like total strangers one morning across the breakfast table, both realizing that a one-sided identification with parenting deprived them of a deeper relationship with each other as husband and wife, as plain people.

Issues pertaining to the individuation process are dreamed about throughout the entire life of an individual. Dreams will point out false role choices made by the ego as the development of the psyche unfolds. False role choices can lead to neurotic suffering since they would be produced by an ego that is living and operating out of sync with its true identity, a state that dreams are always trying to comment upon and rectify. The psyche will stand only so much of misguided falsehood. The dream life of the individual will reveal the inner revolt and attempt to set things straight.

The individuation process encouraged by Jungian psychology involves a continuous openness on the part of the ego toward the deeper voice of the Self that is heard so clearly and incessantly in dreams and fantasies, albeit in a specialized, "foreign" language. Aligning the ego with the will of the Self is a life-long process, one that needs to forge a link between the personal and transpersonal within ourselves. This means that the dream state ought to take on the most vital importance for us in our lives if the individuating truth they express is to be meaningfully and satisfactorily ingested as "food for conscious thought."

What we dream normally seems just as real as what we experience during our waking hours. Occasionally the dream-ego realizes that it is experiencing a dream, a reality different from the ego's waking state, but this does not normally happen, although it is desirable for this phenomenon to take place as often as possible.

Another interesting occurrence is that the dream-ego can sometimes shift its identity from one character to another or even to a totally neutral position, which permits a more objective observation of dream characters and events. Incidentally, yoga teaches that after much training the waking-ego would be able to do similar things, also making for a multifaceted view of things.

We still do not precisely understand the biological basis for dreaming. Dreams may come from many sources, from the body itself (including the various parts of the composite brain) and the stimulated senses, from emotions and from all kinds of conscious and unconscious reactions to things, from attempts to psychically "digest" past events and from apprehensions and musings about future events. Some dreams emanate solely from the personal unconscious and others from the collective unconscious. The various parts of the brain, with their various "concerns" and views, are involved in this dream process on the biological level, as was discussed in the previous chapter.

Jung observed that dreams are beyond the categories of time, space and the usual dynamics of cause and effect. The dream expresses itself in a puzzling manner in a language that is archaic, symbolic and prelogical—even in its reviewing of already lived experiences and events. Closer examination always reveals that the dream is looking at things with its own slant, from an angle far removed from that of the waking-ego. One exception to this is a dream that is produced by a psychic or physical trauma, such as experienced during wartime or a physical assault. This type of dream repeats itself until the traumatic stimulus plays itself out to exhaustion. Only patience and sensitive emotional support on the part of loved ones or a therapist can make the relived trauma somewhat bearable until it wears itself out. The word "patience" classically implies a willingness and resignation to suffer what cannot be avoided or changed. "With your patience you shall possess your souls" (Luke 21:19). Is there really any other way?

Compensation and Complementation

As a purposive activity, dreams try to regulate the entire psyche, checking here, balancing there. This orchestration is achieved by the dream through the processes known as compensation and complementation.

Jung stated: "The more one-sided [the] conscious attitude is, and the further it deviates from the optimum, the greater becomes the possibility that vivid dreams with a strongly contrasting but purposive content will appear as an expression of the self-regulation of the psyche" (*General Aspects of Dream Psychology, Collected Works*, vol. 8, p. 488).

We may dream of a person whom we totally idealize—for example, the perfect grandmother emanating unconditional love from every pore of her body, ever doling out handfuls of delicious goodies. Another dream, however, may paint a picture of her as an absolutely evil shrew and hag. The compensatory purpose of such a dream would be to bring us to a more realistic perception of who our objective, historical, human grandmother really was. When we wake up, we are usually shocked that we had such a dream, but over time its message and balancing capacity sink in and adjust our perspective to a viewpoint that is less idealistic perhaps but closer to reality.

Dream compensation is unfortunately not always as clear-cut as the preceding example. A young boy may dream of his father, with whom he has the most cordial and loving relationship. In a dream, he may see his father as a profligate drunkard who is neglectful of his son. The father may even die in the dream. The dream would seem to blaspheme the objective, congenial nature of the actual father. There could be hidden unconscious animosity on the part of the son for the father, but for all practical purposes the relationship would appear to be one of genuine affection and mutual respect. Why would the boy's unconscious try to discredit his beloved and respected father? This can be very difficult to ascertain. If we remember that dreams are compensatory to conscious attitudes, we might intuit that the purpose of the dream was to break an overly dependent attitude on his father on the part of the son, to offer the son a rite of passage toward independence and individuation. The "father" would have to take on less importance in the boy's mind and even "die" so that the son could begin esteeming his own talents and qualities if he is too enthralled with those of his father. To come to such an understanding of this specific, subtle type of compensation would naturally require a thorough knowledge of the historical facts of this specific father and son duo.

Dreams are not easy to fathom with the logical mind. Jung stated: "It is not easy to set forth any sort of special rules for the type of dream interpretation. Its character depends at times upon the innermost character of the individual's whole being. The possibilities of compensation are countless and inexhaustible, although, with increasing experience, certain fundamental traits will gradually be crystallized out" ("General Aspects of the Psychology of the Dream," *Spring* [magazine], 1956, pp. 15–16).

Compensation usually portrays in an exaggerated way views and attitudes that are polar opposites of those held by the conscious mind. It does so in order to balance out the rigidly held, one-sided conscious views and attitudes.

Complementation, on the other hand, simply supplies missing aspects that perhaps have resulted from a lack of perception of an outer life situation or inner psychic state. These missing bits of information are not necessarily indicative of any polar opposites of a compensatory nature. The complementary dream may simply provide us with more details pertaining to a specific life issue. It makes us pay attention to areas of reality that our conscious minds resisted becoming aware of.

A person may desire to become a famous actor or actress instead of waiting on tables in a restaurant. This individual may mistakenly believe that appearing in a Broadway musical is all glamor, big money and smiles. A dream may come along illustrating the glamor of acting on Broadway but ignoring the drudgery of performances repeated day in and day out, month after month, as well as the in-fighting, jealousy, politics and everything else that makes the life of a Broadway star fully human. In short, the dream completes the half-illustrated, false picture held by the conscious mind and provides the

missing features of the longed-for career in all its blatant
reality.

Dreams of the Past and Future

Besides compensation and complementation, dreaming may
function reductively or prospectively.

For Freud dreams are reductive in that they bring up the
primitive, instinctual, infantile sources of psychic motivation,
reducing current issues and problems to their presumed origins
in the dreamer's past life. This deterministic view of the psyche
tries to see behavior only in terms of causality, of motivation
and influence engendered uniquely by past events, happenings
and traumas. Jung considered this Freudian view to be partially
true but incomplete. Jung stated: "The psychology of an individual can never exhaustively be explained from himself
alone. . . . No psychological fact can ever be explained in
terms of causality alone; as a living phenomenon, it is always
indissolubly bound up with the continuity of the vital process,
so that it is not only something evolved but also continually
evolving and creative" (*Psychology Types, Collected Works*, vol.
6, par. 717).

Jung realized early in his career that what a patient might
tell the therapist ought not always be regarded as historically
true but possibly only as subjectively true. Subjective truth
may be just as painful, psychologically speaking, as historical
truth, but the point is that one is never sure about what has
caused a specific conflict. All we know is that the conflict
must be resolved in the here and now and that dreams can
offer insights on how we can progress out of our problems and
move forward.

Jung therefore disapproved of using only the reductive
method that connects the unconscious dream production to
past causes. He disapproved because therapeutically what we
call the past is a living entity. Memories as living entities in

our psyches are in a perpetual state of evolution, as are all other things in Nature. The present value of a dream may be lost to the dreamer if he or she has been programmed to believe that everything in life is totally and irrevocably conditioned by past events and is only an echo of the past.

Freud's views, and the now-fashionable Eastern idea of karma (i.e., you will reap what you have sown), are often understood too simplistically by Westerners and Easterners alike. The concept of karma is strictly reductionist in its belief that the present moment is caused only by past actions or events. Even in Asian thought karma does not destroy the powers of the Divine, which can intervene at any moment in the life of a human being in order to offer a particular grace or boon that has been neither earned nor merited by some past behavior or deed. For centuries in the West the term *causa finalis* ("the causative action of the goal") has been used to describe the idea of inherent psychic purposiveness, which molds events to intentionally bring about certain goals. Inherent in the DNA of an apple seed is an apple tree. The DNA has a goal in mind, namely an invisible picture of an as-yet-unrealized future event called an apple tree.

Goals as inherent ideas have this power to bring about specific events. Archetypes, which are of the same nature as inherent ideas and which are beyond time and space, are the formative agents that activate certain goals within the framework of time and space. In everyday life there are expressions such as "meeting one's destiny," which everyone seems to understand without any difficulty. The idea is that the Self or cosmos has something "in mind" about our future that might or might not correspond to our own intentions or awareness or even karma. In short, something bigger is at play in our lives than our own individual egos.

In any event, life presents challenges that have not been caused by past events but that arise to pull us forward to some goal set up by the Self.

If one wishes to become muscular, one exercises, does push-ups, lifts weights, and so on, all of which can be a painful experience. The pain is not caused by a past action but rather by a present one that is surrendered to willingly for the purpose of reaching a future goal, namely, enjoying a strong, healthy and muscular physique.

Jung did not discard reductionist views concerning dreams, but he saw that they were valid only part of the time, since dreams also possess a prospective function, indicating the developmental direction in which the dreamer is heading. This is so because of the bipolarity of everything psychic. If dreams are reductive, they are also prospective, since past and future are always intimate parts of every present moment.

Accenting this prospective side helps the dreamer progress beyond the past and the status quo forward toward some positive future development. Jung considered it best to deal with dreams from all three angles—past, present and future—since each is part of the overall picture of an individual dreamer's psychic development and evolution.

Many Jungian analysts are unconsciously guilty of overreductionism when they continuously see archetypes or complexes as causes or producers of certain dreams. We should not forget that dreams, although from some other dimension, are the pictorialization of living processes in action of all psychic components experienced in the here and now. Within every present moment there is a past and a future; likewise with dreams. Jung attributes great importance to uncovering the dreamer's present conscious situation, since the ordering dynamic of the unconscious is always in sync with the conscious activity of the moment in its habitual role of keeping the psyche in balance.

We must never feel that our understanding of a particular dream has been total. Subsequent dreams may throw more light on a psychic situation and modify our understanding radically. Dreams are best studied in a series, in any case, to see the full impact of a new wave arising from the oceanic unconscious depths. If worked with assiduously, each successive dream will produce statements correcting misunderstandings or mistakes in interpreting previous dream messages.

Clusters of Meaning

In their attempt to elucidate a given topic, dreams do not necessarily assume a logical, chronological order. Dreams cluster around a "nucleus of meaning" that wants to be made conscious and from which the dreams radiate like the spokes of a wheel. Each dream appears as a piece of a jigsaw puzzle, one piece or dream fitting the upper-right corner, the next dream completing the lower-left or middle, another dream the lower center, etc. Keeping a record of as many dreams as possible is essential, as each dream is an intricate part of a larger picture of meaning.

Even when dreams are not interpreted, often their power has a marked effect upon waking consciousness. Individuation is hindered, however, when dreams are resisted and consistently go unheeded. When he or she works with the help of an expert who is empathetic, knowledgeable, intuitive and astute and who possesses a certain *je ne sais quoi* culled from years of experience, the dreamer can develop what the French call *l'intelligence du coeur*, an "understanding on the heart level," which allows for personal interaction with our unconscious parts without the constant help of a professional. This independent stance is one of the goals of formal analysis.

If one is undergoing analysis, many dreams may focus on the therapeutic relationship between analyst and analysand (the client or patient), which it is vital to understand if further exploration of the unconscious is to continue smoothly. The therapeutic relationship is a sort of alchemical process in which the consciousnesses of both analyst and analysand interact and change in the subtlest of ways. The relationship is from ego to ego, as well as from unconscious to unconscious, as well as from one's ego to the other's unconscious and vice versa. Jung states that the analyst can take the analysand only as far psychically and spiritually as he or she has gone personally. Choosing an appropriate therapist, therefore, is essential. Equally important is for the analyst to only accept to work with someone that the analyst feels he or she can help. This may take a couple of sessions to determine.

How one sees one's therapist, what one projects onto the therapist, is called transference. Transferential dreams are quite common and must be dealt with. One can project something positive or something negative. Often the Self (i.e., God), which contains all pairs of contradictory opposites, is projected onto the analyst. Sometimes a demonic side is projected. For therapeutic reasons all projections must eventually be resolved by being owned up to by the analysand. Transferential dreams cover a whole range of issues and require considerable skill on the part of the therapist. The dream truly belongs to the dreamer in more ways than one, and so it is ultimately up to the dreamer to decide about the truest interpretation of a dream, transferential or otherwise. Interpretations must always "feel right" to the dreamer.

The analyst may have counter-transferential dreams regarding a particular analysand. At his or her discretion the analyst decides whether to discuss the counter-transferential dream or not. The goal is for the analyst to become conscious of what qualities are being projected onto the analysand and to consciously work through the counter-transferential material.

In dreams we experience personal myths and fairy tales that describe the deepest dynamics in our unconscious, which have repercussive influences in our everyday existence. We ought not forget that if there is no witch or dragon to kill in the fairy tale, there is no fairy tale. Without a negative element to overcome, there would be nothing to produce a heroic act or deed and thus no hero or heroine could appear at the end of the story. Witchiness and dragon-ness are, alas, necessary realities in our lives; without challenges, life is boring and futile. No evolution can take place without them.

How to Remember and Understand Your Dreams

Before retiring for the night, the ego should prepare to encounter its own deeper nature. This should be done in a spirit of great expectancy, for instance by leaving an open dream book or diary and a pen next to your bed. The ego might pose specific questions for the unconscious to answer. Next morning, the moment you awaken, record the current dream exactly as you remember it. Do not move more than necessary before writing down the dream—don't go to the bathroom first or have a cup of coffee to wake up. If when you first awake you have only the tiniest part of the dream in your memory, pull the dream back by that corner; in other words, bring that dream-bit fully into your memory, then push a corner of it farther along into the dream, remember the action just before, and bit by bit you will remember the full dream. As you write down the dream, you may remember the one preceding it and even the one preceding that. With training, you can remember all of your nightly dreams, especially if you attach great importance to them, which is the motivating factor in remembering them.

Dreams show a certain familiar structure much on the lines of ancient Greek theater, which comprised the following elements:

A *cast of characters, time and place*. These aspects should be noted at once when recording a dream.

An *exposition* that states the issue(s) to be dealt with. The dream will generally reply or attempt to reply to these "announced" issues.

The peripeteia reveals the ups and downs of the plot moving toward a climax, a transformatory process of some kind.

The *lysis* is the outcome of the dream, whether meaningful or not, which is meant to be a temporary or permanent solution to the dilemma put forth and portrayed. The ending may be tragic or may provide no solution at all; in either case the dream would show and warn about a truly problematical and critical situation.

In recording dreams, it is useful to remember all of these four parts, recalling that every interpretation is only an attempt at understanding, since the dream itself is its own best interpretation.

What does not appear in the dream is just as important as what does. Living in a grass hut is not living in a crystal palace or a brick-and-stone villa by the sea or a skyscraper. Understanding a dream symbol by contrasting it with what does not appear brings out more of the meaning of what is actually there in the dream.

Dream symbols are polyvalent, meaning they have many values that are not immediately perceived. They are *expressive* of psychic processes in emotionally charged pictorial form, and they are *impressive* as images full of artistry. They impress and impact on our ego-consciousness, influencing intrapsychic processes and creating a flow of energy in the psyche as a whole. In their expressive and impressive characteristics, symbols are the real transformers of psychic energy in the human psyche. In addition to writing down dreams, painting or drawing dream motifs and symbols will truly intensify the impressive and transformative activity of the unconscious in very practical ways.

It is highly advisable for very neurotic and psychotic patients not to work with their dreams at all, because they may open a door they may not be able to close due to all the forces coming through. Instead they can paint or draw whatever comes to mind in order for the analyst to discern the nature of their unconscious processes without any interpretation being necessary for the patient. All of us must cultivate an awareness that psychic productions are sacred in character. If we paint dream persons, motifs or symbols, they ought not be trivialized by using them as mere decorations on walls or as conversation pieces lying around the house. If our psyches and psychic dream expressions are not sacred, then where else is the sacred to be found? Our inner images are such an intimate part of ourselves that displaying them casually for all to see would be akin to showing our private parts in public. This advice is meant to raise our general consciousness to an increased aware- ness of the specialness of what we are dealing with.

Individuation is a truly sacred event. None of us would want to keep the door open to the consultation room while pouring out our hearts during a therapeutic session. Likewise we ought to treat all dream productions, such as paintings and drawings, in a sacred manner. This attitude keeps the fire of the thera- peutic process contained and makes it more efficacious. If we keep taking off the cover on a boiling pot to look inside, the heat escapes and the cooking process takes much longer. The same holds true for all inner work. The worst game to play is the "my therapist says" game. Each person is unique; what is counseled to one individual ought not be construed as general advice that is applicable to everyone else. Sharing dreams with unfamiliar people also falls into the same breach of sacredness. In America, where we are taught to be "up front" in typical extraverted fashion, this may appear as hard advice for extra- verts to follow and may be considered as being overly cautious. Introverts generally need no explanations concerning such protocol.

All aesthetic evaluations should be eschewed in examining dreams, as they will hinder deeper psychological understanding of the depicted dream symbols, whether painted or simply written down. We should take care to depict the dream motif exactly as it appeared in the dream, without beautifying it. The ego always wants to edit out whatever it does not find flattering to its persona ideals, so we have to be ruthlessly faithful in recording material from the unconscious, exactly as it originally appeared, warts and all.

The more we record our dreams and try to relate with their contents, the more we can see one batch of motifs leading to a completely new set. Initially the motifs are generally colored by personal experience, from early childhood up to the present. If we are persistent in our dream work, the farther we journey and the more we penetrate the deeper unconscious layers, the more symbolic and the more archetypal the motifs will begin to appear, and the more charged with pure psychic energy and awesome numinosity they will be. In sum, we move from a very personal world and go deeper and deeper to something that is more impersonal or transpersonal and sacred. A strong ego is needed to face this deepest inner world. It is similar to taking a trip to outer space: The farther from Earth we get, the less human but more divine things seem to become.

In dreaming, for instance, about our mother, we generally move gradually toward a vaster image of Woman in all her cosmic and mystical aspects, all of which eventually leads to the realm of the Goddess and onto more abstract forms of the Feminine such as deep oceans, dark caves in the bowels of the Earth, or the pregnant darkness of the Great Void.

Encountering these realms within ourselves in a slow, rhythmic, organic way is more maturing and infinitely less dangerous than any artificial means that many impatient people wish to try. The task is not to flood the waking state with material from the unconscious, but rather to integrate these contents slowly into an organic state of conscious wholeness. There is a lot for waking consciousness to ingest and digest, and the process is best accomplished a little at a time, slowly but surely.

Fertilization is perhaps a more graphic word to describe the process of integrating the dreams from the unconscious into waking consciousness. The ego truly becomes pregnant with new life when it stops resisting the inner flow and influx. In analysis, the understanding of dreams is never forced on the analysand. The analyst simply follows whatever strong affect or emotion is displayed by the analysand's ego concerns. If the ego is not at a relative state of peace, no journeying into the unconscious can take place. The same is true for meditation: To meditate one needs to be relatively free of overwhelming inner conflicts on the ego-level in order to sit quietly with a serene inward gaze on one's deepest realities. If the kitchen sink is full of dirty dishes, the floor strewn with dirty clothes, books and odds and ends, with dust and grime everywhere, the priority is to do some cleaning up. Likewise, in therapy the ego must first be free of pressing outer problems before it can begin its pilgrimage to the deep psychic center, to the sanctum sanctorum.

Jung's approach to dream understanding is called dialectical because it entails a dialogue between analysand and analyst, and a dialogue between analysand and the various levels of his or her unconscious, aiming at a synthesis that combines and transcends the ego and the non-ego.

The analyst facilitates an approach to the unconscious only if he or she deems that the analysand is ready for this experience, dream-work being only one means of therapy among many.

Jung devised an *association experiment*, which is comprised of a list of one hundred words, each of which can act as a stimulus disturbance to the main complexes hidden in the unconscious. When the analysand is given this "test," it is astounding to see all the unwitting, involuntary physiological reactions to such simple words as "mother," "father," "home," "money," "love." The provoked psychomotor reactions indicate complexes that have been hit by the stimulus words.

Without using the *association experiment* in a formal way to unearth unconscious complexes, even ordinary conversations containing the above-mentioned stimulus words will produce similar reactions in a person. Jung's work with the association experiment was the forerunner to the polygraph test now widely employed by many investigative agencies.

Early in their careers, Freud and Jung both used hypnosis to get the patient to unearth memories surrounding certain disturbing symptoms. Jung abandoned this method for a host of reasons, one of which was overdependency on the therapist by the analysand. Jung also felt that the ego should not be put to sleep via hypnosis but rather make a concerted, personal effort to work on the psyche to become more awake and conscious.

A third therapeutic technique is getting the *anamnesis* ("remembrance," "memories" in Greek) or the historical background and development of a particular symptom or problem. Just talking about the buildup of an issue can in itself be of therapeutic value for an analysand who feels that his or her personal story is falling on sympathetic ears. The analyst's role is not so much to ask leading questions as to mirror back important connections based on the historical data in order to awaken the analysand's awareness. The therapist may also provide certain explanations about basic psychological dynamics that operate in everyone and that might be applicable to the analysand in particular. Therapy is also a learning experience.

Patients who have been conditioned and programmed by a previous classical Freudian experience usually show resentment and annoyance when the Jungian analyst freely interacts and dialogues with them or simply mirrors back some data. They may also find it uncomfortable to sit in a chair facing the analyst during the session. The healing factor, as Jung saw it, is mainly produced by a frank and honest encounter between two individuals on a more or less equal footing, thus the face-to-face seating arrangement with all its psychological implications. But this too is not *de rigueur* in analytical psychology. If the analysand wishes to lie down or sit on the floor, it is his or her prerogative.

The fourth method, actual analysis of the unconscious, is effected through dream-work after the conscious material has been thoroughly sifted through in an effort to determine whether a journey to the realm of the dream is necessary and would be helpful. An analyst always keeps this in mind, not only when dealing with borderline neurotics, psychotics or trauma victims, who are already too attracted by inner dimensions, but especially with youngsters, who basically need to establish themselves in some satisfactory fashion in the outer world with its many concrete demands. Some immature and ill-adapted adults also would do well to leave the unconscious alone, since their egos need working on so they can function in the everyday world. For this reason, working with dreams is not always the primary focus of therapy. The main focus is always centered around the affect-laden issues of the ego with their strong emotional bent and intensity.

When dream interpretation is deemed necessary or of value, the analyst ascertains if a particular dream should or should not be interpreted with the analysand. The waking ego may simply not be ready to acknowledge and assimilate certain information (usually shadow material). The analyst usually feels out the situation by first asking the dreamer what he or she believes the dream to mean and unequivocally respects the dreamer's resistances to discussing certain painful topics. When the analysand is ready to discuss certain things, it will happen automatically and spontaneously. Things need not ever be forced.

Dreams may portray actual persons, living or deceased, known by or close to the dreamer. The appearance of living or dead well-known or close persons in dreams can be said most times to be a direct reference to those outer individuals, but not always. They could simply be symbolizing the dreamer's own persona, shadow sides, complexes, anima or animus, helping or inferior functions or even the Self, projections of all kinds or a whole array of archetypal characteristics. Persons not known in waking life more than likely represent personified aspects of the dreamer's own psyche. Generally speaking, everything in the dream, including inanimate objects such as houses, rooms, gardens and pictures as well as animals and persons reflect aspects of the contents, nature or structure of the dreamer's psyche.

Jung did not employ the method of *free association* in attempting to decipher a dream motif. He believed that one could free associate ad infinitum without getting at all close to what the dream motif means and expresses. He believed that free association "always leads to a complex but we can never be certain whether it is precisely this one that constitutes the meaning of the dream" (*Kindertraumseminar*, 1938–1939).

According to Jung, dreams depict complexes but also provide further detailed information regarding how the psyche is handling and coping with these complexes. One can begin free associating starting with a cereal box top—i.e., one need not even start with a dream motif—and arrive at a given complex that happens to be activated at the time of the exercise. Jung's objection to Freud's habitual use of free association acknowledged that it does indeed lead to complexes, but that it does not unearth their relationship to the specific dream motif that was used as the starting point of the chain of free associations.

Again, Jung does not accept Freud's unfounded premise that dream images always have a hidden or latent meaning. According to Freud, the images are a cover-up and disguise. For Jung dream images are a product of Nature. Consequently the manifest content of a dream is in no way a facade or cover-up but rather is an open expression of what the unconscious wishes to state concerning a given psychic situation. The manifest content of a dream, Jung observed, is an undisguised statement expressing exactly what the unconscious means to say, albeit in a symbolic way, or perhaps even in a comical punsterish way.

If a fox appears in a person's dream, the fact to keep in mind is that Mother Nature produced a dream with a fox in it and not a giraffe or zebra. Mother Nature's intelligence chose the figure of the fox precisely because its specific qualities and characteristics are able to communicate a particular meaning intended by the unconscious. It is up to us to figure out what was intended and meant.

It is important, therefore, to get to the inner meaning of "fox" for the dreamer. This is accomplished not by creating a chain of free associations, which will in all likelihood lead away from the dream product (the fox), but rather by determining what personal meaning foxes hold for the dreamer. Meaning is also achieved by amplification on cultural, folk- loric, mythological and archetypal levels by the analyst, which tells what the fox has symbolized historically in those areas. Amplification of the dream image by the analyst is not an interpretation of the dream symbol, but is only intended as a method to invoke a meaningful response in the dreamer vis- à-vis the dream motif.

The analyst helps the dreamer establish the personal mean- ing of the dream-fox via these archetypal amplifications, gath- ered from myths and elsewhere. The appearance of a fox has something specific to say to the dreamer, making it expedient to examine the personal and mythic ramifications of the sym- bol in question. If the personal association strikes home, then no amplification from mythology, folklore or elsewhere need be supplied.

A clear overview of the dreamer's psychic status, along with ample knowledge of his or her present life issues and pressing conscious concerns, will tremendously facilitate understanding of the contextual aspects of the dream. And with the help of amplification by the analyst the dream motif's significance can be elicited without too much struggle. The amplifications collected from the symbolic portrayals in myths, fairy tales and folklore can also help to underline the universal aspects of life issues faced by every human being from time immemorial. Every personal problem is also a human problem that others before us have had to cope with or solve. We are not alone in our human dilemmas. Others before us have left us a treasury of wisdom just for the taking, but we Westerners must over- come ingrained prejudices that we harbor toward our suppos- edly unenlightened ancestors.

It goes without saying that dreams can be precognitive and prophetic of future events concerning issues that are beyond the control or conscious manipulation of the dreamer. All such events—from earthquakes to political assassinations— may be previewed in dreams.

Contacts with the dead may also take place in dreams. In such dreams, for instance, our long-gone great-grandmother may appear to tell us that if we dig up a pink rose bush she had planted in the family garden before she died, we will find in a little tin box a diamond-and-gold brooch that she wants us to have, along with a note of explanation. We may indeed find the box, brooch and note exactly as our deceased great-grandmother had indicated in the dream. Too many dreams like this take place to require further evidence. The skeptical will in any case believe such dreams exist only if they experience one themselves, so presenting outer proof serves no practical purpose. The human psyche does indeed go beyond time and space via the dream or, to be more accurate, via the unconscious. We should all strive to have our own experiences. Relying on the experiences of others will in no way lead to our own enlightenment. When such dreams occur, they prove to be a great consolation to many of us vis-à-vis such an ultimate and inevitable reality as physical death.

The following books could be very helpful to the interested reader: *Understanding Dreams*, by Mary Ann Mattoon, and *Interpretation of Fairy Tales*, by Marie-Louise von Franz, as well as other books on fairy tales by her. Fairy tales are collective dreams and, as such, can also be understood on a psychological level. Student analysts spend a great deal of time working with fairy tales in preparation for dream analysis. Von Franz approaches dreams with her thinking function, thus making archetypal material understandable to left-brain-oriented psyches. One of Jung's closest disciples for many decades, she is an astute teacher, author and analyst. Another book is *Jungian Dream Interpretation*, by James A. Hall, who takes a practical, thorough, simple and interesting approach.

Much more can be said about dream understanding. For such a vast field, one chapter is hardly sufficient even to scratch the surface. The reading material mentioned should help fill the gaps left by the limited scope of this basic introduction. Formally working in analysis with one's own dreams over a long period can be considered to be the only truly adequate training in understanding dreams. This is the reason why each Jungian therapist in training is obliged to undergo formal personal analysis for many years before being graduated from a training institute. Personal experience is the best teacher.

Chapter 12

Active Imagination

Recording and understanding dreams is not necessarily the end-all in personal psychological mending or even in becoming more conscious.

Jung developed a special means for altering and modifying negative inner situations that are initially depicted in dreams. These special methods also help bring out and enhance positive inner forces. He taught these skills, calling them "active imagination." This indispensable method brings about almost total autonomy for the individual practicing it, because there is no need for a therapist or other knowledgeable person.

Recording a dream in detail gives us a perception of what is happening in the unconscious. Evaluating the dream motifs by applying Jung's symbolical approach allows us to understand the dynamics of the unconscious. "Active imagination" takes a dream image or dream figure after it has been initially dreamed and encourages the dreamer's ego to interact with the image or figure with the intention of transforming its energy or enhancing it through conscious interaction, or simply to get a better comprehension of it. Again, it is not for psychotic persons.

Jung succinctly summarized, in a letter, how he meant this exercise to be conducted. Beginning with the image or figure

that has already been dreamed, he directed: "Contemplate
and carefully observe how the picture begins to unfold or to
change. Don't try to make it into something, just do nothing
but observe what its spontaneous changes are. Any mental
picture you contemplate in this way will sooner or later change
through a spontaneous association that causes a slight alter-
ation of the picture. You must carefully avoid impatient jump-
ing from one subject to another. Hold fast to the one image
you have chosen and wait until it changes by itself. Note all
these changes and eventually step into the picture yourself,
and if it is a speaking figure at all then say what you have to
say to that figure and listen to what he or she has to say."*

Active imagination begins by consciously re-imagining
(i.e., consciously hallucinating) a motif or figure that has
previously appeared in a dream. The intention is to get more
information from it and about it and, through conscious re-
engagement with it, to somehow come to terms with it in a
fuller, more salient way.

If the active imagination is of short duration, we usually
can wait until it is finished before writing down the inner
dialogue. For longer exercises it is best to write things down
as we go along.

We might want to take up the exercise where a dream left
off. If a big cobra was about to sink its fangs into us when we
suddenly awoke, we might want to re-imagine the same serpent, at a very safe distance, to be sure, to ask it a few pertinent
questions. Perhaps it really did not mean to bite us after all;
perhaps it initially appeared for other reasons. *Dreamer*: "Who
are you? Why did you appear in my dream? Why did you try
to bite me?" *An answer may come flooding in*: "I am not just an
ordinary cobra. I am the imaginary cobra you used to play with
as a child. Don't you remember? You were not afraid of me
then. But after you started school, you began putting me out

*C. G. *Jung Letters*, vol. I, Gerhard Adler, Aniela Jaffé (eds.), trans. by R.F.C. Hull,
Bollingen Series XCV: 1, Princeton University Press, Princeton, N.J., 1973.

of your mind, as you did with other imaginary animals and spirit people who were also your friends. You have abandoned us, but we have not abandoned you. I am the wisdom of Mother Nature and have always whispered wise sayings to you all of your life, whether you were aware of it or not. You need me more than ever now. I have come to heal you with the secrets of Nature that are in my possession. Listen carefully to what I have to say. If I appeared to want to bite you, it was simply to reconnect with you, to fill you with my energy in the only way I know how. To heal, to become whole, you must die to your hyperintellectual and critical self. Only then can you reconnect to a new life filled with the feminine wisdom of Mother Nature, whose humble servant I am. It is the Goddess herself who wishes to inspire and heal you, for you are her very own child, whom she dearly loves."

Active engagement in fantasizing is an "alchemical" work, though it may seem to some to be mere madness, since it involves actively and consciously mixing elements from the unconscious with ego-consciousness for purposes of personal transformation and furthering our psychic evolution. It is allowing "cobra-energy," i.e., the wisdom of Nature, to permeate everyday consciousness. In fairy tales this type of animal is known as a helping animal, a personification of an instinct. Some will object that all of this is just a figment of one's imagination, therefore unreal and of no intrinsic value in understanding or transforming ourselves. If our imaginations are not reality, if our psyches are not reality, then how are we to determine what reality is? What we all fear is deluding ourselves. This is natural and something to be avoided. The ego may lie to itself, but in Jung's observations the unconscious, through dreams, will eventually and in no uncertain terms make the ego more than aware of any self-deception. This has been proven time and again by those who pay close attention to the outpourings of their unconscious.

In active imagination, one simply allows the fantasy to unfold under the scrutiny of ego-consciousness, writing down whatever happens, either during or after the exercise is completed. In a way we are allowing ourselves to dream while awake, but we are dreaming about a topic we choose to dream about. What we must avoid is conscious interference while the fantasy images grow and unfold, except, of course, when we converse with them. This exercise trains the ego to be more attentive, more alert to the incessant activities of the unconscious, and to begin differentiating our waking state from our dream state and our dream state from our dreamless sleep state, by consciously "witnessing" and actively relating to what we are witnessing. "Conscious introspection" is another term for this liberating activity.

The exercise with the cobra is a classical example of reconnecting with natural instinct after academic pursuits have done their best to cut the dreamer off from the inherent wisdom of Nature as expressed in the dream. There are countless treasures in the innermost depths of our beings, but few people are genuinely interested or willing to gather them up.

On a more superficial level, within our personal unconscious various voices are always dialoging with each other and with our egos. Some dialogues are harmonious, others are not. It is beneficial for the ego to identify the inner parties engaged in these inner conversations and interactions. In this way we no longer remain in a state of possession or identity with them. If we are totally unaware of them, we are held in their grip and become identical with them due to their being so unconscious. When we become aware, by witnessing, that these voices are autonomous, we begin to differentiate our ego-consciousness from them and set ourselves free from their power over us.

We might notice that there are various voices of persons we have absorbed, introjected and begun merging with. Introjections are the opposite of projections. Introjections are the living impressions other people have made in our innermost psyches, where they take on a life of their own. We all have many of them, such as our mother's opinions battling against our own, our father's typical way of looking at situations contrasting perhaps with our culture's way of viewing the same situations, a favorite teacher's voice agreeing with us and encouraging us in some pursuit in life.

The next step is to ask the introjected mother *aloud* if she ever saw things differently, asking the introjected father, *also out loud,* what his own father used to say about similar topics, asking the introjected teacher if more advice can be given. Their answers must be written down so that we can concretize these elusive inner voices that we all have within us.

This exercise tends to strengthen the ego, to give it more "definition" and differentiation from the dozens of inner voices and figures. Many times an inner voice can become identified only as we repeatedly read over many times what was written down during the exercise.

Some people consider active imagination to be "just talking to yourself" and consequently a form of madness or self-deception. In a way, it is "talking to ourselves," but, in point of fact, we talk to the various parts of ourselves all the time but are generally unaware of this phenomenon. Active imagination simply makes this process conscious, but it requires great effort and self-discipline on our part to reap a reward from this activity. As the old Chinese proverb says: "We only get out of our tea bowl what we put into it." If we put our hearts and minds into active imagination, we benefit greatly from it.

To illustrate, we might look at a practice among the Hindus called *upasana* in Sanskrit. The four Vedas, the sacred Hindu scriptures, describe the religious use of conscious psychic projection of an invisible inner spiritual reality onto a concrete outer object in order to worship the invisible via the five senses, after which the projection is taken back consciously into one's own soul again.

The practice of *upasana* consists, for example, in superimposing the Goddess of Learning upon the River Ganges and offering "her" flowers, milk, rice and floating lights. After this ritual worship the Goddess is re-introjected into the deep inner recesses of one's own being. This ancient practice is living proof that the Hindu spiritual masters knew about basic psychic dynamics and how to use them "alchemically" to bring about personal transformation by having the ego interact with inherent archetypal forces. The offerings of flowers, milk, rice and floating lights are visual symbols used to express psychic nurturing and energizing of the deity out of her slumber in the unconscious. It is active imagination involving a living figure of a collective dream and mythology of an entire people.

Active imagination requires insight as to its intricate workings and efficacy, as well as great discipline and determination, first, because what is unconscious wants to be kept that way by Mother Nature, who created the split between conscious and unconscious in the first place. Second, most of us do not believe we have the power to overcome old patterns and entrenched habits by and through the psyche itself, which produced the irritating patterns and habits to begin with. Much effort is needed to get past the inertia of such false beliefs about ourselves concerning what we are capable or not capable of doing. This is where the assistance of deep psychological knowledge is most needed. Third, as Westerners our culture is not conducive to such exotic "yogic" practices.

Most of us underestimate the power of our imaginations, no less the power of our *active* imaginations because we fail to see that the images and voices in our psyches are what really create the nature of our lives for us. The stark simplicity of this truth somehow is too elusive for extraverted minds to grasp. If we feel we would like to "alchemically" change our lives for whatever reason, we would first need to change or transform the unconscious images and subpersonalities that pattern and give them form. This change is accomplished through active imagination, the tool Jung formulated as an efficacious therapeutic method for accomplishing just this.

The main thing is not to examine too closely or analyze what is happening during active imagination while it is taking place. It is important to keep a "normal flow" as much as possible while the alchemical exchange is occurring. After it is completed, we can examine the written material that has been recorded in detail.

Active imagination is not always easy because our extra-verted culture does not encourage what it considers to be magical and occult activities, and also because it takes a lot of practice. Nothing in our academic education fosters active fantasizing or sees the value in actively daydreaming. The practice actually strikes fear in the minds of the typical hyper-rational, extraverted Apollonian Westerner, who is caught up in the three-dimensional world of ego-concerns.

Interacting consciously with dream characters, however, is what allows for mutual understanding between the conscious and unconscious and for mutual growth and change. Because the reconciliation between conscious and unconscious forces does not readily happen on its own, we must actively seek it. It is not simply a question of watching the activities of the unconscious psyche. We must actively engage in a living, gut-level relationship with these inner events and figures in a truly human fashion—and this implies "talking things over," while giving free rein to these inner figures and subpersonalities to talk back to us in any way they want, and remembering and taking seriously what they have to say.

For example, a man and woman have been dating steadily for a year or two. Somehow the question of marriage never arises until one day a mutual friend asks, "Well, when are you two going to tie the knot?" At that moment one or both partners may realize they feel an incredibly strong inner resis-tance to the idea of marriage and commitment. This is the moment for each person to talk to his or her own personified resistance, which might respond: "If my mother were alive today, she would just never approve," or "I like so and so a lot, but I'm just not in love," or "So and so really bores me, but I suppose having someone around is better than having no one around!" The answers may come as a surprise, but at least each partner will be conscious of why the "inevitable" has never taken place and probably never will.

Jung did not invent active imagination. He merely observed that certain individuals in history have used this method successfully in coming to terms with their inner selves, and it was he who realized that, when mastered, it was an immensely practical tool for psychological use.

The point to remember is that active imagination is *active* and not passive. For a more detailed, readable account of this simple alchemical method of personal empowerment, the reader may consult *Inner Work*, by Robert Johnson. Active imagination will be seen as the principal Jungian tool for psychic transformation. It ought not to be taken lightly, and one should get some professional advice before initiating the use of this powerful practice, to ward off possible self-deceptions. After some time, we may engage in active imagination totally on our own.

Jung taught his student and collaborator Barbara Hannah about active imagination, and he eventually attended the courses she offered on the subject at the Jung Institute of Zurich. Her excellent book *Encounters with the Soul: Active Imagination as Developed by C. G. Jung* is one of the most thorough and classical treatments of the subject.

Epilogue

Books offer useful information, but information is useless unless it is applied to real-life situations. It is hoped that *Jung to Live By* has roused some enthusiasm for the everyday application of the concepts and methods of analytical psychology.

The ideas of Jung are finally filtering out across the world and reaching the mainstream of the general public. This is known from the yearly rise in sales of books by and about Jung and his school of psychotherapy and by the demand for Jungian lecturers and speakers in nations that recognize the ability of Jungian thought to save what is best in their ancient cultures.

Much in this work has been presented in a simplified manner so that those not initiated in psychology might be encouraged to pursue self-knowledge with less fear and trepidation and more confidence. May this work help in enlightening and in restoring peace of mind and a joyful heart.

The whole goal of our search—contented at-one-ment—is very elusive to us, but, then again, it is as close to us as our own breath. We look hither and thither inside and out, high and low, and ultimately it is really a question of the looker looking for the Looker.

The Buddhist legend of Enyadatti may help us remember

this basic truth. Enyadatti was a woman who was convinced she had lost her head. She looked for it everywhere with great intensity but without any luck. She shocked people when she told them what she was looking for. There was no way to convince her that indeed she had not lost anything at all. She just would not listen. She remained anxious and adamant in her search until one day she met Tara, an old school friend, who noticed Enyadatti roaming along the road, obviously perturbed in her search for something.

Tara greeted Enyadatti and, after some preliminary chatter, asked her friend what she was looking for. Enyadatti casually replied that she was looking for her head. Quicker than a flash, Tara gave Enyadatti a good, hard slap square in the middle of her head, which made Enyadatti scream out in pain and in fright. Tara laughed and said, "There's your head, Enyadatti! Right on top of your shoulders!" Enyadatti held her throbbing head and, though still startled and in shock, managed to mutter some halting words of gratitude under her breath.

Tara's behavior is typical of a genuinely concerned, caring and wise friend. Her act of loving-kindness was a spontaneous urge to help another human being in need. It flowed from her unwavering knowledge and certainty of the inner oneness of all beings. The experience of this soulful solidarity always results in the simple capacity to feel the suffering of others as one's very own and to extend a helping hand. It also makes us realize that compassion and empathy do not issue forth from a feeling of mental or spiritual superiority but more truly from the wisdom that sees our essential equality with all others. Wisdom and compassion are ever intimately linked in this way.

When all is said and done, it is not the *what* in psychology that is important. Like Enyadatti, all of us have one thing or another that needs to be solved. What is really important is *how* we deal with the what. Having feelings of anxiety or of having lost one's mind is the what. Talking to and relating with all of our different whats in a skillful, sensitive, empathetic way via active imagination is how Jung advises us to deal with all the multiple issues of our lives. This implies a belief that we are not powerless pawns in a world of chaos.

Individuation does not imply being or becoming nonhuman, unfeeling or humorless, or never having to face trying times. Even the world's cultural and spiritual heros and heroines had obstacles of one kind or another to surmount and trials that tested their mettle. Trials skillfully dealt with are what make us heroes and heroines. Although few of us will be written up in history as saints or practitioners of superhuman heroic virtue, each of us has a personal obligation to ourselves and to the world to trod the path of individuation, the process of becoming more truly human in the context of our own originality. In so doing, we find that we begin experiencing within and behind our very humanity the ever-present hidden, silent, effulgent, blissful One who abides in all things and in whom all things abide, our own Higher Self. It is at this point that we discover that the real journey begins.

Our journey will be pleasant or unpleasant, successful or unsuccessful, depending on what we consciously and unconsciously hold to be true or false.

Everything that we allow to happen in our lives is a result of what we believe or do not believe. All of our achievements are a direct consequence of our most cherished belief system. Some beliefs are limiting, creating conditions that make us suffer such things as sickness, poverty and unhappiness. Other beliefs are liberating, allowing us to revel in well-being, an abundance of all that we need to grow and develop on this planet in a general atmosphere of peace and serenity.

The Olympic games began in Greece in classical times and have been revived in our modern era. Careful records are kept of all the events, the names of the participants and especially of the records they set for each sporting competition. Each year the records of the previous years are broken; new achievements are attained in the same old events. Each year newcomers to the games bring new beliefs about what they are capable of achieving, sure they can surpass the records already set—and they succeed. We long believed that no one could run the mile in under four minutes, until someone came along who thought he could run it in less time. The world of sports has to keep adjusting its belief system, thanks to Olympic record-breakers.

When the steam locomotive was invented, the government scientific patent office in Washington, D.C., closed down because the directors believed that science had achieved its highest possibilities and goals with that invention, and that there could be no further need or requests for scientific patents. As we approach the twenty-first century, we can look back with a smile at this charming but absurd anecdote of our ancestors' naiveté. Our personal and collective naiveté, however, in the long run stops being charming and begins being insidious and harmful, and then downright murderous. We believe cars must be run on oil, so we send huge sums of money to foreign oil powers, pollute our air and destroy our health. The government of Brazil believes cars can burn home-grown sugarcane alcohol, produce no pollution in the atmosphere and allow Brazilians to keep their money at home instead of sending it abroad to buy oil. Some people believe in fatal diseases, so they let themselves and thousands of others die horrible deaths, all because of the limited consciousness and belief systems they hold concerning the creative powers of the human brain and spirit.

All around us, we hear parroted declarations that there is no cure for cancer, AIDS or heart disease. This belief system does not make for "creative medicine" or patients who could very well survive and overcome untold suffering if only we could escape our limiting beliefs and allow the energies of new, record-breaking Olympic-style points of view to flood through our consciousness. Marvels would take place. Many times they do, but they are squelched by such elements as a greedy pharmaceutical "cancer industry" that makes fortunes from dying and suffering human beings while keeping them ignorant about the possibilities of creative medicine.

Shadow forces are ever at play, even when beliefs turn very positive. Simple oxygenating or ozoning of blood, use of foods as medicine and other modalities are used by individuals in countries whose belief systems are positive and who are not enslaved by greed—another negative belief system centered around issues of controlling one's personal security at the expense of everyone else's. Nature produces diseases as well as the cures for them. As all archetypes, Nature has a light and dark side, so we need not look far afield for cures. The illness itself gives us clues. Homeopathic medicine is based on the premise that "like cures like."

Many books and volumes may be written about belief, and the powers of intellect and spirit it is capable of releasing into our lives. All of the knowledge in this book will better enable us to discern those hidden archetypal forces in our unconscious that make us believe a thousand and one different things. Ultimately what is needed to combat negative beliefs is moral strength, which can be achieved only through contact with the Self, with the Transcendent Spirit that we really are. Even this is conditioned by our personal belief systems, but if we look closely at the heart and core of every religion and spiritual tradition, we will generally find the perennial Truths that will set us free.

The word "creed" means "belief." It is very important to know what creed we adhere to. Seeing a creed in written form is helpful in making our personal and collective creeds more conscious. We are also able to change them and consequently our lives by altering the words, sentences and ideas used in expressing these creeds. Even more important and powerful is to state aloud in the presence of others the positive beliefs that we hold and wish to affirm. Many intellectuals think this a childish activity. It is not negative childishness but rather positive, childlike behavior. Unless we become childlike and open to new ideas and new ways of seeing and evaluating reality, we become fossilized and spiritually dead. Children are full of life and renewing energy, and we would be wise to reconnect with our own inner child on a conscious daily basis.

To quote Jung: "Psychotherapy only helps us to find the way to the religious experience that makes us whole" (*Letters*, vol. 2, p. 265).

Whatever is the highest perfection of human consciousness, may we all realize it for the benefit of all that lives.

Suggested Reading

Bernhardt, Patrick. *The Secret Music of the Soul.* Imagine Records and Publishing, Sainte-Adèle, Quebec, 1991.

Bolen, Jean S. *Goddesses in Every Woman.* Harper & Row, San Francisco, 1984.

———. *Gods in Every Man.* Harper & Row, New York, 1989.

———. *The Tao of Psychology.* Harper & Row, San Francisco, 1979. On synchronicity.

Brewi, Janice, and Anne Brennan. *Celebrate Mid-life: Jungian Archetypes and Mid-life Spirituality.* Crossroad, New York, 1990.

Briggs Myers, Isabel. *Gifts Differing.* Consulting Psychologists Press, Palo Alto, California, 1990. On typology.

Bruns, J. Edgar. *God as Woman and Woman as God.* Paulist Press, New York, 1973.

Buzan, T. *Use Both Sides of Your Brain.* E. P. Dutton, New York, 1976.

Campbell, Joseph. *The Masks of God: Primitive, Oriental, Occidental, and Creative Mythology* (four volumes). Viking Press, New York, 1959.

———. *Myths to Live By.* Viking Press, New York, 1973.

———, ed. *The Portable Jung.* Viking Press, New York, 1971.

———, with Bill Moyers. *The Power of Myth.* Book: Doubleday, New York, 1998; video: Mystic Fire Video, Montauk, New York, 1989.

Capra, Fritjof. *The Tao of Physics: An Exploration of the Parallels between Modern Physics and Eastern Mysticism.* Shambhala, Boulder, Colorado, 1975.

Cooper, J. C. *An Illustrated Encyclopedia of Traditional Symbols.* Thames and Hudson, London, 1978.

————. *Jung and Reich: The Body as Shadow.* North Atlantic Books, Berkeley, California, 1988.

————. *Yin and Yang: The Taoist Harmony of Opposites.* Aquarian Press, Wellingborough, United Kingdom, 1981.

Cunningham, Donna. *An Astrological Guide to Self-Awareness.* CRCS Publications, Reno, Nevada, 1978.

Davis, Bruce. *Monastery without Walls: Daily Life in the Silence.* Celestial Arts Publishing, Berkeley, California, 1990.

De Castillejo, Irene Claremont. *Knowing Woman.* G. P. Putnam's Sons, New York, 1973.

De Laszlo, Violet S., ed. *The Basic Writings of C. G. Jung.* Modern Library, New York, 1959.

————, ed. *Psyche and Symbol: A Selection from the Writings of C. G. Jung.*

Diallo, Yaya, and Mitchell Hall. *The Healing Drum: African Wisdom Teachings.* Inner Traditions, Rochester, Vermont, 1990.

Edinger, Edward. *Anatomy of the Psyche: Alchemical Symbolism in Psychotherapy.* Open Court, La Salle, Illinois, 1985.

————. *Ego and Archetype: Individuation and the Religious Function of the Psyche.* Penguin Books, Baltimore, 1973.

Edwards, Betty. *Drawing on the Right Side of the Brain.* J. P. Tarcher, Los Angeles, 1979.

Ellenberger, Henri F. *The Discovery of the Unconscious: The History and Evolution of Dynamic Psychiatry.* Basic Books, New York, 1970.

Evans, Richard. *Jung on Elementary Psychology: A Discussion between C. G. Jung and Richard Evans.* E. P. Dutton, New York, 1976.

Fierz, Heinrich K. *Jungian Psychiatry.* Translated by Stephen Waller. Daimon Verlag, Einsiedeln, Switzerland, 1991.

Fordham, Michael. *Children as Individuals: An Analytical Psychologist's Study of Child Development.* Hodder & Stoughton, London, 1969.

Frey-Rohn, Liliane. *From Freud to Jung.* G. P. Putnam's Sons, New York, 1974.

Furth, Gregg M. *The Secret World of Drawings.* Sigo Press, Boston, 1988.

Grateful Members. *The Twelve Steps for Everyone.* Comp Care Publishers, Minneapolis, 1975.

Hall, James A. *Jungian Dream Interpretation.* Inner City Books, Toronto, 1983.

Hannah, Barbara. *Encounters with the Soul: Active Imagination.* Sigo Press, Santa Monica, California, 1981.

———. *Jung: His Life and Work.* G. P. Putnam's Sons, New York, 1976. Biographical memoir.

———. *Striving Towards Wholeness.* Sigo Press, Boston, 1988. On individuation.

Haule, John R. *Divine Madness: Archetypes of Romantic Love.* Shambhala, Boston and Shaftesbury, 1990.

The Herder Symbol Dictionary. Translated by Boris Matthews. Chiron Publications, Wilmette, Illinois, 1986.

Hillman, James. *Suicide and the Soul.* Hodder & Stoughton, London, 1964.

Hopcke, Robert H. *A Guided Tour of the Collected Works of C. G. Jung.* Shambhala, Boston and Shaftesbury, 1989.

———. *Jung, Jungians and Homosexuality.* Shambhala, Boston and Shaftesbury, 1989.

———. *Men's Dreams, Men's Healing.* Shambhala, Boston and London, 1990.

Hutt, Corinne. *Males and Females.* Penguin Books, London, 1972.

Jacobi, Jolande. *The Way of Individuation.* Translated by R.F.C. Hull. Hodder & Stoughton, London, 1967.

————, and R.F.C. Hull, eds. *C. G. Jung, Psychological Reflections: A New Anthology of His Writings.* Princeton University Press, Princeton, New Jersey, 1978.

Jaffe, Aniela. *From the Life and Work of C. G. Jung.* Harper & Row, New York, 1971.

James, George G. M. *Stolen Legacy.* Julian Richardson Associates, San Francisco, 1985.

Jocelyn, John. *Meditations on the Signs of the Zodiac.* Multimedia Publishing Corp., Blauvelt, New York, 1970.

✳ Johnson, Robert. *Inner Work: Using Dreams and Active Imagination for Personal Growth.* Harper & Row, San Francisco, 1983.

————. *We: Understanding the Psychology of Romantic Love.* Harper & Row, San Francisco, 1983.

Jung, C. G. *Analytical Psychology: Its Theory and Practice: The Tavistock Lectures.* Random House, New York, 1970.

————. *Memories, Dreams, Reflections.* Pantheon Books, New York, 1963. Autobiography.

————. *Modern Man in Search of a Soul.* Harcourt Brace, New York, 1933.

————, et al., *Man and His Symbols.* Aldus Books, London, 1964.

Kalweit, Holger. *Dreamtime and Inner Space: The World of the Shaman.* Shambhala, Boston and London, 1988.

Keirsey, David, and Marilyn Bates. *Please Understand Me.* Prometheus Nemesis Book Co., Del Mar, California, 1984. On typology testing.

Kiepenheuer, Kaspar. *Crossing the Bridge: A Jungian Approach to Adolescence.* Translated by Karen R. Schneider. Open Court, LaSalle, Illinois, 1990.

Kroeger, Otto, and Janet Thuesen. *Type Talk.* Delacorte Press, New York, 1988.

Larousse Encyclopedia of Mythology. Hamlyn, London, 1959.

Larson, Martin A. *The Story of Christian Origins.* Village Press, Tahlequah, Oklahoma, 1977.

Leonard, Linda. *Witness to the Fire: Creativity and the Veil of Addiction.* Shambhala, Boston, 1989.

———. *The Wounded Woman: Healing the Father-Daughter Relationship.* Swallow Press, Athens, Ohio, and Chicago, 1982.

LeShan, Lawrence. *How to Meditate.* Bantam, New York, 1974. Audio cassette: St. Martin's Press, New York, 1987.

Lockhart, Russell A. *Cancer in Myth and Dream.* Spring Publications, Zurich, 1977.

Mattoon, Mary Ann. *Understanding Dreams.* Spring Publications, Dallas, 1986.

McGaa, Ed. *Mother Earth Spirituality: Native American Paths to Healing Ourselves and Our World.* HarperCollins, San Francisco, 1990.

Moir, Ann. *Brain Sex.* Michael Joseph, London, 1984.

Neumann, Erich. *The Child: Structure and Dynamics of the Nascent Personality.* Harper Colophon Books, New York, 1976.

Niehardt, John G. *Black Elk Speaks.* University of Nebraska Press, Lincoln, Nebraska, 1961.

Noble, Vicki. *Shakti Woman: Feeling Our Fire, Healing Our World: The New Female Shamanism.* HarperCollins, San Francisco, 1991.

Oken, Alan. *Complete Astrology.* Bantam, New York, 1988.

Perry, John Weir. *The Far Side of Madness.* Prentice-Hall, Englewood Cliffs, New Jersey, 1974. On schizophrenia.

Samuels, Andrew, Bani Shorter, and Fred Plant. *A Critical Dictionary of Jungian Analysis.* Routledge & Kegan Paul, London and New York, 1987.

Sanford, John A. *Evil: The Shadow Side of Reality.* Crossroad, New York, 1981.

———. *Healing and Wholeness.* Paulist Press, New York, 1977.

———. *The Invisible Partners.* Paulist Press, New York and Mahwah, New Jersey, 1980.

Schechter, Harold, and Jonna Gormely Semeiks. *Patterns in Popular Culture.* Harper & Row, New York, 1980.

Schwartz-Salant, Nathan. *Narcissism and Character Transformation.* Inner City Books, Toronto, 1982.

Sedlar, Jean W. *India and the Greek World.* Rowman and Littlefield, Totowa, New Jersey, 1980.

Segaller, Stephen, and Merrill Berger. *Wisdom of the Dream: The World of C. G. Jung.* Shambhala, Boston, 1989. Video: Border Televisions, Stephen Segaller Films, 1989.

Sheldrake, Rupert. *A New Science of Life: The Hypothesis of Causative Formation.* J. P. Tarcher, Los Angeles, 1981.

Springer, Sally, and Georg Deutsch. *Left Brain, Right Brain.* W. H. Freeman, San Francisco, 1981.

Stein, Murray. *In Midlife: A Jungian Perspective.* Spring Publications, Dallas, 1983.

————, ed. *Jungian Analysis.* Open Court, LaSalle and London, 1982.

Stevens, Anthony. *Archetypes: A Biological Basis of Jung's Theory.* Quill, New York, 1983.

Stone, Merlin. *When God Was a Woman.* Harcourt Brace Jovanovich, New York, 1976.

Van der Post, Laurens. *Jung and the Story of Our Time.* Random House, New York, 1977.

Von Franz, Marie-Louise. *C. G. Jung: His Myth in Our Time.* Trans. by W. H. Kennedy. G. P. Putnam's Sons, New York, 1975.

————. *The Feminine in Fairy Tales.* Spring Publications, Irving, Texas, 1982.

————. *Individuation in Fairy Tales.* Shambhala, Boston, 1991.

————. *Interpretation of Fairy Tales.* Spring Publications, Zurich, Switzerland, 1973.

————. *Shadow and Evil in Fairy Tales.* Spring Publications, Zurich, Switzerland, 1974.

Ware, Kallistos. *The Orthodox Way.* St. Vladimirs, Crestwood, New York, 1979.

Index

About the Author

Eugene Pascal is an American born in 1942. He has two degrees in philosophy from the Institut catholique de Paris, where he did all of his college training. In November 1978, he was graduated from the C. G. Jung Institute of Zurich, Switzerland, where he studied for four years. He did his practicum program at the Clinique psychiatrique de Bel-Air in Geneva.

In 1979 he returned to New York to establish a private practice in analytical psychology. In 1985 he was graduated from the New Interfaith Seminary of New York, where he was also dean of studies for a time.

He is a member of the New York Association for Analytical Psychology, the Association of Graduate Analytical Psychologists of the C. G. Jung Institute of Zurich and the International Association for Analytical Psychology. He has taught at the Institut féminin de l'Institut catholique de Paris, the New School for Social Research, Fordham University and the New York Open Center, and he has lectured at several colleges in Bombay, India. He lectures in many countries on Jungian psychology and on his thesis topic, "Jung and the Art of Dream Interpretation among the Hindus and Buddhists of Asia," a pioneering work. He has traveled to more than forty-five countries over the years. He presently lives in New York and in the American Southwest with his adopted son, from India, his daughter-in-law and his four grandchildren. His goal is to make known the basics of Jungian thought to laypersons around the world. He welcomes all invitations to lecture abroad and wishes to see Jungian training institutes set up in Third World countries to help preserve native cultures.